Preventing Reading Failure

An Examination of the Myths of Reading Instruction

Patrick Groff, Ph.D.

San Diego State University

NATIONAL BOOK COMPANY
A Division of
Educational Research Associates
A Nonprofit Research Corporation
Portland, Oregon 97205-3784

1088

Graphics and Production   John Kimmel

Editorial and Computer Coordination   Mark Salser

ISBN 0-89420-252-9

341150

Educational Research Associates would like to express its appreciation to the U.S. Department of Education's National Advisory Council on Educational Research and Improvement for its unflagging support of reading research, in general, and Dr. Patrick Groff's work, in particular.

The work upon which this publication is based was performed pursuant to Contract No. NIE-P-0005 of the National Institute of Education, U.S. Department of Education. It does not, however, necessarily reflect the views of that department.

TABLE OF CONTENTS

Preface

When the National Commission on Excellence in Education, commissioned by Secretary of Education T. H. Bell on August 26, 1981, reported recently it found "...Our nation is at risk...the educational foundations of our society are presently being eroded by a rising tide of mediocrity that threatens our future as a Nation and a people... If an unfriendly foreign power had attempted to impose on America the mediocre educational performance that exists today, we might well have viewed it as an act of war."

Evidence of the need for educational reform cited by the Commission included:

. On 19 academic tests administered internationally, American students never scored first or second, and they were last on seven tests when compared to other industrialized nations;

. Approximately 23 million American adults, 13% of all 17 year olds, and up to 40% of all minority youth are functionally illiterate by the simplest of tests;

. One fourth of recent Navy recruits cannot read the minimum needed to understand written safety instructions.

Correlation does not imply causality, as is well known. However, it cannot escape notice that our prisons are full of illiterate and semi-literate men and women whose lives might have been very different had they experienced more success in school.

Estimates of the dollar cost of illiteracy are staggering. And often those figures fail to take into account the cost of retaining children who have "failed" (been failed by) a grade. When one child is in school an extra year, it costs the taxpayers well over $1500 on the average. It also delays by a year the time when that student becomes an employed taxpayer and thus shortens by a year his or her productive work life. Surely no one disputes that inability to read is the major cause of retention.

Estimates of the dollar cost of illiteracy are staggering.

To attribute the decline in American education solely to inadequate methodology of teaching reading would be simplistic; but to refuse to recognize the dramatic improvement that would result if all children were more easily and efficiently taught to read would be foolish.

Learning to read is the sine qua non *of a successful school experience.*

Learning to read is the *sine qua non* of a successful school experience. One can only speculate about the cumulative personal frustration and pain directly attributable to reading failure. How is it that a nation with the resources of the United States stands seemingly bewildered and help-less to teach its citizens basic skills?

Very simply, we have been using the wrong techniques of reading in-struction. It seems incredible that the education establishment could have persisted in the folly of inappropriate reading methodology over so many years and with so many millions of failures. Had we not known how to teach children to read easily and well, this persistence in ineffec-tive methods would have been more understandable. However, we have had highly successful methods, programs, and techniques for many, many years. Not only have we had successful programs, but we have had ample and conclusive research evidence of their efficacy.

Groff's Preventing Reading Failure *is a superb analysis . . .*

Groff's *Preventing Reading Failure* is a superb analysis of twelve falla-cious beliefs that are responsible for the perpetuation of ineffective and inappropriate approaches to reading instruction. Understanding that these myths are patently and demonstrably false is the first step toward increased literacy in our nation. The next step is overthrowing these myths. Dr. Groff has also shown us how this can be done. All of us who believe that learning to read our primary language is a necessary and early step toward constructive and meaningful participation in the world around us will be delighted by Groff's analysis. It is welcome in proportion to the magnitude and seriousness of the problem it addresses.

Let us hope that Groff's message is spread far and wide, and that just perhaps it will be truly heard and heeded. Our nation urgently needs a more literate citizenry. While that would be no guarantee of our sur-vival, it would certainly be a step in the right direction.

Barbara Bateman, Ph.D., J.D.
Professor of Education
University of Oregon

Introduction

The term, *myth,* in the title of this volume refers to a belief about reading instruction the truthfulness of which apparently has been accepted uncritically. The *Myths of Reading Instruction* that this book confronts as erroneous therefore are examples of articles of faith among reading educators. These suppositions nonetheless have been used as evidence for many years to justify certain aspects of reading instruction.

The purpose of *Preventing Reading Failure* is to make a reasonable case against these longstanding, highly-regarded (and yet unsupported) notions about reading instruction. The goal of this volume is to help dispel the influence that these contentions have had on reading instruction.

The reader of *Preventing Reading Failure* is advised that this book is not intended to be a complete description of a recommended or optimum program of reading instruction. The book therefore does not comment on all the varied aspects that go to make up a modern reading program. Although this text often refers to phonics teaching in its pages, it is not designed to be a detailed or comprehensive account of this instruction.

Neither does the book describe the many interrelationships that exist between the varied and numerous aspects of an optimum reading program. It makes no pretense at being a standard textbook on the teaching of reading. The book, instead, sets for itself a more modest goal: an analysis of a carefully selected group of reading practices that, while they have been strongly supported by certain reading experts, do not have support form the research findings on reading instruction.

Preventing Reading Failure *is intended for a wide audience.*

Preventing Reading Failure is intended for a wide audience. First, it was written to inform *reading teachers* about certain instructional practices they currently may use which are in need of reform. Second, the book addresses *teacher educators* at all levels: the college, school district, and state or federal levels. Since teachers generally practice what they have been taught this text is especially pertinent for the teachers of teachers.

Third, *school boards and other citizen groups* interested in school practices, but who are not reading professionals, need to know about teaching that is not in the best interests of children, if they are to properly supervise or criticize reading instruction. This text provides them such information.

Finally, the book is directed to *legislative bodies* who are in a position to influence school policies. How these legislative bodies can help reform the teaching of reading is described in the sections of this book called "Why the Myths of Reading Instruction Prevail" and "Can the Myths of Reading Instruction be Dispelled?"

Dangers of the Myths

A waste of teacher time and effort results . . .

The principal danger of using unsubstantiated assumptions as guidelines for the teaching of reading is immediately apparent. A waste of teacher time and effort results when wrongful presumptions are made about this instruction. Teaching time is a precious commodity in the modern school. The time that can be given to reading instruction always must compete with demands for the teacher's attention made from numerous other school subjects. Misuse of the limited time available for reading instruction in schools thus invariably has a negative effect on the rate at which children acquire reading skills.

In short, nothing retards pupils' acquisition of reading ability as much as ineffectual teacher efforts.

Without fear of contradiction, it can be said that erroneous notions by teachers as to how reading is best taught finally result in poor pupil performance on reading tests. In short, nothing retards pupils' acquisition of reading ability as much as ineffectual teacher efforts.

The Myths and Phonics

It will become increasingly clear to the reader of *Preventing Reading Failure* that the misapprehensions about reading instruction that it describes stem basically from the negative views about the direct, intensive, systematic, and early teaching of phonics* held by many reading educators since the turn of the century.

Direct teaching of phonics is instruction given to pupils in a deductive, straightforward manner. Here the teacher explains or demonstrates to children exactly what they are to learn. It is expected that these learners will acquire the precise phonics knowledge that the teacher plans for them to attain.

Intensive phonics teaching is that given on a regular basis, at least daily, often more than once a day. Special times are set aside for this instruction, and much time is given over to practice and drill on what is to be learned.

To teach phonics *systematically* to children is to arrange the subunits of this body of knowledge into a hierarchy of difficulty. According to this procedure, children first learn the aspects of phonics that are seen to be the least difficult to acquire. The teaching of each successive unit of phonics is carefully integrated with what has previously been taught.

By the *early* teaching of phonics is meant the initiation of this teaching to children as soon as they enter elementary school. The evidence of children's readiness for this learning is obtained through their responses to this teaching. Reteaching of phonics skills is a common practice here, since individual children respond to the early teaching of phonics in different ways.

*Phonics is information about the relationships between the way we speak words and the way we spell them. English is an alphabetic language that, when written, uses letters to represent speech sounds (e.g. //kat/ = *cat*). Instruction in phonics includes teaching pupils to consciously identify the speech sounds and to recognize that letters are used to represent them. Pupils are trained to use this phonics information to decode the names of unknown written words.

Direct teaching of phonics is instruction given to pupils in a deductive, straightforward manner.

By the early *teaching of phonics is meant . . .*

History of Opposition to Phonics

The history of opposition to the early, intensive teaching of phonics is almost as old as the origin of phonics itself.[1] Disagreements with the phonics method came within less than a century after it was proposed in 1527. Lubinus offered the essence of the *whole word* or *look-and-say* method in 1614.

By 1779, there had appeared even stronger defenders of the whole-word method. In Germany, Gedike argued that it is neither necessary nor useful for children to begin reading with a knowledge of the individual letters; that it is not only far more pleasant but also far more useful for the child if it learns to read entire words at once, he insisted.

To this effect, Jacotot (in 1823) suggested that pupils first memorize the words in a sentence. Shortly thereafter a whole-word method surfaced in the USA.

To Worcester belongs the distinction of being the first American author, in 1828, to advocate the whole-word method.[2] He believed that beginning readers should first learn to read words by seeing them, hearing them pronounced, and having their meaning illustrated. Only after this would the child learn to analyze words or name the letters of which they are composed.

The early whole-word methods did concede that phonics should be taught -- but only after beginning readers had first learned to recognize a number of whole words by "sight," as this form of identification later came to be called.

The battle for the ascendancy of the whole-word method was not won in the 1800's, however.

The battle for the ascendancy of the whole-word method was not won in the 1800's, however. It is true that this method was accepted by a few other writers of basal readers during Worcester's time, and even some prominent educators of the period saw its value. Horace Mann, for instance, believed that there were many advantages in beginning with whole words. Despite endorsements of this kind, the whole-word method found no widespread support in the nineteenth century. The loyalty of teachers up to this point stayed, instead, with phonics-based instructional materials, especially the McGuffey Readers, or with a spelling method. In the latter method, children were taught to recognize words by spelling them aloud.

It was a handful of influential educators at the turn of the century who rescued the whole-word method from the doldrums into which it had fallen. There is no question but that the man most responsible for the word method triumph in the twentieth century was Colonel Francis Parker, first director of the University of Chicago School of Education.[1] Parker, along with John Dewey and G. Stanley Hall, realized that the whole-word method fitted well into their notion of "progressive" education, as did the Progressive Education Association (which was founded by their followers). After 1912, progressivists in elementary education also tended toward a belief in Gestalt psychology, which had tenets compatible with those of the whole-word method. For example, Gestalt psychology of that time held that our experience is always perceived by us as a totality.

From at least 1908 onward, there was further strong support for the notion of delaying any instruction in phonics from the textbooks on reading methodology. In that year, it was suggested that new words are best learned by hearing or seeing them in context. Phonics was condemned as dangerous before the age of eight or nine.[3] The writers who wrote the textbooks on reading methods in the present century were also the authors of our popular look-say basal readers and their teachers' manuals. These were basal readers in which recognizing words as "wholes" was the prime means of word recognition, and in which phonics was usually buried under masses of other material (Chall,1967).*

The "progressive" teacher educators of this period warned teachers that to be a phonics teacher was to become a mechanical taskmaster who compulsively drives pupils through parrot-like, even bizarre, drills on connecting letters in isolation, with facsimile speech sounds. Classes on phonics were described as repulsive, fear-ridden places, the disreputable depths into which teachers would inevitably fall if they phonics early and intensively.

*References given as numbers (1, 2, etc.) are found at the end of each chapter. References given as names (e.g., Chall, 1967) are found in the Bibliography at the end of the book.

The "progressive" teacher educators of this period warned teachers that to be a phonics teacher was . . .

The indifference of reading researchers in the first half of this century to challenging the validity of the whole-word method also abetted its dominance. Before 1958, these researchers appeared to have little or no interest in finding an answer to the question "If words are recognized by wholes, how are the wholes recognized?" The researchers had no more interest in this than did the authors of the textbooks for teachers on reading methods and of the basal readers of this time.

"If words are recognized by wholes, how are the wholes recognized?"

During the years 1924-35, 654 studies on reading were published. There appears to be only one study during that period designed to discover the cues that beginning readers use to recognize words. From 1938-57, no such studies were made. Between 1921 and 1957, there were 3,450 published studies in reading. Only one of them dealt with the question, "How are whole words recognized -- if they are so identified?"

Protests Against Look-Say Reading

The best-known protest in this century to the whole-word method was made by Flesch, in 1955.[4] His contention that the whole-word method was inferior to phonics for the development of the beginning reading skills was later confirmed by Chall's 1967 and 1983 reviews of the research on this question. The Bibliography of this volume presents many other reviews of the research on this issue, which come to the same conclusions as did Chall.

The best-known protest in this century to the whole-word method was made by Flesch, in 1955.

There are other negative criticisms that can be made of the assumptions made by advocates of delayed phonics. As noted, the advocates of the whole-word method in the present century came to rely on Gestalt psychology for an affirmation of their beliefs. This reliance was influenced by early studies that found that mature readers could recognize whole words as fast as, or faster than, single letters. From this finding it was concluded, but wrongly so, that beginning readers, as well as mature readers, see words as "wholes."

The advocates of the word method have continued to misjudge the studies made of the eye movements . . .

The advocates of the word method have continued to misjudge the studies made of the eye movements of young children while reading. The distorted view of these findings is demonstrated when they say that confirmation of the value of a whole-word method comes form early eye-movement studies in reading. The facts are that the data on eye movements of beginning readers in no way confirm the belief that these children see words as wholes. Later studies of the eye movements of children find that a child cannot be expected to recognize, within a single eye-fixation, more than one or two letters of the size usually used in a primer.[5]

Today there is impressive empirical evidence that children, in fact, do use letters as cues to word-recognition from the time they learn to read words. There is no evidence, however, to support the notion that the whole-word method enables beginning readers to look at a word and say it without going through any kind of analysis.[6] So, to argue that the beginning reader uses no cues for the recognition of an unknown word, except in a meaningful sentence context, begs the question, "How were the other words in the sentence recognized?" Consequently, the major premise of the whole-word method -- that beginning readers first see words only as wholes, through an exclusive use of context cues -- is a non sequitur.

The New Anti-phonics Movement

This short history of the traditional objection to phonics helps put into perspective the ideas of more recent group of opponents to phonics. This latter group of negative critics of phonics has appeared in the wake of Chall's report in 1967 of the research on the relative merits of phonics. This present group is spearheaded by Frank Smith,[7] whose books on reading provide the theory and the rationale for this new anti-phonics movement, and by Kenneth Goodman,[8] who censures phonics in most of his writings about the techniques of reading instruction.

Smith makes clear his belief that phonics is the great fallacy of beginning reading instruction. One of his twelve easy ways to make learning to read difficult is to ensure that phonics skills are learned and used. Goodman[8] agrees that phonics (in any form) in reading instruction is at best a peripheral concern. Obviously, the new anti-phonics evaluates the usefulness of phonics in a way fundamentally different than its traditional opponents. The latter opposed only the teaching of phonics early and intensively in the reading program.

The members of the new anti-phonics movement, which came into being after 1967, have made many negative remarks about phonics teaching. These criticisms are voiced in a confident-sounding, authoritative manner. It will be demonstrated in *Preventing Reading Failure,* however, that these critics of phonics can find little or no support for their view from the empirical research.

For example, the new detractors of phonics teaching claim that too much emphasis has been placed on phonics and that its teaching makes reading a difficult or incomprehensible task.[9;10;11;12;13] The critics of phonics further argue that phonics teaching is likely to do more harm than good, since it is impossible for children to identify the name of a word from the speech sounds that its letters represent.[14;15;16;17] Children's inabilities to learn to read are not caused by phonics problems, it is said, because it is not difficult to find children who over-rely on phonics.[18;19;20;21;22;23] Reading teachers are thus advised not to be concerned with words, letters, and word recognition.[24;25;26]

Some negative critics of the intensive teaching of phonics say that only a "little dab" of phonics is needed by children. They believe that more phonics instruction will simply make the poor reader worse off.[27;28;29;30;31] Such critics see the intensive teaching of phonics as an "overemphasis" of this instruction.[32;33;34;35]

There are many reading experts who judge that this "overemphasis" on phonics, as they call it, interferes with children's abilities to comprehend what they read.[36;37;38;39;40;41;42;43;44;45;46;47] They contend that remedial reading classes are filled with children who know how to use phonics quickly and accurately.[48;49]

The opponents of phonics also distrust it because they believe English is spelled so unpredictably that phonics, even if learned, cannot function.[28;50;51;52;53] They see phonics as almost useless for sounding out words, since each letter in a word represents to many speech sounds.[12]

A final argument against phonics teaching is that children learn to read as naturally and as easily as they learned to understand speech and to speak. Why should direct teaching of phonics be undertaken, they aver, when children will develop their own rules for learning to read, much as they did when they learned to speak?[54;55;56;57;58]

It is not uncommon to read such critical remarks about phonics, even though they have not been corroborated by research evidence. These erroneous comments about phonics are found in many educational journals, in books written for teachers on the methodology of reading in-

The critics of phonics further argue that . . .

It is not uncommon to read such critical remarks about phonics, even though . . .

struction, and even in monographs on reading instruction sponsored by the two largest organizations in the world concerned with the development of literacy -- the International Reading Association and the National Council of Teachers of English.

The extent and frequency of these denunciations of phonics and the prestigious sources that publish them doubtlessly have mislead numerous reading educators into believing in their validity.

As an example of the intense publicity given to the new anti-phonics point of view, I found that during one recent five-year period, the *Reading Teacher,* an official organ of the IRA, published at least twenty-eight articles which were complimentary to the new anti-phonics position. During this extended period, the journal did not publish one article that was negatively critical of the anti-phonics viewpoint. Then, in recent national conventions, the NCTE and the IRA have scheduled few, if any, sessions on phonics, among the many hundreds of such meetings that they sponsor at their well-attended conclaves.

From these signs of condemnation and deemphasis of phonics, the naive, uninformed, or easily persuaded reading educator doubtlessly would assume that phonics has become increasingly discredited as a valid aspect of reading instruction.

Goals of this Book

The justification for *Preventing Reading Failure* rests on the degree to which intensive phonics teaching has been wrongly criticized by the new anti-phonics movement. This volume will serve its intended purpose as it demonstrates that the notions about reading instruction held by the new anti-phonics movement are the result of misinterpretations or neglect of the findings demonstrated by empirical research on phonics and other matters. If the material in this book helps dispose of certain widespread yet undocumented notions about phonics, it is apparent that the quality of reading instruction in our schools could be enhanced as a result.

The National Commission on Excellence in Education[59] reported that in 1983 there were 23,000,000 American adults in America who were functionally illiterate, with the percentage of illiteracy running as high as 40 percent among our minority youth. The Commission was correct in con-

The justification for Preventing Reading Failure *rests on the degree to which . . .*

The National Commission on Excellence in Education reported that in 1983 there were 23,000,000 American adults . . .

cluding that among the essential changes needed to help overcome this horrendous problem is "our better understanding of learning and teaching and the implication of this knowledge for school practice." *Preventing Reading Failure* is dedicated to the accomplishment of that goal.

References

1. Mathews, M. M. *Teaching to Read.* Chicago, IL; University of Chicago, 1966.

2. Smith, N. B. *American Reading Instruction.* Newark, DE: International Reading Association, 1965.

3. Huey, E. B. *The Psychology and Pedagogy of Reading.* Cambridge, MA: MIT, 1968 (first published in 1906).

4. Flesch, R. *Why Johnny Can't Read.* New York, NY: Harper, 1955.

5. Gaspar, R. and Brown, D. *Perceptual Processes in Reading.* London: Hutchison Educational, 1973.

6. Groff, P. "The Topsy-Turvy World of 'Sight' Words." *Reading Teacher,* 1974, 27, 572-578.

7. Smith, F. *Understanding Reading and Psycholinguistics and Reading.* New York, NY: Holt, Rinehart and Winston, 1971 and 1973.

8. Goodman, K. S. "Do You Have to be Smart to Read? Do You Have to Read to be Smart?" *Reading Teacher,* 1975, 28, 625-632.

9. Goodman, Y. and Altwerger, B. "Reading-How Does It Begin?" In G.S. Pinnell (Ed.), *Discovering Language with Children.* Urbana, IL: National Council of Teachers of English, 1980. p. 84.

10. Fleming, J. T. "Review of Development in Children's Language and Composition." in S.W. Lundsteen (Ed.), *Help for the Teacher of Written Composition: New Directions in Research.* Urbana, IL: ERIC Clearninghouse on Reading and Communication Skills, 1976. p. 21.

11. Ferreiro, E. and Teberosky, A. *Literacy Before Schooling.* Exeter, NH: Heinemann Educational, 1982. p. 276.

12. Smith, F. *Understanding Reading.* New York, NY: Holt, Rinehart and Winston, 1978.

13. Cushenbery, D. C. and Gilreath, K. J. *Effective Reading Instruction for Slow Learners.* Springfield, IL: Charles C. Charles, 1972. p. 84.

14. Hall, M. and Ramig, C. J. *Linguistic Foundations for Reading.* Columbus, OH: Charles E. Merrill, 1978. p. 53.

15. Cunningham, J. W.: Cunningham, P. M. and Arthur, S. V. *Middle and Secondary School Reading.* New York, NY: Longman, 1981. p. 4.

16. Hittleman, D. R. *Developmental Reading: A Psycholinguistic Perspective.* Chicago, IL: Rand McNally, 1978.

17. Lee, D. and Rubin, J. *Children and Language.* Belmont, CA: Wadsworth, 1979. p. 243.

18. Hoskisson, K. "Successive Approximation and Beginning Reading." *Elementary School Journal,* 1975, 75, 443-451. p. 446.

19. Melvin, M. P. "Psycholinguistics and the Teaching of Reading." *Elementary School Journal,* 1979, 79, 277-283. p. 282.

20. Ammon, R. "Generating Expectancies to Enhance Comprehension." *Reading Teacher,* 1975, 29, 245-249. p. 245.

21. Johnson, D. D. and Pearson, P.D. "Skills Management Systems: A Critique." *Reading Teacher,* 1975, 28, 757-764. p. 759.

22. Menosky, D.M. "The Three Cue Systems: #1-Graphophonic." In P.D. Allen and D. Watson (Eds.) *Findings of Research in Miscue Analysis: Classroom Implications.* Urbana, IL: National Council of Teachers of English, 1976. p. 79.

23. Allen, P. D. "Some General Implications Concerning Specific Taxomonomy Categories." In P. D. Allen and D. Watson (Eds.) *Findings of Research in Miscue Analysis: Classroom Implications.* Urbana, IL: National Council of Teachers of English, 1976. p. 73.

24. Garman, D. "Comprehension Before Word Identification." *Reading World,* 1977, 16, 279-287. p. 286.

25. Smith, E. B.; Goodman, K. S. and Meredith, R. *Language and Thinking in School.* New York, NY: Holt, Rinehart and Winston, 1976. p. 271.

26. Smith, F. and Goodman, K. S. "On the Psycholinguistic Method of Teaching Reading." *Elementary School Journal,* 1971, 71, 177-181. pp. 178-179.

27. Tonjes, M.J. and Zintz, M.V. *Teaching Reading/Thinking/Study Skills in Content Classrooms.* Dubuque, IA: Wm. C. Brown, 1981. p. 152.

28. Weaver, C. *Psycholinguistics and Reading: From Process to Practice.* Cambridge, MA: Winthrop, 1980. p. 90.

29. Lundsteen, S.W. "On Developmental Relations Between Language-Learning and Reading." *Elementary School Journal,* 1977, 77, 190-203. p. 199.

30. Cooper, J. D., et al. *The What and How of Reading Instruction.* Columbus, OH: Charles E. Merrill, 1979. p. 97.

31. Nicholson, T. *An Anatomy of Reading.* Sydney, Australia: Martin Educational, 1982. p. 90.

32. Farr, R. and Roser, N. *Teaching a Child to Read.* New York, NY: Harcourt Brace Jovanovich, 1979. p. 152.

33. Fox, B. C. "How Children Analyze Language: Implications for Beginning Reading Instruction." *Reading Improvement,* 1976, 13, 229-234. p. 233.

34. May, F. B. *Reading as Communication.* Columbus: Charles E. Merrill, 1982. p. 70.

35. Mangrum, C. T. and Forgan, H. W. *Developing Competencies in Teaching Reading. Columbus, OH: Charles E. Merrill, 1979. p. 170.*

36. Hillerich, R. L. "Comprehension Skills: The Question is . . . " *Reporting on Reading,* 1979, 5, 1-3. p. 3.

37. Harris, A. J. and Sipay, E. R. *How to Teach Reading.* New York, NY: Longman, 1979. p. 100.

38. Davis, A. R. "A Historical Perspective." In J. E. Alexander (Ed.), *Teaching Reading.* Boston, MA: Little Brown, 1979. p. 421.

39. Fishbein, J. and Emans, R. *A Question of Competence: Language, Intelligence and Learning to Read.* Chicago, IL: Science Research Associates, 1972. p. 188.

40. Smith, K.J. "Efficiency in Beginning Reading: Possible Effects on Later Comprehension." In S.F. Wanat (Ed.), *Language and Reading Comprehension.* Arlington, VA: Center for Applied Linguistics, 1977. p. 56.

41. Niles, J.A. and Graham, R.T. "Teacher Feedback as a Factor in Children's Oral Reading." *Reading in Virginia,* 1979, 7, 16-19. p. 17.

42. Ladd, E. "Review of Jeanne Chall, *Reading 1967-1977: A Decade of Change and Promise." Reading Teacher,* 1979, 32, 983-984. p. 984.

43. Downing, J. "What is Decoding?" *Reading Teacher,* 1975, 29, 142-144. p. 144.

44. Sherman, B. W. "Reading for Meaning: Don't Let Word Study Blind Your Students." *Learning,* 1979, 8, 40-44. p. 41.

45. Bettelheim, B. and Zelan, K. *On Learning to Read.* New York, NY: Alfred A. Knopf, 1982. p. 193.

46. Nieratka, S. "Miscue Analysis in a Special Education Resource Room." In K. S. Goodman (Ed.), *Miscue Analysis: Applications to Reading Instruction.* Urbana, IL: National Council of Teachers of English, 1973. p. 101.

47. Cunningham, P. "Knowledge for More Comprehension." *Reading Teacher,* 1982, 36, 98-101. p. 98.

48. Artley, A. S. "Psycholinguistics Applied to Reading Instruction." *Reading Horizons, 1980, 20, 106-111. p. 108.*

49. Goodman, K. S. "The 13th Easy Way to Make Learning to Read Difficult: A Reaction to Gleitman and Rozin." *Reading Research Quarterly,* 1973, 8, 484-493. p. 491.

50. Harris, A. G. "Graphic and Phonemic Proximity." In P. D. Allen and D. Watson (Eds.), *Findings of Research in Miscue Analysis: Classroom Implications.* Urbana, IL: National Council of Teachers of English, 1976. p. 31.

51. Artley, A. S. "Phonics Revisited." *Language Arts,* 1977, 54, 121-126. p. 122.

52. Readance, J. E.; Bean, T. W. and Baldwin, R. S. *Content Area Reading: An Integrated Approach.* Dubuque, IA: Kendall/Hunt, 1981. p. 33.

53. Smith, R. *Reading.* New York, NY: Cambridge University, 1978. p. 56; 63.

54. Sampson, M. R. and Briggs, L. D. "What Does Research Say About Beginning Reading?" *Reading Horizons,* 1981, 21, 114-118. p. 117.

55. Harste, J. C. "Children, Their Language and World: Initial Encounters With Print." In A. Humes (Ed.), *Moving Between Practice and Research in Writing.* Los Alamitos, CA: SWRL Educational Research and Development, 1981. p. 43.

56. Watson, D.J. "Helping the Reader: From Miscue Analysis to Reading Instruction." In K. S. Goodman (Ed.), *Miscue Analysis: Applications to Reading Instruction.* Urbana, IL: National Council of Teachers of English, 1973. pp. 104-105.

57. Goodman, K. S. "Miscues: Windows on the Reading Process." In K. S. Goodman (Ed.), *Miscue Analysis: Applications to Reading Instruction.* Urbana, IL: National Council of Teachers of English, 1973. p. 12.

58. Forester, A. D. and Michelson, N. I. "Language Acquisition and Learning to Read." In R. E. Shafer (Ed.), *Applied Linguistics and Reading.* Newark, DE: International Reading Association, 1979. p. 86.

59. National Commission on Excellence in Education. *A Nation at Risk.* Washington, D.C.: U. S. Department of Education, 1983.

Chapter I

Myth #1: Phonics Hinders Comprehension

The purpose of this chapter is to demonstrate that the argument that the acquisition of phonics knowledge hinders the development of pupils' comprehension of what they read is a false one. It will be shown, to the contrary, that the research indicates there is a positive and close relationship between pupils' knowledge of phonics and their comprehension of written materials.

The Attack on Phonics Teaching

Intensive phonics teaching has come under heavy attack over the years from certain reading experts. Prominent among the charges made by reading authorities against the use of phonics instruction is the claim that the intensive teaching of phonics will interfere with the development of children's reading comprehension abilities.

The strongest of the protests against phonics teaching contends that such instruction is a potential and powerful method of interfering in the process of learning to read.[1] Others agree that phonics instruction is likely to do more harm than good.[2] It is said that phonics problems are not the cause of children's inability to read written material.[3]

Other writers are equally severe in their castigations of phonics teaching. There is little relation in much of the phonic instruction to the realities of how beginning readers recognize words, one such critic remarks.[4] Others concur that in phonics teaching the child will be hindered from learning to read.[5] Phonics is said to be the least successful approach to teaching word recognition.[6] Some of the critics thus are sure that applying phonics to unfamiliar words is not likely to lead to their successful identification.[7] One of its leading opponents believes that phonics *in any form* in reading instruction is *at best* a peripheral concern.[8] This conclusion doubtlessly is based on his contention that psychology shows that the child's memory is so constrained that he or she could not possibly comprehend speech and writing if he or she analyzed individual words.[9]

Since it is held that converting letters to sounds accurately . . .

Since it is held that converting letters to sounds accurately is a process not directly related to reading comprehension,[10] it is claimed that whenever the child tries to apply phonics, both fluency and comprehension tend to suffer.[11] At least, some reading experts reflect, phonics decoding at times hinders comprehension. Its application supposedly can result in serious comprehension loss.[12]

Other negative critics of phonics teaching charge that children can learn to decode words fluently but yet cannot comprehend what they decode. One reading expert observes that the child who can decode words but who doesn't know what has been read is a common sight in many classrooms.[13] Others insist that it is not an infrequent occurrence to find a

Myth #1: Phonics Hinders Comprehension

child who can fluently decode words, yet be unable to give an adequate account of what has been read.[14] To this effect it is maintained that children who are at the decoding or word recognition level of reading indeed are not reading, since they are attaching no meaning to what they are reading.[15]

Another writer agrees that many teachers have discovered (among children who could pronounce the words correctly) many who do not know their meaning.[16] Some reading authorities call this condition "phonic disability." They believe that a child with this condition will be able to sound out words but will not be able to understand them.[17] In this case it is believed that a child may read very accurately and not be able to follow ideas in a story.[18] One writer contends that she has observed children who, in spite of their hard-won decoding skills, could not so much as read a page of simple material.[19] Yet another reading expert remarks, some children seem to be able to decode beautifully, but when questioned, apparently understand little of what they have read.[20] Others claim they know very well that some children can read well but do poorly on phonics exercises, while others can do the reverse.[21]

Some reading authorities call this condition "phonic disability."

It is paradoxical, says another writer, to find that the pupils who are the most obedient in following our instructions to sound out words are destined to have the most trouble.[22] He would agree that it is accurate to say that the unfortunate child who fastens too closely upon phonics teaching will likely fixate at this state and go no further.[23] The end result of this situation, it is observed, is that remedial reading classes are filled with youngsters who can sound out words fluently.[24] More than one critic of phonics teaching believes that clinics and special reading programs are filled with children who can sound out words fluently but still cannot construct meaning from what they so decode.[25]

More than one critic of phonics teaching believes that . . .

A careful reading of the recent negative criticisms of phonics teaching reveals that the opponents of this instruction often complain about the overemphasis of phonics teaching. This term usually is used as a synonym for intensive teaching. The detractors of phonics teaching never explain specifically what they mean when they denounce the "overemphasis" of phonics teaching.

A close examination of their comments on this matter makes it clear, nonetheless, that they believe limited amounts of phonics teaching, given in an indirect and incidental manner, are adequate to teach children to read. These critics of intensive phonics teaching would appear to agree with the writer who judged that when it comes to phonics in reading instruction, the motto "Just a little dab will do you" seems appropriate.[26]

Overemphasis upon the teaching of phonics -- that is, the intensive version of this teaching -- often is cited as dangerous. Teachers are warned that emphasis on letter-sound correspondences and phonics may produce readers who are not proficient either at identifying words or at getting meaning.[27] Others agree that far too much emphasis has been placed on the speech sound-letter relationship, as a building block in learning to read.[28] Some reading experts are confident that the use of complex word recognition strategies detracts from children's ability to obtain meaning.[29] This means that a heavy emphasis on decoding in the beginning instructional program supposedly may make comprehension tasks more difficult for large numbers of children.[30] The result: Time spent on teaching extensive word-analysis skills rarely pays off in helping children become avid, fluent readers, it is alleged.[31]

Yet other reading experts reiterate the viewpoint that there is danger . . .

Yet other reading experts reiterate the viewpoint that there is danger that decoding may be overemphasized to the detriment of comprehension.[32] Some allege that as a result of emphasis on phonics, some children may become slow, overly analytic readers.[33] One pair of critics of phonics stress that emphasizing phonics turns reading into a game with rules to follow in order to please the teacher, but robs it of meaning.[34] The danger of overemphasized phonics teaching is ever-present, too, caution some writers. They believe that any sequential intensive phonics program can easily lead to overemphasis on repetition and deadening drill.[35] The reading problems in schools thus derive from too much stress on the decoding of words, it is said.[36] There is danger of misleading children and creating future problems if you overemphasize phonics, one reading expert urges teachers to believe.[37]

These problems cited here are said to be caused by the inherent difficulty . . .

These problems cited here are said to be caused by the inherent difficulty of phonics for children, and by its lack of interest for them. We tend to think we facilitate learning to read by breaking written language into bite-size pieces for learners, one writer relates.[38] Instead, he argues, we turn it from an easy-to-learn language into hard-to-learn abstractions. Phonics teaching is an example where fragmenting and isolating components of written language makes reading an abstract and difficult task, others agree.[39] It is clear, some claim, that learning phonics may be un-

Myth #1: Phonics Hinders Comprehension

necessarily difficult for children, even unnatural and overly difficult for children, because it is an abnormal learning task.[31]

Thus, comprehension may not be the only casualty of phonics instruction, some reflect. Boredom and disinterest may result,[40] since it would be difficult to exaggerate the complexity and unreliability of phonics.[41] Some caution teachers that phonics teaching is a fundamentally incomprehensible aspect of reading instruction, to which children should not be exposed.[42]

It is even argued that phonics teaching may lead children to distrust the strategies for reading words that they have developed themselves from natural, ongoing encounters with written language.[43] If this were so, such teaching would not have long-range usefulness. One writer supports this view when he contends that among those practices which may actually hinder mature reading is to learn certain phonic procedures for sounding out large numbers of words.[44]

This sample of the negative judgments of reading experts, concerning the merit of phonics teaching, makes it clear that many reading authorities believe that this instruction inhibits reading comprehension. Moreover, they maintain that it is common to observe children who can decode fluently but who cannot comprehend the words that they decode. This same group of reading authorities contends that teaching phonics in an intensive manner to children is dangerous, because it inherently is a difficult and boring subject.

Research on the Phonics-Comprehension Connection

It is immediately noticeable, however, that these negative views of phonics teaching are seldom accompanied by any reference to empirical research. For example, one can readily find statements by reading experts to the effect that it is common to identify children who can decode fluently, but who cannot then comprehend the reading material that they so easily decode. Unfortunately, these statements do not provide references to experimental research in support of these conclusions. They appear to be opinions about this instruction, and not reflections of what the research says about this issue.

There have been many reviews of the published research on the relationships of phonics teaching and reading comprehension, since Jeanne

It is even argued that phonics teaching may lead children to distrust . . .

This same group of reading authorities contends that teaching phonics in an intensive manner . . .

Chall completed the first full-scale survey of this evidence in 1967. Chall's analysis of the research on this matter, from 1910 to 1965, led her to conclude that "The long-existing fear that an initial code [phonics] emphasis produces readers who do not read for meaning or enjoyment is unfounded."

"On the contrary, the evidence indicates that better results in terms of reading for meaning are achieved with the programs that emphasize code at the start" (p.307). Later,Chall (1979, p. 33) wrote: "Would my conclusion regarding the benefits of code-emphasis be the same today -- after 10 more years of research? I would tend to say 'yes,' since I do not see any viable data to disconfirm it." In 1983 Chall brought her review up to date, and made the same conclusion.

Since 1967, the continuing reviews of the research on the relationship of phonics instruction and reading comprehension largely have come to the same conclusions as did Chall on this matter. (Chall and the references to follow are a sample of those on this issue, included in the Bibliography at the end of this volume.)

Wardhaugh concluded that valid research evidence to support look-and-say and other whole-word methods over phonic methods does not exist and fair comparisons nearly always show phonics instruction to result in the development of superior reading achievement.

Gough and Cosky agree that the letter-by-letter (phonics) hypothesis is the strongest . . .

Gough and Cosky agree that the letter-by-letter (phonics) hypothesis is the strongest (i.e., the cleanest and the richest) idea anyone has had about word recognition. Gibson offers her support when she writes that the heart of learning to read would seem to be the process of mapping written words and letters to the spoken language. Vellutino echoes the idea that the child's task in learning to read is to decode print to his spoken language. Weigl goes further. To him, written language can be learned only as a consequence of the rule-governed correspondence between graphic and acoustic structures. The research evidence on phonics that Nickerson surveyed led him to conclude that perhaps there are no better ways to teach reading.

Downing and Leong found that the research findings suggest that facility in decoding and extraction of word meaning are related. Less skilled comprehenders are deficient or inefficient in the utilization of decoding skills. Perfetti and Lesgold agree that the research indicates

Myth #1: Phonics Hinders Comprehension

that general verbal coding facility is substantially correlated with reading achievement. Johnson and Lefton interpret the research similarly. In summary, they say, it appears that poor decoding skills can contribute significantly to poor comprehension.

The reviewers of the research on the relationship of phonics instruction and reading comprehension are especially convinced that the above conclusions apply to beginning reading. Resnick and Beck concluded that the large majority of scholars -- both psychologists and linguists -- argue that a fundamental task of initial reading is learning the structural relationship between written and spoken language, i.e., the grapheme-phoneme mapping. His survey of the evidence led Glushko to the conclusion that it seems undeniable that phonic or analytic instruction works for beginning readers.

To Ehri (1980) the research indicates that the task of beginning readers is to assimilate the word's printed form to its phonological structure. Liberman and Shankweiler agree that the child's fundamental task in learning to read is to construct a link between the arbitrary signs of print and speech. Kintsch has no doubts about this connection. He believes that, obviously, decoding here is crucial. The evidence which suggests the importance, for the early reader, of decoding the graphemic information into a phonological form, that McCuster, Hellinger, and Bias consulted, doubtlessly was that also read by Stanovich. He also reports that there is considerable evidence that phonemic segmentation and analysis skills that depend on explicit phonemic awareness are related to early reading success.

Recalling that the average English-speaking high school student can name 50,000 different written words, while the Chinese scholar can name only 4,000 logograms, Rozin and Gleitman reflect that it is no wonder that poor reading and poor phonological recoding skills are found to be so highly correlated among young readers.

Yet another survey of empirical data dealing with the question (Fowler, 1981) indicates that the sound system must be critically involved in the reading process independently of the reading level of the learner.

Golinkoff's (1978) critique of these data drew her to the conclusion that phonemic awareness skills -- both analysis and synthesis -- have been shown in a number of studies to be predictive of early and extended

. . . that poor decoding skills can contribute significantly to poor comprehension.

. . . the average English-speaking high school student can name 50,000 different written words, while the Chinese scholar can name only 4,000 logograms . . .

reading achievement. The research on this matter tells Layton that phonics is one of the truly independent reading techniques that will serve children into adulthood. Baron reports that the research indicates that it is important to use the rules relating to spellings and sounds because they are used in fluent reading. Those who wrote the influential *Bullock Report* for Great Britain's Department of Education and Science also found that the empirical evidence supports the conclusion that competence in phonics is essential both for attacking unfamiliar words and for fluent reading.

Some reviewers of the research contend that the empirical findings suggest that there are special ways that phonics knowledge and its application aids in the comprehension of reading. Barron (1978) believes that the evidence indicates that phonetic recoding plays a critical role in the comprehension of printed connected discourse by providing the reader with a strategy for maintaining in memory the wording of, for example, a sentence long enough for that sentence to be comprehended. Allport agrees that phonological coding in reading provides additional temporary storage after lexical access, until the meaning of larger syntactic units (phrases and sentences) has been satisfactorily analyzed. Levy's review of the research came to the same conclusion: Phonemic representation is important in reading largely because it acts as a good memory representation from which message comprehension can occur.

Allport agrees that phonological coding in reading provides additional temporary storage . . .

To Liberman, et al. (1977) the research findings offer the possibility that working from a phonetic base is natural and necessary if the reader (including even one who is highly practiced) is to take advantage of the primary language processes that are so deep in his experience and, indeed, in his biology. While Banks, Oka, and Shugarman concur that speech recoding seems to be one mechanism by which words are kept available for short periods, they see another possible role for phonics teaching: For determining the supra-segmental phonemes, rhythms, and stress patterns that mark phrase boundaries in speech but are not perceived in written text.

As noted, many reading experts are convinced that the intensive teaching of phonics, the overemphasis of this instruction, as they call it, is a dangerous practice. The experts in reading who have surveyed the research come to a different conclusion, however. To this effect, Holland indicates that *intensive,* systematic decoding programs result in better reading achievement than do other kinds of beginning reading programs.

Myth #1: Phonics Hinders Comprehension

Wallach and Wallach (in their review of the research) acknowledge that the child must be thoroughly trained to "break" the code, to transform the visual forms of letters into the sounds they represent. In short, declares Resnick, the charge that too early or too much emphasis on the code depresses comprehension finds no support in the empirical data.

Lesgold and Curtis' review of the existing research evidence affirms the conclusion that there is no data to substantiate any strong claim that children having trouble learning to read will, if taught in a phonics-loaded program, become "word callers." Indeed, to the contrary, Adams reports that children who have been taught to read *without* due emphasis on the mechanics of decoding are found to be at a disadvantage in the long run. Baron references research indicating that the child must learn phonics rules eventually if he is to have a full battery of reading skills. Since this is an inevitable requirement, there appears to be no reason that it should not be attained as soon as possible through intensive teaching. The fact that second- and third-grade pupils in code-emphasis instructional programs are at least as capable in reading comprehension as those whose instruction has been characterized by delayed, gradual phonics instruction, as reported by Dykstra, is yet further evidence that the intensive teaching of phonics does not have the dangerous shortcomings attributed to it by some reading experts.

Baron references research indicating that the child must learn phonics rules eventually . . .

The premise that the rapid, accurate, and automatic application of any skill requires extensive practice as a precursor to its accomplishment is a widely-held psychological principle. Keeping this principle in mind, one can identify several reviews of reading research that contradict the notion that the intensive teaching of phonics is dangerous. That is, several reviewers of research on phonics and reading comprehension have discovered that these findings indicate that the rapid, accurate, and automatic application of phonics is closely related to reading comprehension. To this effect, Samuels and Schachter explain that one important prerequisite is the development of decoding skills. These skills must be brought beyond the level of mere accuracy to the level of automaticity. When these skills become automatic, the student is able to decode the printed symbols without the aid of attention, thereby freeing attention for the all-important task of processing meaning.

These skills must be brought beyond the level of mere accuracy to the level of automaticity.

Barron (1978) agrees that one of the reasons phonics knowledge (decoding skill) correlates so highly with success in learning to read is that good decoders are individuals who can rapidly and accurately convert printed words into phonetic representations. Their review of the pertinent research led Gibson and Levin to the conclusion that decoding must become smooth and automatic before attention can be strongly concentrated on the meaning to be extracted.

Other critiques of the empirical evidence concur that fast decoding is critical (Perfetti, 1977), that good comprehenders decode accurately and rapidly (Carnine and Silbert), that teachers should be sure that word recognition skills are developed to the point they are automatic (Weaver), and that good readers seem to have automatized basic decoding skills (Golinkoff, 1975-1976).

It is unlikely that the rapid, accurate, and automatic application of phonics skills (found to be closely related to reading comprehension) could best be developed by incidental rather than intensive instruction. It is also improbable, therefore, that this intensive teaching incorporates the dangers claimed by the negative critics of phonics instruction.

The charge from the negative critics of intensive phonics instruction that there are children who can apply phonics in a rapid, accurate, and automatic manner and yet cannot understand the words they so decode is never accompanied by a reference to supporting published data. These pupils are called "word callers," or children who "bark at print."

In reality, however, there is no evidence to substantiate any strong claim that children having trouble learning to read will, if taught in a phonics-loaded program, become word callers (Lesgold and Curtis). Danks and Fears note, in fact, that there is considerable dispute over whether word callers really exist and over what the criteria should be for so labeling a child.

The notion that remedial classes are filled with children who have the skills needed . . .

They judge that there is serious question whether so-called word callers read aloud as fast and with the same number and type of errors as do other children, or read with normal intonation. The notion that remedial classes are filled with children who have the skills needed to effectively apply phonics knowledge also has been dispelled.

Groff[45] asked the directors of university reading clinics in thirty-four different states "Approximately what percent of remedial readers have such skills?" The median answer here was 10 percent.

Myth #1: Phonics Hinders Comprehension

One finds no support in reviews of the research literature for the charge that phonics teaching interferes with the development of children's reading comprehension, because it inherently is difficult and boring. The conclusions drawn from these surveys of the empirical evidence imply, to the contrary, that children are capable of learning and applying phonics; i.e., that they do not find it overly difficult to learn or distractingly irksome.

To this effect, Carroll and Walton[46] cite research showing that segmentation skills can be critical in learning to use phonics cues and that they are quite easily taught to nearly all children. Calfee[47] adds that working on phonics is an acceptable task to more children. In short, it seems illogical to assume that knowledge and skill of phonics, which relate so closely to success in reading acquisition, could be so difficult to learn and so unattractive to the leaner that it impedes the attainment of reading ability.

Conclusions

The charge that the teaching of phonics, and especially the intensive version of this instruction, interferes with the development of children's reading comprehension skills obviously is a serious and crucial accusation. All reading experts agree that gaining command of comprehension skills in reading is the ultimate and most important goal of instruction in this subject. Thus, any teacher behavior in the reading program that acts to inhibit the growth of comprehension is to be avoided by all means.

Thus, any teacher behavior in the reading program that acts to inhibit the growth of comprehension is to be avoided by all means.

It appears safe to say, however, that the rejection by teachers of intensive phonics instruction, in the hope that this would foster the development of children's reading comprehension, is foolhardy. The claims that this teaching interferes with the attainment of reading comprehension are not supported by research on this issue. To the contrary, the reviews of research on this matter confirm that intensive phonics instruction is a justified practice.

There are varied and numerous reasons why phonics teaching aids in the acquisition of reading skills, including comprehension of what is read. English writing is based on the alphabetic principle. That is, the speech sounds in our language are represented, in relatively predictable ways, by letters of the alphabet. Once children understand the workings of this code, they can decode, on their own, the names of unfamiliar written words. With continued practice in the use of this code, such decoding of written words becomes automatic -- easy, quick, and effortless. Without instruction in this code, however, children have difficulty learning to read.

The present discussion displays another example of an unfortunate aspect of the advice that has been given teachers. Displayed in this discussion is contradictory advice given to teachers on a vital aspect of instructional practice. As unfortunately has been the case elsewhere in the educational literature, the present discussion indicates that teachers have been given directly contrary recommendations for the teaching of reading. This conflicting advice stems largely from two mutually exclusive sources -- opinion and research findings.

On the one hand, it is the opinion of some reading experts that intensive phonics instruction is a hindrance to the development of children's reading comprehension. On the other hand, it is the conclusion of the reviewers of the research on this issue that phonics is closely related to reading comprehension, and therefore that it should be taught intensively, so that its learners can apply it in a rapid, accurate, and automatic way.

Venezky has noted that educators justify particular practices on the authority of the particular reading god they worship.

Venezky[48] has noted that educators justify particular practices on the authority of the particular reading god they worship. For the sake of effective reading instruction, teachers must resist this temptation. Instead, they should use for this purpose the facts offered by empirical research. Reasonable minded teachers will accept the advice that this research advances. In this way we can satisfactorily resolve the unnecessary controversy that now rages over phonics and reading comprehension.

Myth #1: Phonics Hinders Comprehension

References

1. Smith, F. *Psycholinguistics and Reading.* New York, NY: Holt, Rinehart and Winston, 1973.
2. Lee, D. M. and Rubin, J. B. *Children and Language.* Belmont, CA: Wadsworth, 1979.
3. Menosky, D. M. "The Three Cue Systems: #1--Graphophonic." In P. D. Allen and D. Watson (Eds.), *Findings of Research in Miscue Analysis: Classroom Implications.* Urbana, IL: National Council of Teachers of English, 1976.
4. Hittleman, D. *Developmental Reading: A Psycholinguistic Perspective.* Chicago, IL: Rand McNally, 1978.
5. Hoskisson, D. "Successive Approximation and Beginning Reading." *Elementary School Journal,* 1975, 75, 443-451.
6. Tonjes, M. J. and Zintz, M. V. *Teaching Reading/Thinking/Study Skills in Content Classrooms.* Dubuque, IA: Wm. C. Brown, 1981.
7. Readence, J. E.; Bean, T. W.; and Baldwin, R. S. *Content Area Reading: An Integrated Approach.* Dubuque, IA: Kendall/Hunt, 1981.
8. Goodman, K. S. "Do You Have to be Smart to Read? Do You Have to Read to be Smart?" *Reading Teacher,* 1975, 28, 625-632.
9. Smith F. and Goodman, K. S. "On the Psycholinguistic Method of Teaching Reading." *Elementary School Journal,* 1971, 71, 177-181.
10. Sherman, B. W. "Reading for Meaning: Don't Let Word Study Blind Your Students." *Learning,* 1979, 8, 40-44.
11. May, F. B. *Reading as Communication.* Columbus, OH: Charles E. Merrill, 1982.
12. Lapp, D. and Flood J. *Teaching Reading to Every Child.* New York, NY: Macmillan, 1978.
13. Cunningham, P. "The Clip Sheet: Knowledge for More Comprehension." *Reading Teacher,* 1982, 36, 98-101.
14. Niles, J. A. and Graham, R. T. "Teacher Feedback as a Factor in Children's Oral Reading." *Reading In Virginia,* 1979, 7, 16-19.
15. Blumberg, H. M. *A Program of Sequential Language Development.* Springfield, IL: Charles C. Thomas, 1975.
16. Davis, A. R. "A Historical Perspective." In J. E. Alexander (Ed.), *Teaching Reading.* Boston, MA: Little Brown, 1979.
17. Fishbein, J. and Emans, R. *A Question of Competence: Language, Intelligence and Learning to Read.* Chicago, IL: Science Research Associates, 1972.
18. Nieratka, S. "Miscue Analysis in a Special Education Resource Room." In K. S. Goodman (Ed.), *Miscue Analysis: Applications to Reading Instruction.* Urbana, IL: National Council of Teachers of English, 1973.
19. Chomsky, C. "When You Still Can't Read in Third Grade: After Decoding What?" In S. J. Samuels (Ed.), *What Research Has to Say About Reading Instruction.* Newark, DE: International Reading Association, 1978.
20. Hillerich, R. L. "Comprehension Skills: The Question is . . . " *Reporting on Reading,* 1979, 5, 1-3.
21. Johnson, D. D. and Pearson, P. D. "Skills Management Systems: A Critique." *Reading Teacher,* 1975, 28, 759-764.
22. Sherman, B. W. "Reading for Meaning: Don't Let Word Study Blind Your Students." *Learning,* 1979, 8, 40-44.
23. Henderson, E. H. "Reading is not Decoding." *Reading World,* 1978, 17, 244-249.
24. Goodman, K. S. "The 13th Easy Way to Make Learning to Read Difficult: A Reaction to Gleitman and Rozin." *Reading Research Quarterly,* 1973a, 8, 484-493.

25. Artley, A. S. "Psycholinguistics Applied to Reading Instruction." *Reading Horizons,* 1980, 20, 106-111.

26. Lundsteen, S. W. "On Developmental Relations Between Language-Learning and Reading." *Elementary School Journal,* 1977, 77, 190-203.

27. Weaver, C. *Psycholinguistics and Reading: From Process to Practice.* Cambridge, MA: Winthrop, 1980.

28. Fleming, J. T. "Review of Development in Children's Language and Composition." In S. W. Lundsteen (Ed.), *Help for the Teacher of Written Composition: New Directions in Research.* Urbana, IL: ERIC Clearinghouse on Reading and Communication Skills, 1976.

29. Mangrum, C. T. and Forgan, H. W. *Developing Competencies in Teaching Reading.* Columbus, OH: Charles E. Merrill, 1979.

30. Ladd, E. "Review of Jeanne Chall, *Reading 1967-1977. A Decade of Change and Promise." Reading Teacher,* 1979, 32, 983-984.

31. Melvin, M. P. "Psycholinguistics and the Teaching of Reading." *Elementary School Journal,* 1979, 79, 277-283.

32. Harris, A. J. and Sipay, E. R. *How to Teach Reading.* New York, NY: Longman, 1979.

33. Hall, M.; Ribovich, J. K.; and Ramig, C. J. *Reading and the Elementary School Child.* New York, NY: D. Van Nostrand, 1979.

34. Bettelheim, B. and Zelan, K. *On Learning to Read.* New York, NY: Alfred A. Knopf, 1982.

35. Aukerman, R. C. and Aukerman, L. R. *How Do I Teach Reading?* New York, NY: Wiley, 1981.

36. Collins, A. and Haviland, S. E. *Children's Reading Problems.* Urbana, IL: University of Illinois Center for the Study of Reading, 1979.

37. May, F. B. *Reading as Communication.* Columbus, OH: Charles E. Merrill, 1982.

38. Goodman, K. S. "Miscues: Windows on the Reading Process." In K. S. Goodman (Ed.), *Miscue Analysis: Applications to Reading Instruction.* Urbana, IL: National Council of Teachers of English, 1973b.

39. Goodman, Y. and Altwerger, B. "Reading--How Does it Begin?" In G. S. Pinnell (Ed.), *Discovering Language with Children.* Urbana, IL: National Council of Teachers of English, 1980.

40. Bush, C. L. and Huebner, M. H. *Strategies for Reading in the Elementary School.* New York, NY: Macmillan, 1970.

41. Smith, F. *Reading.* New York, NY: Cambridge University, 1978a.

42. Smith, F. *Understanding Reading.* New York, NY: Holt, Rinehart and Winston, 1978b.

43. Harste, J. C. "Children, Their Language and World: Initial Encounters with Print." In A. Humes (Ed.), *Moving Between Practice and Research in Writing.* Los Alamitos, CA: SWRL Educational Research and Development, 1981.

44. Smith, K. J. Efficiency in Beginning Reading: Possible Effects on Later Comprehension. Arlington, VA: Center for Applied Linguistics, 1977.

45. Groff, P. "Views on Phonics of Reading Clinicians." *Reading World,* 1977, 17, 93-98.

46. Carroll, J. B. and Walton, M. "Has the Reel Reeding Prablum Bin Lade Bear?" In L. B. Resnick and P. A. Weaver (Eds.), *Theory and Practice of Early Reading,* Vol. III. Hillsdale, NJ: Lawrence Erlbaum, 1979.

47. Calfee, R. C. "Memory and Cognitive Skills in Reading Acquisition." In D. D. Duane and M. B. Ransom (Eds.), *Reading, Perception and Language.* Baltimore, MD: York, 1975.

48. Venezky, R. L. "Harmony and Cacophany From a Theory-Practice Relationship." In L. B. Resnick and P. A. Weaver (Eds.), *Theory and Practice in Early Reading,* Vol. II. Hillsdale, NJ: Lawrence Erlbaum, 1979.

Chapter II

Myth #2: Unpredictable Spelling Invalidates Phonics

There is not an entirely regular matchup in English between the letters of the alphabet and the speech sounds that they represent. This fact leads some opponents of phonics to conclude that unless the application of a phonics rule results in the totally accurate pronunciation of words, it should not be taught to pupils learning to read. Recent research is discussed which disputes this contention. This research suggests that rather than putting limits on the number of phonics rules that are taught, as many of these rules should be taught as is possible.

Background of the Issue

In 1963, Clymer[1] reported on the first influential study of how frequently the application of various phonics rules would result in the true pronunciation of words. In the course of this study, Clymer asked the question: "Which phonics generalizations are useful?" Clymer decided that if a pupil applied a given phonics rule to twenty words, this rule would be considered useful if it aided the pupil in getting the correct pronunciation in fifteen of the twenty words. Thus came into being the now widely accepted 75 percent standard for utility of phonics rules.

Other reading researchers have accepted the validity of Clymer's 75 percent standard regarding the degree of utility of phonics rules. Since 1963, other studies of the extent to which phonics generalizations meet the Clymer 75 percent level of utility have been carried out.[2,3,4] The findings from these later studies were similar to Clymer's. Most significantly, these studies also rejected phonics rules which did not meet the Clymer standard for utility.

In short, their findings were deemed to confirm Clymer's notions about the utility level of phonics generalizations. According to some reading experts, the findings of these later studies do not change Clymer's implications in the slightest.[5]

Many authors of texts on the methods of reading instruction have accepted Clymer's proposition. They contend that unless the application of phonics rule results in the accurate pronunciation of a written word 75 percent of the time, that this application should not be considered useful.

A pair of these writers says that Clymer's type of study has been most useful in clarifying this aspect of the phonics program.[6] Others agree that some phonics rules should not be taught, since they are not useful. They advise teachers to consider 75 percent utility generalizations as helpful to children. Even recent texts for teachers (those concentrating solely on the teaching of phonics) accept this conclusion. One writer of such a book judges that "' research such as Clymer's has raised serious doubt about the validity of the phonics generalizations commonly included in courses, texts, and teaching materials.[7]

Thus came into being the now widely accepted 75 percent standard for utility of phonics rules.

Myth #2 - Unpredictable Spelling Invalidates Phonics

Those who oppose the teaching of phonics in general also use Clymer's evidence (as to the frequency with which the application of phonics rules results in the authentic pronunciation of written words) as a means to attack phonics. One leading opponent of phonics calls it the great fallacy of reading instruction, one of the twelve easy ways to make learning to read difficult. He sees phonics as a potential and powerful method of interfering in the process of learning to read. These conclusions stem from his conviction that the first objection to phonics as a way of reading is that it is conspicuously unreliable.[8]

Reading experts who agree with this so-called "psycholinguistic" approach to reading instruction add to the complaint that English spelling is so irregular that the application of phonics rules is not a useful practice. To this effect, some reading experts believe that speech sound-spelling relationships are tenuous at best.[9] They agree that these relationships are not consistent enough to make it possible to use phonics with any degree of regularity. They contend that there are so many exceptions to phonics rules that their application becomes trying and confusing, since the spellings of English do not always directly indicate the pronunciations of words.[10] They thus insist that it is misleading for the teacher to try to teach the child phonics.[11] Since they believe that the frequently taught phonics rules are not consistent enough to make it worthwhile to teach them, they argue that phonics rules can be successfully applied so seldom that it is questionable to have students learn them.[12]

Opinion to the Contrary on Phonics Rules

A few reading experts have challenged these assertions. They observe that mispronunciations produced by rules that relate letters to speech sounds are easily detected and corrected in context.[13] Others maintain that since one purpose of phonics teaching is to yield an approximate pronunciation of the unknown word, there is no need for letters to be completely determinative of sounds, in order for the knowledge of typical letter-speech-sound relationships to be enormously useful to the child.[14]

It is held that there is a powerful advantage to learners if through the use of phonics knowledge they can (at least to a rough approximation) pronounce a word that they have never before either heard or read.[15]

It is held that there is a powerful advantage to learners if through the use of phonics knowledge they can . . .

Even if the application of a phonics rule does not lead to precise pronunciation, it may still effectively lead a child to word recognition, it is said. That is, if at least some of the letter-speech-sound relationships are known and recognized, then! there will be enough glue to secure the visual symbols in one's memory.[16]

In addition, it is seen, perfectly predictable correspondences are not necessary because the reader has other cues to work with.[17] Even though the rules of English are far from perfect in their capacity to specify a pronunciation uniquely, they are usually good enough, especially with the help of context.[18]

In short, phonic analysis is seen as a tool to use ...

In short, phonic analysis is seen as a tool to use in making an intelligent guess as to the oral equivalent of the printed word.[19] One advocate of this point of view reasons that this phenomenon operates in the following way: As letters in a word are identified, an entire neighborhood of words that share the same spelling features is activated in one's memory, and the pronunciation of the given word emerges through the coordination and synthesis of many partially activated phonological representations.[20] None of these writers could cite any empirical evidence for their defenses of the value of gaining approximate pronunciations of words through phonic analysis, however. The absence of any published research findings on this issue helps explain this noticeable omission. It is clear, on the one hand, that these opinions about the usefulness of gaining the approximate pronunciations of words through the application of phonics rules were based on personal observations or logical reasoning, but not on research findings.

New Evidence on the Issue

It is just as obvious, however, that the reading experts who have demanded Clymer's 75 percent utility for phonics generalizations, if they are to be seen as useful, have not paused to reflect: "If a child can gain an approximate pronunciation of a written word through the application of phonics rules, can he or she then infer and produce the true pronunciation of this word?" Because of the absence of research finding on either side of this issue, I designed a study to investigate whether pupils who hear a word mispronounced,so as to follow phonics rules, in a story-like context, can infer and reproduce the true pronunciations of

Myth #2 - Unpredictable Spelling Invalidates Phonics

these words.[21] For example, if pupils hear find pronounced /fĭnd/, can they infer and reproduce its correct pronunciation?

The major assumption of my study was that the mental activity that pupils undertake when they infer and reproduce the true pronunciations of irregularly-spelled words that have been mispronounced according to phonics rules is analogous to the mental processing they use to decode irregularly-spelled written words.

For example, it is surmised that as pupils decode *head*, using phonics rules, they will pronounce the word as /hēd/. It further is deduced that after this point in the decoding of *head*, pupils can infer and correct their mispronunciation of *head* through the use of context and semantic cues that are available in connected discourse.

My study postulated that this description of how pupils decode irregularly-spelled words is an acceptable one. Therefore, the inferences made by pupils to correct the mispronunciations of irregularly-spelled words read aloud to them should be comparable to the inferences they make when they decode irregularly-spelled written words.

For support of this hypothesis one can appeal to the substantial empirical evidence that has dealt with the question: Does reading require the same kind of memory representation as speech? A review of this research concludes that we may expect reading to share many processes in common with the perception of speech.[15] In both these forms of communication it appears that the perceiver makes use of a phonetic representation in order to comprehend the message.

In another analysis of the research relevant to this question it was convincingly demonstrated that reading is the process of comprehending in print what is already understood when spoken. This reviewer[22] maintains that the research suggests how reading and listening with comprehension use the same language signals. Reading uses the same language and conceptualizing skills and knowledges that are used in listening with comprehension. The parallels of mental processing in the apprehension of written and spoken messages has been documented in the research.[23]

The internal language signals that are derived from listening to speech thus seem to be highly similar to the internal language signals that are

A review of this research concludes that . . .

The parallels of mental processing in the apprehension of written and spoken messages has been documented in the research.

19

It therefore appears reasonable to assume that second-grade children . . .

developed from reading written language. It therefore appears reasonable to assume that second-grade children, such as those in my study, when presented with words mispronounced according to phonics rules, in sentence contexts, would use similar mental processes to infer their correct pronunciation, whether these mispronounced words were the results of reading or listening.

Each of the forty-nine second-graders in my study was examined in a standardized fashion. First, each pupil was released from his or her classroom so as to meet individually with me out of the hearing and visual range of his or her classmates. At this point, each pupil was read aloud an identical set of instructions and other material to which the pupil had been requested to listen.

To this effect, I said to each of the pupils in the study: "I am going to read you a story. Listen carefully. One of the words in each sentence of the story will sound funny. You tell me how to say that word." At the end of each sentence read aloud, the investigator paused to allow the individual child to respond. Each of the forty-nine pupils in this study heard, one at a time, the following story-like discourse:

> A boy (girl) is hurt on the playground. He (she) goes to see the nurse. The nurse says, "Which room are you *from*? Do you *have* a headache? Did you bump your *head*? Were you hit by a *ball*? I'll *give* you a pill. I can *find* a pill for you. Take *both* of these pills. Take the *paper* off each pill. *Put* them into your mouth. Now lie on the *bottom* bed. Rest now, and listen to the *music*. Remember. Always tell the *truth* to the nurse. Don't keep a *secret* from the nurse. Try to help *her* to help you.

During this oral reading, the fourteen italicized, irregularly-spelled key words in the above discourse were pronounced as if they conformed to phonics rules. Accordingly, the key words were mispronounced in these ways:

> *from* as /frŏm/; *have* as /hāv/; *head* as /hēd/; *ball* as /băl/; *give* as /gĭv/; *find* as /fĭnd/; *both* as /bŏth/; *paper* as /păpər/; *put* as pŭt//; *bottom* as /bŏtəm/; *music* as /mŭsik/; *truth* as /trŭth/; and *secret* as /sĕkrĕt/ and *her* as /hĕr/.

Myth #2 - Unpredictable Spelling Invalidates Phonics

The data gathered in my study suggest that by the end of their second grade of schooling pupils can readily infer and produce the correct pronunciations of irregularly-spelled, high-frequency words that have been mispronounced so as to conform to specified phonics rules.

Only fifty-one, of 7.4 percent, of the 686 responses given by the pupils in my study (to these mispronounced words) resulted in incorrect reproductions of these words. The findings of this study suggest, however, that it is significantly more difficult for beginning readers to make similar inferences with certain irregularly-spelled words such as *ball*, *find*, *paper*, and *her*. Apparently, the vowel phoneme-grapheme correspondences in these words are more difficult to infer than are the correspondences in other words examined in my study.

The findings of this study suggest, however, that it is significantly more difficult . . .

The findings of my study do not support the conclusions drawn first by Clymer, and later by other reading experts, that the application of a phonics rule must result in the true pronunciation of a written word 75 percent of the time for this rule to be deemed a useful one.

My study assumed that it is reasonable to deduce that beginning readers will make similar kinds of inferences about the pronunciations of irregularly-spelled written words that they decode as they did of the mispronounced words I read to them in the present investigation. If this assumption is correct, the only kind of phonics rules that could be classified as not useful for word recognition would be those in which the application results in mispronunciations that pupils cannot correctly reproduce as true pronunciations.

In my study, the only phonics rules that might be considered as having lesser utility would be those that pertain to the vowel sounds in *ball*, *find*, *paper*, and *her*. I found that 18, 22, 20, and 16 percent of the pupils in my study, respectively, failed to infer and reproduce the correct pronunciations of these words.

In my study, the only phonics rules that might be considered as having lesser utility . . .

Implications of the Study

Despite the fact my study found that a few mispronounced vowel sounds were relatively difficult for children to reproduce accurately, its main finding was the generally high rate of success that young children had with this task. In fact, my study, apparently the first of its kind, suggests that there is a far greater usefulness to be found in the teaching of phonics than even its most fervent advocates had previously imagined.

If it is true that the application of phonics rules in general will result in approximate pronunciations of words (close enough to their true pronunciations that children can correctly infer and reproduce the true pronunciations of these words), the importance of teaching phonics obviously is supported and reinforced. The findings of my study suggest that rather than teaching a few phonics rules we should teach as many as possible. Bliesmer and Yarborough[24] concluded from their research that the number of phonics rules taught should be of a sufficiently large number that pupils are equipped with the means for independent decoding of words.

Furthermore, my study appears to explain why it is critical that such a goodly number of phonics rules should be taught. And, if it is crucial that a large set of phonics rules be successfully taught, it is also highly likely that the best way to achieve this goal is to teach these rules in an early, intensive, direct, and systematic fashion.

Such teaching requires the setting up of a hierarchy of phonics skills beginning with those thought to be the easiest for children to learn. There is general agreement among intensive phonics programs that predictable speech sound-letter correspondences that occur in monosyllabic words be taught first. This phonics teaching is scheduled to take place on a regular daily basis. Careful records are made of pupil progress so that any necessary reteaching can be undertaken promptly. Such instruction should proceed in a deductive manner. That is, it is made clear to pupils what they are to learn and they are given much practice in this skill attainment procedure.

Furthermore, my study appears to explain why it is critical that such a goodly number of phonics rules should be taught.

Myth #2 - Unpredictable Spelling Invalidates Phonics

References

1. Clymer, T. "The Utility of Phonic Generalizations in the Primary Grades." *Reading Teacher*, 1963, 17, 252-258.
2. Bailey, M. H. "The Utility of Phonic Generalizations in Grades One through Six." *Reading Teacher,* 1967, 20, 413-416.
3. Burmeister, L. E. "Usefulness of Phonic Generalizations." *Reading Teacher,* 1968, 21, 349-356.
4. Emans, R. "The Usefulness of Phonic Generalizations Above the Primary Grades." *Reading Teacher,* 1967, 20, 419-425.
5. Spache, G. D. and Spache, E. B. *Reading in the Elementary School.* Boston, MA: Allyn and Bacon, 1977. p. 380.
6. Dauzat, J. A. and Dauzat, S. V. *Reading: The Teacher and the Learner.* New York, NY: John Wiley, 1981. p. 122.
7. Mazurkiewicz, A. J. *Teaching About Phonics.* New York, NY: St. Martin's, 1976. p. 105.
8. Smith, F. *Psycholinguistics and Reading.* New York, NY: Holt, Rinehart and Winston, 1973. p. 1986.
9. Harris, A. G. "Graphic and Phonemic Proximity." In P. D. Allen and D. Watson (Eds.), *Findings of Research in Miscue Analysis: Classroom Implications.* Champaign, IL: National Council of Teachers of English, 1976.
10. Artley, A. S. "Phonics Revisited." *Language Arts,* 1977, 54, 121-126.
11. Chomsky, C. "Language and Reading." In R. E. Shafer (Ed.), *Applied Linguistics and Reading.* Neward, DE: International Reading Association, 1979.
12. Friedman, M. I. and Rowls, M. D. *Teaching Reading and Thinking Skills.* New York, NY: Longman, 1980.
13. Gough, P. B. and Hillinger, M. L. "Learning to Read: An Unnatural Act." *Bulletin of the Orton Society,* 1980. 30, 179-196. p. 186.
14. Wallach, M. and Wallach, L. *Teaching All Children to Read.* Chicago, IL: University of Chicago, 1976. p. 161.
15. Liberman, I. Y. and Shankweiler, D. "Speech, the Alphabet, and Teaching to Read." In L. B. Resnick and P. A. Weaver (Eds.), *Theory and Practice of Early Reading,* Vol. II. Hillsdale NJ: Lawrence Erlbaum, 1979. p. 111.
16. Ehri, L. C. "The Development of Orthographic Images." In U. Firth (Ed.), *Cognitive Processes in Spelling.* New York, NY: Academic, 1980. p. 313.
17. Venezky, R. L. "Theoretical and Experimental Bases for Teaching Reading." In T. A. Sebeok (Ed.), *Current Trends in Linguistics.* The Hague: Mouton, 1974. p. 2074.
18. Baron, J. "Mechanisms for Pronouncing Printed Words: Use and Acquistion." In D. LaBerge and S. J. Samuels (Eds.), *Basic Processes in Reading: Perception and Comprehension.* Hillsdale, NJ: Lawrence Erlbaum, 1977. p. 205.
19. May, F. B. *Reading as Communication.* Columbus, OH: Charles E. Merrill, 1976. p. 69.
20. Glushko, R. J. "Principles for Pronouncing Print: The Psychology of Phonography." In A. M. Lesgold and C. A. Perfetti (Eds.), *Interactive Processes in Reading.* Hillsdale, NJ: Lawrence Erlbaum, 1981. p. 62.
21. Groff, P. "A Test of the Utility of Phonics Rules." *Reading Psychology,* 1983. 4, 217-225.
22. Sticht, T. G., et al. *Auding and Reading: A Developmental Model.* Alexandria, VA: Human Resources Research Organization, 1974. p. 209.

23. Guthrie, J. T. and Tyler, S. J. "Psycholinguistic Processing in Reading and Listening Among Good and Poor Readers." *Journal of Reading Behavior,* 1976. 8, 415-46.

24. Bliesmer, E. P. and Yarborough, B. H. "A Comparison of Ten Different Beginning Reading Programs in First Grade." *Phi Delta Kappan,* 1965. 56, 500-504.

Chapter III

Myth #3: Sight Words

Examined in this chapter is the validity of a highly consequential contention of the new anti-phonics movement. This is the issue of "sight" words. Those who negatively criticize phonics teaching base their opposition to this instruction largely on a supposition that young pupils do not need to learn to decode words via phonics because they can recognize them more easily and quickly on "sight" as "wholes." This chapter demonstrates that the idea of "sight" words is not supported by the research, and appears to be based solely on subjective judgment.

Sight Words: A Popular Supposition

The notion that children learning to read should be taught, first of all, to recognize whole words, or "sight" words, as they are commonly called, persists to the present time. As was so in the past, today's teachers of reading are told the first step of any reading program should be to train children to recognize a certain number of "whole" words. "Whole-word" identification supposedly will enable a child to look at a word and say it, without going through any types of analyses.[1]

In reading sight words, some writers profess, the child goes through no evident analytic process as his eye sweeps across each word.[2] Sight words thus are words which readers purportedly learn to recognize without having to analyze them.[3] Some reading experts insist that there are hundreds of words which cannot be sounded out by applying letter-speech sound analysis.[4] Children learning to read in this way have no choice but to learn such words as wholes, it is claimed.

The use by the child of the configuration, overall outline, shape, or length of a sight-word as an aid to its recognition is approved of. Today's advocates of sight words remain convinced that these words be learned from their general shape, configuration, or contour.[5] Children may be taught to recognize a word on the basis of configuration as a sight word, it is claimed.[6] Learning words by their shapes, as they appear, is the first stage in the sequence of phonics, one reading expert says.[7]

The special advantages or values of sight words generally are thought, by their advocates, to be self-evident. That is, their defenders rarely go beyond the basic defense made for sight words -- that is, the beginning reader has to know them in order to begin analyzing words and using other word-attack approaches to meaning and recognition.[8] Sight words, it is said, are useful since they form the basis for studying phonetic and structural elements of words.[9]

Sight words are needed, it is argued, when the phonics principles involved are not yet within the child's grasp and he needs the word for immediate use.[10] Sight words come first. Later pupils combine meaning, phonic, and possibly structural clues -- but not at the outset.[3] This sequence is judged best in most circumstances.[11]

Children learning to read in this way have no choice but to learn such words as wholes, it is claimed.

Often repeated is the traditional notion that the acquisition of an initial sight vocabulary is one of the first steps the child takes in a successful reading program. It provides the foundation on which to teach word attack and other vital reading skills.[12] Word recognition thus begins with acquisition of a large repertoire of immediately recognized words.[13] Reading instruction should begin with teaching children a core of sight words;[14] without it, there will be little, if any, progress in learning to read, it is claimed.

Supposedly, it is also as easy for the beginning reader to learn to identify sight words as it is to identify letters.[15] Then, the learning of sight words is said to minimize the time the child spends on word recognition, and thus acts to get children reading immediately.[16] Sight words keep meaning in the limelight.[11] Besides acknowledging that such learning leads to immediate success in the interpretation of meaning, some declare that it lengthens the eye span, increases speed at the outset, and gives the beginner early satisfaction.[10]

The general procedure for the teaching of sight words remains in force, say many of today's defenders of this idea. No visual analysis supposedly is made of sight words in the course of the beginning reader's recognition of them. It is necessary, therefore, that a student has repeated exposures to a word he/she is to learn by sight.

It is emphasized, however, that the teacher does not call attention to any of the letters in a sight word, nor have the learner use letters as cues to its recognition.[17] The whole word method of teaching reading usually involves heavy repetition as one of the important teaching strategies.[18]

The whole word method of teaching reading usually involves heavy repetition as one of the important teaching strategies.

One writer says there must be thirty-eight repetitions in order for the average individual to recognize a single sight word.[14] Here, however, the defenders of sight words cannot agree. Some advise teachers not to develop them by repetition of words, with the notion that frequency of contact is an aid to retention.[19] A sight vocabulary grows spontaneously. There is little need to control the introduction of words, they argue.

One writer says there must be thirty-eight repetitions in order for . . .

The up-to-date proponents of sight words maintain that children need to learn frequently occurring words as early as possible. This early learning, they contend, is done faster through sight word teaching (the simple, repeated exposure technique) than through systematic phonics instruction. The quickest way to learn the high frequency words is to memorize them, they insist. These reading authorities claim that this look-say approach better develops pupil independence and reading comprehension than does phonics instruction.[20] And, sight words are easy to learn, they aver. It is often not necessary to provide special lessons on sight words. The child talks. It is written down. The child reads it back and thus learns sight words. The child simply knows them because the child has said them, explains one reading expert.[7]

The Issue Becomes Confusing

Which words should be selected for teaching as sight words?

Which words should be selected for teaching as sight words? The answers to this question vary. Some simply say these should be frequently used words.[8] Others contend there are fifty-four sight words: those that do not follow the common phonetic principles of the language.[21]

Some regard a sight word as a high frequency word that has an irregular spelling pattern and a high emotional content.[2] One gets lost on the way from the latter two criteria, however, to the examples these writers provide as a demonstration. Supposedly these are legitimate sight words: *after, but, didn't, his, much, must,* and *not.*

Other writers also appear to get confused at this point. Sight words (all the various parts of speech), one writer says, are irregular words that cannot be successfully recognized by word attack. Yet he offers as examples: *small, bat, bun, bone, skip, skunk,* and *bump.*[16]

To yet others the sight words to be taught first should be those that represent the smallest linguistic unit that can stand alone and that has meaning.[11] This would mean, of course, that any word with an affix, or any inflected word, could not be a sight word used in the first stage of reading instruction. All derivations and compound words therefore would be excluded as sight words, In short, only free morphemes could be sight words.

To his question, "Which words should be included in a list of sight words to be taught?" one writer answers, "function words."[22] These are the parts of speech other than nouns, verbs, adjectives, and adverbs (e.g., *in, an, and*). These are the proper sight words, he contends, since they are small in number, are stable, constitute 30 to 50 percent of all running words, and are phonetically irregular and difficult to pin a lexical meaning on.

This confusing argument among their supporters as to what sight words actually are persists. While some would restrict them to words whose spellings are irregular to some degree,[13] others believe that words on any list of basic words call for rote learning, as the strategy for instruction.[23] To the contrary, says another expert, who believes that there is no single sight vocabulary.[12] Sight words to her include those that occur frequently in print and those that children speak.

By far, the longest specific list of sight words has been about 900. One immediately is confronted by the contradictions in this presentation, however. It is said children may not be able to learn long words, like *nightingale* or *superintendent*, as sight words, but the words which may be effectively taught as sight words include: *pneumonia, phlegm, mnemonic.*[24] The largest group of potential sight words, however, were those offered by the writers who say sight words are any words that children cannot remember.[25]

The various opinions regarding the different aspects of sight word recognition contrast sharply with the lack of attention writers give to the critical issue concerning this matter. This is: What research evidence is there to substantiate the assorted statements made in the defenses of sight words?

One of the very few who venture an answer to this question suggests that confirmation of the value of a whole-word method came from early eye-movement studies in reading.[26] These investigations supposedly indicated that in a single eye fixation the reader recognizes whole words. The studies cited here are invalid as justification for teaching sight words, however. These studies showed that on occasion mature readers may have such eye movements, but not children learning to read.[27]

Some writers note that extensive studies have been devoted to the cues children can and do use in order to recognize words.[2] Which studies they believe those to be, and how they support a trust in sight words, are not divulged, however.

Others admit they don't know exactly how a given individual will remember sight words. They concede that beyond seeing the word in

Some writers note that extensive studies have been devoted to the cues children can and do use in order to recognize words.

meaningful context, a careful study of the visual components of the word is necessary.[9] Doing the latter analysis violates the usual definition of seeing a word by sight, of course. One writer concludes that efforts to discover how a beginning reader can read by sight have not been completely fruitful.[3] To what extent any of these "efforts" are "fruitful" confirmations of his faith in sight words, he does not reveal.

Research Clears the Air

In 1967, Jeanne Chall voiced the first well-publicized rejection by a professor of education . . .

In 1967, Jeanne Chall voiced the first well-publicized rejection by a professor of education of the notion that in beginning reading children first read words by sight. As she pointed out, the acceptance of this assumption was seldom questioned through the period covered by her study of reading practices. Her search through the studies on reading, which extended to before the turn of the century, thus revealed an important fact about sight words. Seldom has it been thought important by the experts in teaching reading to challenge the validity of the common suppositions about sight words. It becomes obvious, therefore, that experts before 1967, and since then, generally have accepted the speculations about sight words at their face value.

The research carried out related to this matter does not give comfort for such beliefs, however. This was research that in effect posed the question: If words are recognized as wholes, how are the wholes recognized? What does the reader look for, and in what way is his knowledge of what a whole word looks like stored? It is no answer to say he has already learned what every word looks like. That is the basic question -- What exactly does the reader know if he knows what a word looks like?

Attempts to answer such questions can be traced at least back to the 1920s. At this time, studies showed that beginning readers make eye fixations that could not be interpreted to mean they were seeing whole words.[27] These patterns of eye fixations instead suggested that beginning readers look at letters within a word in order to recognize it. Other studies reported that children frequently appear to learn words by observing some minute detail.[28] One researcher concluded from her study that certain letters or small groups of letters were the chief cues these young children used in reading words.[29]

In the 1930s, it was found that the beginnings and endings of words were most frequently observed and used as cues by children learning to read.[30] The children studied in this decade were letter conscious in the early stages of their reading progress.[31] The evidence from such studies seems to point to early and clear attention by young children to letter form and sounds as basic elements of, and keys to, reading, it was concluded.

A dearth of research on sight words characterized the next twenty years.

A dearth of research on sight words characterized the next twenty years. A significant return to this problem came in the 1950s. From a study of the growth of word perception abilities in children, one study concluded there is no support for the assumption that a sight vocabulary of seventy-five words should be established before word analysis instruction is given.[32]

In the 1960s, interest in determining the validity of sight words had sharply increased. It was reported that children who were learning to read words gave greater attention to the first letter or two and the middle letters were given less attention than any other part of the word.[33] This finding corroborated those of earlier research.[28;34;30] Research in the 1970's also found this is so.

This evidence explains that children in the early stages of learning to read a word tend to get the initial segment correct.

This evidence explains that children in the early stages of learning to read a word tend to get the initial segment correct. They fail on subsequent ones because they do not have the conscious awareness of phonemic segmentation needed specifically in reading.[35] Others found that kindergarten children discriminate among similar length words of different shape on the basis of specific letter differences.[36] It was discovered when kindergarten children were asked to match letters, versus words, that matching all of the single letters of the words to be learned later was superior to training in matching the same words.[37]

From a study of first graders' perception of word elements, it was concluded that growth in recognition vocabulary, in beginning reading, is related to perception of word elements.[38] Also indicative that young children pay attention to letters in words was the finding of a significantly higher correlation between reading achievement and the ability to rearrange the letters of scrambled words of grade two pupils ($r = .73$) than of grade six pupils ($r = .53$).[39]

The 1960s also were distinguished by other studies that refuted the validity of sight words. In one of these it was found that training that forces attention to each letter is less likely to lead to subsequent reading

It was also found that first graders' abilities to recognize letters in words does have a significant effect on the rate at which children learn words.

errors than training that permits the child to identify whole words on the basis of a single feature.[40] It was also found that first graders' abilities to recognize letters in words does have a significant effect on the rate at which children learn words.[41]

A most useful means for determining whether children read sight words was an intricately designed study in which kindergarten and first grade children matched a given pseudoword (for example, VEJAT) to one of five other pseudowords. Each of these five other words contained only one cue from the first word. They each were the same as the first word in only one way. For example, VEJAT was shown to the child. Then the child looked at the following five words.

Beyond the first letter, these five words are the same as VEJAT only in the indicated way: VOPUF (shape); VETEP (second letter); VHJUO (third letter); VUMAG (fourth letter); and VISHT (fifth letter). The child matched one word out of the five he thought was the same as VEJAT. It was found that the least-used cue in reading these pseudo-words, and other three-letter pseudowords, was shape. Shape was a significantly more limited cue than the next weakest cue, the fourth letter.

Another study of a similar design with children from the kindergarten and the first grade again found shape was chosen by these children significantly less often (as cues to the recognition of pseudowords) than first and last letters. The principal conclusion here was that children do not match words on the basis of configuration as much previous data and a good bit of lore would have it.[43] Yet another study of this design found first graders attending more to features of letters in words than to total word shape.[44]

At least three other studies of the 1970s reinforce this conclusion. In one of these, the researchers found their results supporting the general conclusion that prereading children depend to a great extent on features of individual letters in making discrimination among words.[45] In a second study, it was found that by the first grade children begin to extract the spelling structure of words -- for instance, they say that *tup*, *dink*, *besks*, or *blasps* are "more like a real word" than *nda*, *xogl*, *mbafr*, or *lkiskr*.[46] Then, by testing first graders' abilities to identify letters, others found beginning readers used information from one part of a word to facilitate the identification of other parts or letters of a word.[47]

Finally, the notion, held by some advocates of sight words, that it is as easy for a child to learn a whole word as it is a letter has been effectively confronted. For example, it has been found that training in the discrimination of letter-like forms is quite effective at the very start of kindergarten.[48] Another study found that first graders needed twice the time to learn a letter-sound relations as they did a letter-name relationship.[49]

One researcher found that at first grade entrance almost every child is able to match letters correctly.[50] Kindergarten children are capable of learning to discriminate letters, studies show.[51] One study obtained a correlation of .87 between first grade children's abilities to match lower case letters and their reading ability.[52] The teacher who thinks that words are recognized by young pupils holistically, just because they are presented to them to learn as wholes, thus is not in conformity with the research which indicates that beginning readers recognize words letter-by-letter.[53]

Conclusions

The striking conflict between the opinions given by some experts in reading methodology about sight words and the pertinent research findings on this matter are demonstrated here. Assuming that attempts at the improvement of reading instruction are best served by a reliance on empirical evidence, rather than on hearsay or traditional beliefs, the following seem to be inescapable conclusions about this matter.

The statements made by many modern writers about how children recognize sight words generally are wrong. The shape of a word is the least-used cue to its recognition by beginning readers. This explanation of how sight words are read thus is discredited. Children discriminate parts of words from the time they begin to learn to read, the research reveals. The assumption that they make no such analyses is faulty. Moreover, this assumption misleads teachers of reading into the wasteful and ineffectual practice of teaching sight words, which permits and even fosters a number of problems, including inaccurate word perception.

To certify beyond doubt that the sight word supposition is faulty, it is necessary to explain how pupils, learning to read, successfully apply

One researcher found that at first grade entrance almost every child is able to match letters correctly.

Children discriminate parts of words from the time they begin to learn to read, the research reveals.

phonics knowledge to decode unpredictably spelled words, such as *small* and *been*.

According to phonics rules, these words would he decoded so as to be pronounced /smal/ and /ben/. In the discussion on the decoding of unpredictably spelled words, in the preceding chapter, it was revealed that recent research[54] has suggested that if young pupils learning to read discover, through the application of phonics rules, the approximate pronunciation of an unpredictably spelled word, they then can successfully infer its correct pronunciation.

For example, pupils pronouncing small as /smal/ (the result of the application of the rule that *a* in closed syllables is /a/) in the sentence, *The boy's shoes were too small for him*, would likely correct this pronunciation to /smol/.

In short, if the application of a phonics rule to an unpredictably spelled written word results in an approximate sounding of this word, the pupil then can successfully infer and produce its accurate pronunciation. This seems the most reasonable explanation so far of why it is that pupils trained in phonics are so relatively adept at decoding unpredictably spelled words, both monosyllabic and multisyllabic.

The evidence presented appears to substantiate the opinion that teaching each while word as a single entity is currently in rather bad repute, and deservedly so.

The evidence presented appears to substantiate the opinion that teaching each whole word as a single entity is currently in rather bad repute, and deservedly so. It appears in agreement with the theory that the novice reader is forced to analyze all the constituents of the surface appearance of words. It is important to conclude, therefore, that future advice as to how children recognize letters and words must take into account all that is known from research about the ways young children develop their powers of word identification.

When one understands that the idea of sight words is not based on research evidence (It is significant that sight word proponents almost never refer to research for confirmation of this idea), an explanation emerges for the confusing and often contradictory manner in which this purported phenomenon is discussed. Without objective information with which to support their existence, it is little wonder that the advocates of sight words cannot even agree as to what these words are, or what their relationship to phonics is.

Nonetheless, it is clear that reading experts presently cling to the discredited notion of sight words. This loyalty to sight words probably is best illustrated by the inclusion of this term in the recent *A Dictionary of Reading and Related Terms.*[55] The accuracy of this dictionary (which represents a five-year effort to clarify the meanings of reading terms) was judged by an editorial staff that consisted of fifty-three prominent reading experts. These reading authorities concurred that sight words (like *and* and *have*) are those which beginning readers best learn to identify as whole units, without the application of any form of word analysis.

There are probably several interconnected reasons why many of today's reading experts continue to ignore the empirical evidence regarding the invalidity of sight words. They simply may be unaware of this information. Because a reading professor has published an article or a textbook on reading methodology does not, unfortunately, always ensure that he/she has knowledge of the research that pertains to all of the varied items it describes. Also, some reading experts may have found it too uncomfortable to admit that they have been wrong in the past about sight words. This admission may be too embarrassing or ego-deflating a confession to make. Some authorities on reading also are reluctant to forcibly question fixed or traditional practices, such as the teaching of sight words.

The erroneous notion that any given method of teaching reading has about as much inherent value as any other method may contribute, as well, to the perpetuating support for sight words. And lastly, the recent emergence among reading experts of a strong anti-phonics movement doubtless has reinvigorated the traditional allegiance shown for sight words.

Whatever the reasons may be, the notion of sight words persists to the present time. Any such justifications of this idea obviously cannot add to its respectability. It needs to be reiterated, therefore, that a reform in the thinking about sight words among certain reading experts still is badly needed. Their continued circulation of misinformation about this matter obviously is unfortunate. Worse yet, however, is the danger that teachers will be, or are, convinced by these reading experts that the teaching of sight words is a useful and effective practice in beginning reading, and/or that this teaching can replace instruction in phonics. This latter consequence clearly is the least tolerable of all.

Nonetheless, it is clear that reading experts presently cling to the discredited notion of sight words.

Any such justifications of this idea obviously cannot add to its respectability.

References

1. Durkin, D. *Teaching Young Children to Read.* Boston, MA: Allyn and Bacon, 1972.
2. Harris, L. A. and Smith, C. B. *Reading Instruction Through Diagnostic Teaching.* New York, NY: Holt, Rinehart and Winston, 1972.
3. Karlin, R. *Teaching Elementary Reading.* New York, NY: Harcourt Brace Jovanovich, 1971.
4. Heilman, A. W. *Principles and Practices of Teaching Reading.* Columbus, OH: Charles E. Merrill, 1977.
5. Arnold, R. and Miller, J. "Word Recognition Skills." In P. Lamb and R. Arnold (Eds.), *Teaching Reading.* Belmont, CA: Wadsworth, 1980.
6. McNeil, J. D.; Donant, L. and Alkin, M. C. *How to Teach Reading Successfully.* Boston, MA: Little, Brown, 1980.
7. Veatch, J. *Reading in the Elementary School.* New York, NY: John Wiley, 1978.
8. Bush, C. and Huebner, M. H. *Strategies for Reading in the Elementary School.* New York, NY: Macmillan, 1970.
9. Hafner, L. E. and Jolly, H. B. *Patterns of Teaching Reading in the Elementary School.* New York, NY: Macmillan, 1972.
10. Jones, D. M. *Teaching Children to Read.* New York, NY: Harper and Row, 1971.
11. Dechant, E. V. *Improving the Teaching of Reading.* Englewood Cliffs, NJ: Prentice-Hall, 1970.
12. Wynn, S. J. "Development of Sight Vocabulary." In J. E. Alexander (Ed.), *Teaching Reading.* Boston, MA: Little, Brown, 1979.
13. Hittleman, D. R. *Developmental Reading: A Psycholinguistic Perspective.* Chicago, IL: Rand McNally, 1978.
14. Stoodt, B. D. *Reading Instruction.* Boston, MA: Houghton Mifflin, 1981.
15. Zintz, M. V. *The Reading Process.* Dubuque, IA: Wm. C. Brown, 1970.
16. Wallen, C. J. *Competency in Teaching Reading.* Chicago, IL: Science Research Associates, 1972.
17. Dauzat, J. A. and Dauzat, S. V. *Reading: The Teacher and the Learner.* New York, NY: John Wiley, 1981.
18. Fry, E. B. *Elementary Reading Instruction.* New York, NY: McGraw-Hill, 1977.
19. Stauffer, R. G. *The Language-Experience Approach to the Teaching of Reading.* New York, NY: Harper and Row, 1980.
20. Mangrum, C. T. and Forgan, H. W. *Developing Competencies in Teaching Reading.* Columbus, OH: Charles E. Merrill, 1979.
21. Duffy, G. G. and Sherman, G. B. *Systemtic Reading Instruction.* New York, NY: Harper and Row, 1972.
22. Savage, J. F. *Linguistics for Teachers.* Chicago, IL: Science Research Associates, 1973.
23. Aukerman, R. C. and Aukerman, L. R. *How Do I Teach Reading?* New York, NY: John Wiley, 1981.
24. Lapp, D. and Flood, J. *Teaching Reading to Every Child.* New York, NY: Macmillan, 1978.
25. May, F. B. and Eliot, S. B. *To Help Children Read.* Columbus, OH: Charles E. Merrill, 1978.
26. DeBoer, J. J. and Dallmann, M. *The Teaching of Reading.* Englewood Cliffs, NJ: Prentice—Hall, 1970.
27. Buswell, G. T. *Fundamental Reading Habits: A Study of Their Development.* Chicago, IL: University of Chicago, 1922.

28. Gates, A. I. and Boeker, E. "A Study of Initial Stages in Reading by Preschool Children." *Teachers College Record,* 1923, 24, 469-477.

29. Meek, L. H. *A Study of Learning and Retention in Young Children.* New York, NY: Teachers College, Columbia University, 1925.

30. Hill, M. B. "A Study of Word Discrimination in Individuals Learning to Read." *Journal of Educational Research,* 1936, 29, 487-500.

31. Wilson, F. T. and Fleming, C. W. "Letter Consciousness in Beginners in Reading." *Journal of Genetic Psychology,* 1938, 53, 273-285.

32. Olson, A. V. "Growth in Word Perception Abilities as It Relates to Success in Beginning Reading." *Journal of Education,* 1958, 140, 25-36.

33. Diack, H. *Reading and the Psychology of Perception.* New york, NY: Philosophical Library, 1960.

34. Wiley, W. E. "Difficult Words and the Beginner." *Journal of Educational Research,* 1928, 17, 278-289.

35. Shankweiler, D. and Liberman, I. Y. "Misreading, a Search for Causes." In J. F. Kavanagh and I. G. Mattingly (Eds.), *Language by Ear and by Eye.* Cambridge, MA: MIT, 1972.

36. Muehl, S. "The Effects of Visual Discrimination, Pretraining with Word and Letter Stimuli on Learning to Read a Word List in Kindergarten Children." *Journal of Educational Psychology,* 1961, 52, 215-221.

37. King, E. M. "Effects of Different Kinds of Visual Discrimination Training on Learning to Read Words." *Journal of Educational Psychology,* 1964, 58, 325-333.

38. Murphy, H.A. "Growth in Perception of Word Elements in Three Types of Beginning Reading Instruction." *Reading Teacher,* 1966, 19, 585-589.

39. Elkind,D.; Horn, J. and Schneider, G. "Modified Word Recognition, Reading Achievement and Perceptual De-centration." *Journal of Genetic Psychology,* 1965, 107, 235-251.

40. Samuels, S. J. and Jeffrey, W. E. "Discriminability of Words and Letter Cues Used in Learning to Read." *Journal of Educational Psychology,* 1966, 57, 337-340.

41. Galocy, J. C. "The Effects of Pretraining in Transfer and Letter Naming on the Rate Children Learn." *Dissertation Abstracts International,* 1972, 30, 5339A-5340A.

42. Marchbanks, G. and Levin, H. "Cues by Which Children Recognize Words." *Journal of Educational Psychology,* 1965, 56, 57-61.

43. Williams, J. P.; Blumberg, E. L. and Williams, D. V. "Cues Used in Visual Word Recognition." *Journal of Educational Psychology,* 1970, 61, 310-315.

44. Timko, H. G. "Configuration as a Cue in the Word Recognition of Beginning Readers." *Journal of Experimental Education,* 1970, 39, 68-69.

45. Nodine, C. G. and Hardt, J. B. "Role of Letter-Position Cues in Learning to Read Words." *Journal of Educational Psychology,* 1970, 61, 1-15.

46. Rosinski, R. R. and Wheeler, K. E. "Children's Use of Orthographic Structure in Word Discrimination." *Psychonomic Science,* 1972, 26, 97-98.

47. Lott, D. and Smith, F. "Knowledge of Intrawood Redundancy by Beginning Readers." *Psychonomic Science,* 1970, 19, 343-344.

48. Williams, J.P. "Training Kindergarten Children to Discriminate letter-like Forms." *American Educational Research Journal,* 1969, 6, 501-514.

49. Jenkins, J. R.; Bausell, R. B. and Jenkins, L. M. "Comparison of Letter Name and Letter Sound Training as Transfer Variables." *American Educational Research Journal,* 1972, 9, 75-86.

50. Nicholson, A. "Background Abilities Related to Reading Success in First Grade." *Journal of Education.* 1958, 140, 7-24.

51. Wheelrock, W. H. and Silvaroli, N. J. "Visual Discrimination Training for Beginning Readers." *Reading Teacher,* 1967, 21, 115-120.

52. Smith, N. B. "Matching Ability as a Factor in First Grade Reading." *Journal of Educational Psychology,* 1928, 19, 560-571.

53. Samuels, S. J.; LaBerge, D. and Bremer, C. "Units of Word Recognition: Evidence of Development Changes." *Journal of Verbal Learning and Verbal Behavior,* 1978, 17, 715-720.

54. Groff, P. "A Test of the Utility of Phonics Rules." *Reading Psychology,* 1983, 4, 217-225.

55. Harris, T. L. and Hodges, R. E. *A Dictionary of Reading and Related Terms.* Newark, DE: International Reading Association, 1981.

Chapter IV

Myth #4: Reading is Best Taught in Sentences

This chapter discusses what advocates of teaching reading by a "sentence method" (rather than a phonics method) propose. It is shown that there is no convincing research evidence that the sentence method is as effective, however, for developing beginning reading ability, as is instruction that stresses individual word recognition. This finding does not imply that sentence context cues have no usefulness in reading. The research does indicate that both word recognition skills and sentence context cues are important in learning to read. The latter has distinctive limitations, however, as is shown in Chapter 5.

Past Support for the Sentence Method

The idea that learning to read should proceed on a whole-task basis has been with us for a long time. A "sentence method" of teaching reading was seriously advanced at least 150 years ago. Indeed, in 1823 Jacotot advised teachers to have pupils memorize complete sentences as the initial stage of their reading skill development.[1] At present, there are advocates of what can be called "new" sentence methods. It turns out that these are variations of the traditional look-say method.[2] There is little support in research for the supposition that the whole-task method should displace teaching the child to recognize individual words through the use of a combination of phonics and context cues (see Bibliography).

The notion that children learning to read have little need to recognize individual words has grown in intensity over the past few years, moving out from the academic circles which first propagated this conception of reading. School reading specialists now have come to accept certain reading professors' negative criticisms of word reading. One such field practitioner of reading lately gave testimony of her conversion to this belief.[3] Reading instruction, she said, should move away from the precise and purely visual domain, away from letters, sound-symbol associations, and word recognition. The concern of the teacher should not be with words, doubtless would be her answer to reading teachers in her school district, wondering how to best conduct this instruction. The thesis that words are not the correct content to use to teach children to read is no new concept, it can be recalled.

Around 1870 in the U.S., George Farnham was the earliest crusader for this new analytic sentence method.[4] In his 1905 manual for reading teachers (one of the first of such guides), Farnham proposed that the sentence is the unit of expression, and therefore that the sentence -- if properly taught -- will be understood, as a whole, better than if presented in detail.

Farnham advised that the sentence should first be presented as a whole, after which the words are discovered. Later, others described in yet more detail how this teaching specifically was to be accomplished.[5]

First, it was said that the attention to letters, elementary sounds, words, and word-meanings must be displaced by attention to sentence wholes

A "sentence method" of teaching reading was seriously advanced at least 150 years ago.

40

and sentence meanings. One method of generating such sentences was to have pupils dictate sentences or short stories to their teacher, who recorded them in written form. It was noted that the child soon can read such sentences, although not at first knowing the place of a single word.

Nevertheless, the important thing, it was said, is to begin with meaning wholes and sentence wholes, make thought lead, and thus word secure natural expression, letting word analysis follow in its own time. Out of this instruction, children will notice certain words and certain sentence structures on their own, it was believed. And finally, the sentence-wholes are gradually analyzed into their constituent words and these again, in time, into their constituent sounds and letters. No systematic, intensive, or early teaching of word analysis was felt necessary, however.

The New Sentence Method

Currently, some authorities in reading continue to endorse the hypothesis of the sentence method. Some find sentences of the highest usefulness in beginning reading. One expert contends that, initially, most children have little else on which to rely. Later they combine meaning, phonic, and possibly structural clues--but not at the outset.[6]

Some find sentences of the highest usefulness in beginning reading.

One recent attempt to revive the notion that the sentence is the proper written context with which to begin reading instruction is called "assisted reading" or "reading by immersion."[7]

It is said that "assisted reading" qualifies as a means of giving children the experience in reading they need in order to use their knowledge of the language and their cognitive skills in learning to read in the natural way they learned their spoken language. Children taught by this method are said to learn reading by being "immersed" in reading in a manner similar to the way they learned to speak. Children should learn to read by reading, just as they learn to speak by speaking, it is claimed.

It is said that "assisted reading" qualifies as a means of giving children the experience in reading they need in order to . . .

In "assisted reading," the teacher reads, and the child reads after him or her, either phrase-by-phrase or sentence-by-sentence. When children recognize words from the story read aloud, the teacher reads aloud but leaves out words she thinks the children will recognize because of the many times the children have repeated the words. Since none of the cues used in word identification are taught directly, a word may have to be repeated many times before it is recognized.

Finally, it is said that children have enough words to do the initial reading themselves. That is, beginning readers now say aloud the sentences given them, while the teacher anticipates the words the children will not know and supplies the words.

Supposedly, each child here determines his/her own readiness for each of these three stages.

Supposedly, each child here determines his/her own readiness for each of these three stages. The child moves to Stage 3 when he or she asks the teacher to say the words. The teacher's role in determining if and when a child moves to or from one of the three stages of assisted reading is indeterminant, since it is insisted the child alone is in a position to determine when he/she is ready to read.

An unspecified level of fluency and complexity in children's oral language is sad to be a sign that most children are probably ready to begin learning to read. If reading instruction is begun before this undefined point is reached, there may be some interference with the acquisition of a child's oral language, teachers are cautioned.

Emerging clearly from this set of beliefs is the conclusion that children solve the reading problem by themselves.[8] It is argued that learning to read is not a process of mastering one skill after another. That is, learning to read is a problem the child must solve, not a set of skills that he or she must be taught. Supposedly, each individual child develops his or her own means for learning to read. It follows, therefore, that no formal hierarchy of reading skills can be imposed on the child. In any case, it is said, too little is known about the reading process itself to insist that children move through a systematic program of reading instruction.[9]

Assisted reading, therefore, supposedly represents a means of teaching reading skills without resorting to formal methods.

Assisted reading, therefore, supposedly represents a means of teaching reading skills without resorting to formal methods. In assisted reading there is no bogging children down with the minutiae of instruction and work sheets, it is avowed. It is said that reading should be fun and remain free of any attempts to teach skills.

In any reading program that teaches reading skills in a sequential manner, the child will be hindered from learning to read, teachers are warned.[7] It is insisted that sequences of reading skills may, by their very nature, be counterproductive to acquiring reading skill. So, under the assisted reading approach, children are not taught, directly, any of the cues to word recognition that research tells us they employ. Instead, they are merely given an opportunity to look for the significant differences between or among words.

These assumptions lead to the conclusion that it would make sense to use the sentence as the main unit in reading.[7] Children will discover the orthographic regularities of the written language only if they are provided with complete stories that are truly representative of the writing system, it is noted. The procedures of assisted reading, it is reiterated, represent the only route open for children to acquire knowledge of the orthographic system. This is because all that may really occur in reading instruction is that sentences are presented to a child and he or she uses them to solve the reading problem. This agrees with the notion that all the teacher can do in reading instruction is provide the raw material, the written word, and its "name."

It follows, in assisted reading, that no controls are put on the types of vocabulary, syntax, or concepts in the written contexts used in this approach. It is noted that when a child learns to speak, there is no formal attempt to limit what the child hears. Therefore, it would be wrong in reading instruction, it is concluded, to try to control the length of words provided young children, or to pay attention to whether they are frequently used ones, or are spelled predictably. An unlimited linguistic environment is provided the child learning to speak. Assisted reading purports to do the same thing. Thus, no restrictions based on the level of difficulty of vocabulary or syntax would be placed on the selection of books read in this new sentence method.

The New Sentence Method Falls Short

It is clear that what the advocates of assisted reading call an economical, efficient, and effective program does not in fact deserve this tribute. There are several severe weaknesses regarding the claims for assisted reading that one can point to.

There is no convincing empirical evidence indicating that assisted reading, or any of the other versions of look-say methodology, are as effective for developing beginning reading skills as is a systematic, direct, early, and intensive teaching of decoding or phonics. The overwhelming amount of research indicates that look-say or "meaning" approaches to beginning reading instruction are inferior to a systematic, intensive

There are several severe weaknesses regarding the claims for assisted reading that one can point to.

teaching of phonics. Many comprehensive reviews of such research have been made (See Bibliography).

We are assured that in assisted reading a child does not experience failure, but when comparisons are made to decoding or phonics methods, the research finds that look-say methods, like assisted reading, result in more failures than do decoding methods. The advocates of assisted reading undercut themselves when they concede that for a child to recognize a word in assisted reading, the word may have to be repeated many times. There are systematic decoding programs that have better records for success in individual word recognition than this.

There is no reason to approve "immersing" beginning readers in the full stream of written materials, as assisted reading does. It is doubtful wisdom to ignore the range of concepts found in this full choice of materials. It is foolhardy to be unconcerned about syllabic lengths or unpredictable spellings. It is rash to disregard the complexity and length of the sentences that occur in unrestricted reading materials. There is impressive evidence to suggest that unpredictably spelled words are easier for beginning readers to recognize,[10] and that the syllabic length of words[11] and the complexity and length of sentences[12] is of concern in reading instruction.

The fact is that the well accepted formulas for predicting readability use both the syllabic length of words and the complexity of sentences as key elements in determining the relative difficulty of reading materials. Even the "language experience" approach to reading instruction carefully controls the kind of language the child sees in writing.[13] This deliberate and systematic attempt to eliminate certain vocabulary and syntax not in the child's oral language contrasts sharply with the casual attitude of assisted reading toward these linguistic matters.

Without this mastery of subskills, no fruitful combining of them -- necessary for comprehension -- can take place.

One can find little if any data from the research on reading to support the notion that the best reading instruction requires that the teacher should intervene as little as possible, so that children are allowed to teach themselves to read. This hypothesis minimizes unduly the difficulty children have in mastering the subskills of the complex act we call reading. Without this mastery of subskills, no fruitful combining of them -- necessary for comprehension -- can take place.

Myth #4: Reading is Best Taught in Sentences

The advocates of assisted reading would have us leave this critical matter totally to the impulses of the child learner. Common sense tells us this is far too risky. As well, there is impressive research to suggest that learning to read predominantly by discovery techniques is less efficient than if the reading teacher takes on a deterministic role.[14]

Those who defend assisted reading overestimate the cause-and-effect relationship between children's oral language development and their reading achievement. It is true that one can find research studies that support such a cause-and-effect relationship. One can just as frequently point to studies which have discovered no such connection.[15] Accordingly, we must not accept the notion that early systematic instruction in phonics will hinder the development of children's oral language. To the contrary, at present we cannot say with confidence if any certain level of fluency and complexity of children's oral language is necessary for beginning reading instruction to be successful.

There remain far too many ascertainable differences between written materials (and how we learn to read them) and speech (and how this is mastered) to assume that children best learn to read in precisely the same manner as they learned to talk.[12] It is observable that the three stages of assisted reading do not approximate the stages of children's learning to speak. That is, children do not learn to talk by first listening carefully to an adult's sentences and then repeating these sentences verbatim. Children learning to speak are not normally then asked to fill in words in sentences that are purposely deleted by mature speakers.

Finally, children do not ordinarily practice talking by having an adult supply words at given points in all the sentences they speak. It is clear, therefore, that the three stages of assisted reading do not for the child solve the problem of learning to read, just as he solves the problem of learning to speak.

Empirical Evidence on the Issue

The key question to be asked about the new sentence method is whether its use is likely to bring on satisfactory reading gains, especially for primary grade children. As yet, the proponents of new sentence methods have not offered empirical evidence as to the relative effectiveness of their proposals for reading instruction. Nonetheless, we may correctly infer that a method which teaches children only to use sentence

The advocates of assisted reading would have us leave this critical matter totally to the impulses of the child learner.

45

context cues, would fare even less well (in a comparison with phonics method) than would the look-say method (which does teach phonics, albeit in a delayed and incidental manner).

The evidence is clear-cut that an early, systematic, and intensive teaching of phonics results in significantly higher word recognition and comprehension scores in the primary grades than is possible with the use of look-say methodology (See Bibliography). It seems fair to say, therefore, that this result in favor of phonics would also be repeated if the new sentence method were compared to it. The claim by its proponents that the new sentence method will prove to be the most productive of any of the reading methods proposed so far accordingly is put into serious doubt.

Another issue of consequence regarding the new sentence method has to do with whether or not the use of context cues by beginning readers may in fact hinder early reading growth. We know that as children proceed through grade one they increasingly pay more attention to words in sentences than they did to sentence contexts. The earlier in the first grade that children realized they must pay close attention to individual words in a sentence, the more likely they are to learn to read.

Thus, teaching beginning readers to rely too soon and too intensively on sentence contexts can have undesirable consequences.

Thus, teaching beginning readers to rely too soon and too intensively on sentence contexts can have undesirable consequences. The children's early use of contextual information does not appear to greatly facilitate progress in acquiring reading skill. The longer they stay in the early, context-emphasizing phase, without showing an increase in the use of phonics, the more deficient their skills are at the end of the year.[16]

If the major contention of the new sentence method (that comprehension of a written passage is not possible if one reads its individual words) were true, then one would find only small and insignificant relationships between test scores for word reading and sentence or paragraph reading. This has not been proven to be the case, however.

To the contrary, the coefficients of correlation obtained between word reading and sentence or paragraph reading scores in standardized reading tests have been uniformly high. We see r's between these two sets of scores on the Gray Oral Reading Test as .72, .77, and .77 for grades two, three, and four, respectively. An r of .81 has been obtained between the word reading and paragraph reading scores of the Wide

Myth #4: Reading is Best Taught in Sentences

Range Achievement Test, and a similar r for these scores on Spache's Diagnostic Reading Scales.[2] I have found that high r's between word reading and sentence or paragraph reading scores have also been obtained for several other elementary grade standardized reading tests. These r's ranged from .68 to .96, with a median of .85.[2]

Undoubtedly many teachers regularly carry out, without harm, actions similar to stage two of assisted reading. That is, these teachers read a sentence, pausing to allow the child to read a word they expect her or him to be able to recognize, based on the decoding or phonics skills the child has previously been taught. Almost all teachers also have children read aloud, while they listen to supply words the individual child cannot identify.

The use of these activities in no way serves as a confirmation, however, of the view that assisted reading is the most effective procedure available for teaching reading, that only through it will children learn to recognize the spelling regularities of written material, that children best learn to read the way they learned to speak, that sequential or systematic programs for teaching reading skills actually hinder children from learning to read, or that no attention needs to be paid to the range of concepts, sentence lengths or their complexities, or to the predictability of the spellings of words, in the books chosen for beginning reading.

It is these contentions of assisted reading that make it a handicap to success in beginning reading. Seen merely as something teachers practice, certain parts of their otherwise systematic program of instruction in phonics and context cues, the use of assisted reading invites no risk. The acceptance by teachers of assisted reading to replace a sequential and direct teaching of reading skills would be deplorable, however.

Claims for Context Cues

It is apparent that the rationale for teaching reading through sentences is embedded in the notion that the use of context cues is extremely helpful in reading. The importance of context cues for word identification has long been emphasized by reading experts. Some are so convinced of their value, in fact, that they see context cues as all-important to beginning readers. One expert contends that, initially, most children have little else on which to rely for word recognition. Later they combine meaning, phonic, and possibly structural clues--but not at the outset, he

Undoubtedly many teachers regularly carry out, without harm, actions similar to stage two of assisted reading.

The importance of context cues for word identification has long been emphasized by reading experts.

says.[6] This reading authority is wrong, since the research as to the cues beginning readers actually use to recognize words clearly reveals they use letters for this purpose, from the time they first begin reading.[17]

The exaggerations made as to the usefulness of context cues, in word recognition by beginning readers, stem from certain reports made about this matter. The author of one such report claims that he found that first-graders could read in a story context almost two out of three of the words they had previously missed, when attempting to read them as isolated items in word lists.[18]

This single piece of research has been widely quoted as proof for the proposition that if children do not consistently read words in context they will learn to rely solely on visual cues (letters) for word recognition. As a consequence, it is claimed they will become word-callers, that is, to have developed the ability to name words correctly without being able to comprehend their meanings.[18] Despite the fact that the results of this study (concerning the utility of context cues) has been generally accepted by reading experts, the attempts to replicate its findings have not been successful.[19;20;21;22;23] It has been found, in fact, that by the time they are third-graders, children do not make significantly fewer errors when reading a full story than they make when reading words in isolation.[24] One researcher[25] had good readers read the first eight words in various, easy-to-read sentences. He found that only 10 percent of the time could they guess correctly the noun, verb, adjective, or adverb that followed.

The research finds that the usefulness of context cues diminishes as the reading ability of children advances.

The research finds that the usefulness of context cues diminishes as the reading ability of children advances.[26] Context cues are most useful when children still have difficulty recognizing individual words. Children with poor word recognition skills use context cues as a crutch to compensate for their word recognition deficiencies.

It is accurate to say, therefore, that the degree to which context cues aid children in word recognition depends to a great extent on children's reading skill.[27] Beginning readers have few word recognition skills, so they must depend on context cues in order to identify written words. At the same time, if the teacher does not soon wean pupils away from their dependence on context cues, and instruct them in phonics, their early reading growth will be handicapped.[16]

Myth #4: Reading is Best Taught in Sentences

To prove the proposition that context cues have a special value in word recognition, the proposition would have to pass a critical test. It would have to be shown that there is a greater difference between good and poor readers' abilities to recognize words in sentence contexts than in isolation. In studies of this issue, however, good readers have been found to recognize words both in context and in isolation significantly better than poor readers. The difference in the abilities of these two groups to recognize words in sentence contexts is no larger, however, than the difference between their abilities to recognize words in isolation. In short, the addition of context fails to increase the difference between the reading abilities of good and poor readers.[26]

It is clear that modern research suggests that many reading experts give context cues too prominent a place in word recognition instruction. It thus is necessary to put the role of context cues into proper perspective. The usefulness of context cues for children when reading may be narrowed down to helping them decide which of the various meanings of a word -- one they have already recognized -- best fits the sentence being read. Early reading instruction should not stress context cues; the cue system that research suggests may contribute the least to mature reading ability.

Conclusions

It has been noted that context cues are not the only cues available to the beginning reader for identifying words (the advocates of "sight words" in beginning reading to the contrary notwithstanding). While context cues do have a function in word recognition by the beginning reader, the extent of this usefulness must be judged in relationship to the weaknesses for this purpose these cues have been shown to exhibit. There is evidence from both research findings and linguistic analyses to suggest that certain limitations be placed on the values for beginning readers of the use of context cues:

The type of vocabulary used in a reading program will affect the usefulness of context cues.[28] If this vocabulary is chosen on the basis of the phoneme-grapheme similarities among the words involved, then the application of context cues may have a depressing effect on young children's reading growth.

The type of vocabulary used in a reading program will affect the usefulness of context cues.

The use of context cues contributes a relatively minor solution to the problem of comprehension of reading materials faced by the beginning reader.[29] The unknown mental factors that control the acquisition of comprehension far outweigh the influences on this matter the use of context cues can exert.

Many facets of English syntax or grammar hinder the successful use of context cues by the beginning reader.

Many facets of English syntax or grammar hinder the successful use of context cues by the beginning reader.[30] Moreover, the handicaps posed by these aspects of language probably are unaffected by how well the uses of context cues are taught in the beginning reading program.

The length of an unknown word may have some effect on a beginning reader's ability to recognize it via the use of context cues. As yet, it is uncertain precisely what effect a word's length has on word recognition in the primary grades.[31] Word length probably has less effect on the word recognition of middle-grade pupils.

Written syntax that is different from a child's spoken language likely will inhibit his use of context cues.[32] This seems apparent regardless of whether tho child speaks standard or nonstandard English.

The use of context cues may negatively affect the speed with which children recognize words.[33] The need for context-free word recognition abilities is apparent.

Myth #4: Reading is Best Taught in Sentences

References

1. Mathews, M. M. *Teaching to Read.* Chicago, IL: University of Chicago, 1966.
2. Groff, P. "Should Children Learn to Read Words?" *Reading World,* 1978, 17, 256-264.
3. Garman, D. "Comprehension Before Word Identification." *Reading World,* 1977, 16, 279-287.
4. Smith, N. B. *American Reading Instruction.* Newark, DE: International Reading Association, 1965.
5. Huey, E. B. *The Psychology and Pedagogy of Reading.* Cambridge, MA: MIT, 1968 (first published in 1906).
6. Karlin, R. *Teaching Elementary Reading.* New York, NY: Harcourt Brace Jovanovish, 1971.
7. Hoskisson, K. "The Many Facets of Assisted Reading." *Elementary English,* 1975, 52, 312-315.
8. Hoskisson, K. "Reading Readiness: Three Viewpoints." *Elementary School Journal,* 1977, 78, 45-52.
9. Hoskisson, K. and Krohm, B. "Reading by Immersion: Assisted Reading." *Elementary English,* 1974, 51, 832-836.
10. Groff, P. "The New Anti-Phonics." *Elementary School Journal,* 1977, 77, 323-332.
11. Groff, P. "Long Versus Short Words in Beginning Reading." *Reading World,* 1975, 14, 277-289.
12. Groff, P. "Limitations of Context Cues for Beginning Readers." *Reading World,* 1976, 16, 97-103.
13. Hall, M. *Teaching Reading as a Language Experience.* Columbus, OH: Charles E. Merrill, 1970.
14. Bennett, N. *Teaching Styles and Pupil Progress.* Cambridge, MA: Harvard University, 1976.
15. Groff, P. "Oral Language and Reading." *Reading World,* 1977, 17, 71-78.
16. Biemiller, A. "The Development of the Use of Graphic and Contextual Information as Children Learn to Read." *Reading Research Quarterly,* 1970, 6, 75-96.
17. Groff, P. "The Topsy-Turvy World of 'Sight' Words." *Reading Teacher,* 1974, 27, 572-578.
18. Goodman, K. S. "Linguistic Study of Cues and Miscues in Reading." *Elementary English,* 1965, 42, 639-643.
19. Singer, H., et al. "The Effects of Pictures and Contextual Conditions on Learning Responses to Printed Words." *Reading Research Quarterly,* 1973-74, 9, 555-567.
20. Chester, R. D. "Differences in Learnability of Content and Function Words Presented in Isolation and Oral Context When Taught to High and Low Socio-economic Level Students." *Dissertation Abstracts International,* 1972, 32, 3833a.
21. Pearson, P. D. "On Bridging Gaps and Spanning Chasms." *Curriculum Inquiry,* 1978, 8, 353-362.
22. Groff, P. "Children's Recognition of Words in Isolation and in Context." *Reading Horizons,* 1979, 19, 134-138.
23. Negin, G. A. and Mulwauki, M. N. "Students' Abilities to Recognize Words in Isolation adn in Context." *Reading Improvement,* 1981, 18, 73-80.
24. Nicholson, T. and Hill, D. "Good Readers Don't Guess-Taking Another Look at the issue of Whether Children Read Words Better in Context or In Isolation." *Reading Psychology, 1985, 6, 181-198.*
25. Gough, P.B. "Context, Form, and Interaction." In K. Raymer (Ed.), *Eye Movements in Reading: Perceptual and Language Processes."* New York, NY: Academic, 1983.

26. Stanovich, K. E. "Toward an Interactive-Compensatory Model of Individual Differences in the Development of Reading Fluency." *Reading Research Quarterly,* 1980, 16, 32-71.

27. Samuels, S. J. and Kamil, M. L. "Models of the Reading Process." In P. D. Pearson (Ed.), *Handbook of Reading Research.* New York, NY: Longman, 1984.

28. Hartley, R. M. "A Method of Increasing the Ability of First Grade Pupils to Use Phonetic Generalizations." *California Journal of Educational Research,* 1971, 22, 9-16.

29. Groff, P. and Seymour, D. Z. *Word Recognition.* Springfield, IL: Charles C. Thomas, 1987.

30. Schlesinger, I. M. *Sentence Structure and the Reading Process.* The Hague: Mouton, 1968.

31. Groff, P. "The Significance of Word Length." *Visible Language,* 1983, 17, 396-398.

32. Hatch, E. *The Syntax of Four Reading Programs Compared With Language Development of Children.* Los Alamitos, CA: SWRL for Educational Research and Development, 1971.

33. Juel, C. "The Development and Use of Mediated Word Identification." *Reading Research Quarterly,* 1983, 18, 306-326.

Chapter V

Myth #5: Oral Language Test Scores Equal Reading Readiness

It is widely accepted among reading experts that unless children attain a certain level of oral language competency they are not ready to learn to read. Reading instruction should be delayed for children who do not achieve a certain score on an oral language test, it is maintained. Opponents of phonics teaching have used this argument to delay or otherwise limit the introduction of this instruction. The research findings do not support this assumption. There is as much research evidence to suggest there is little or no relationship between oral language test scores and reading readiness as there is data to indicate a positive relationship between these two factors. It appears unreasonable, therefore, to argue that unless children attain some given score on an oral language competency test they will experience difficulty in learning to read.

Research findings on the relationship between children's oral language proficiency, skill, facility, competence or productivity and their reading achievement have been reported in the past to be inconclusive. Oral language proficiency or competence as referred to here, and to follow, is generative or expressive oral language, the verbal fluency, complexity, or effectiveness of this oral language, but not listening nor the articulation or rhythm of speech sounds.

Evidence to 1941

In her review of the research on this matter Gaines[1] in 1941 found there were 8 studies to that time that discovered a significant and positive relationship between children's oral language competency and their reading prowess. On the other hand, she uncovered 5 such studies that suggested that there was no such connection between these two aspects of children's linguistic development. Gaines concluded in 1941 that no definitive decision could be made about this relationship.

. . . a significant and positive relationship between children's oral language competency and their reading prowess.

Evidence to 1975

Groff[2] continued the survey of research on this subject published between 1941 and 1975. He identified 17 studies that found a statistically significant, positive relationship between children's oral language skill and their reading abilities. To the contrary, however, he uncovered 19 studies that concluded there was little, if any, such relationship between these two factors. From the results of his review, Groff believed that the only authentic judgment that could be made in 1977, about children's oral language and their reading, was that this topic remains one of the most unsettled to be found in reading instruction.

Despite the inconclusive nature of the experimental data regarding children's oral language and their reading accomplishment, Groff reported that many reading experts up to 1975 believed that these two factors were closely related. During the time period 1941 to 1975, Groff found only a relatively small group of reading experts who did not support this conclusion.

Myth 5: Oral Language Test Scores Equal Reading Readiness

The Current Situation

An examination of the comments in the 1980s by reading experts about the relationship of children's oral language proficiency and their reading skill reveals that a high percentage of these statements continue to defend the assumption that unless children attain certain levels of oral language proficiency, they will find learning to read difficult. For example, Dallmann, et al.[3] contend there is a close relationship between reading and other language abilities. If a child's oral language is stimulated, they say, he or she will become a more efficient reader. Stoodt[4] echoes this conclusion. A child who does not have a good mastery of oral language will have some difficulty in beginning reading skills, Miller[5] cautions teachers. To this effect, Cheek and Cheek[6] advise teachers there is little doubt that oral language development plays a major role in reading instruction because poor oral language skills negatively affect both word recognition and comprehension skill development. Durkin[7], May[8], and Swaby[9], all appear to share these views to varying degrees.

The development of reading ability so closely parallels children's control of oral language, says Dechant[10], that the teacher must be as interested in the development of good speech as is the speech correctionist. If follows, note Otto, Rude, and Spiegel[11], that in order to enable all students to have a successful beginning when learning to read the teacher must provide numerous appropriate oral language activities. Ringler and Weber[12] concur. It is wrong, then, Hall, Ribovich, and Ramig[13] aver, that in school the attention to written language often overshadows the conscious furthering of oral language competence and performance.

A smaller number of reading experts of the 1980s take a more reserved position regarding this matter. Harris and Sipay[14] believe that for most children entering school oral language abilities are adequate for learning to read English. Moreover, McNeil, Donant, and Alkin[15] reflect, important differences occur between the processing of oral and written information. Kolker[16] also notices this condition. Otto and Smith[17] counsel teachers that whether the cause of a speech defect is also the cause of learning problems in reading is problematical. Then, it is extremely important to separate nonstandard English oral language productions from reading comprehension, warns Knight.[18]

. . . there is a close relationship between reading and other language abilities.

Otto and Smith counsel teachers that whether the cause of a speech defect is also the cause of learning problems in reading is problematical.

The notion that if a child can become an accomplished speaker it is likely he or she will develop into an effective reader . . .

The rarity of, and the restrained nature of such qualifying remarks about children's oral language and reading abilities contrast, however, with the enthusiasm that remains among reading experts, in general, for the idea that the more one can advance children's oral language productivity or fluency, or the complexity of their oral syntax, the greater is the likelihood children will become skilled readers. This point of view is taken even by reading experts who concede that children enter school with vast oral language backgrounds.[19]

The notion that if a child can become an accomplished speaker it is likely he or she will develop into an effective reader obviously has attractiveness for many of today's reading authorities.

The Evidence to Present

As noted, the research through 1975 on the relationship of children's oral language proficiency and their reading attainment was equivocal in its support for the proposition that children need numerous, specially-designed oral language activities in school if they are to learn to read in the most effective fashion possible. Through 1975, there was no clear resolution given by the research on this issue. The research through 1975 offered almost equal numbers of findings that questioned the hypothesis that oral language proficiency and reading achievement are closely related as it did findings that supported this assumption.

Is the research done on this issue since 1975 of a different character? Can the reading experts of the 1980s, who defend the idea that children's oral language and reading development are closely intertwined, legitimately contend that the research since 1975 supports their point of view?

There have been several pieces of empirical research conducted since 1975 that investigated the relationship of children's oral language skill and their reading proficiency. The research of this nature since that date falls into two general groups.

There are 10 reports of this research in *group one*.[20;21;22;23;24;25;26;27;28;29] These investigations found either *(a)* no statistically significant relationship between children's oral language and reading, or *(b)* a positive relationship between only a part of the subtests of the oral language and reading examinations that were made. For example, Hopkins[23] found that only two of the ten subtests of oral language that she administered were predictive of children's reading achievement. This body of researches suggests that it is unwarranted to fear that children who appear to be backward in oral language productivity or proficiency will fail to learn to read in a normal fashion.

There are 13 research reports in *group two* of this research done since 1975.[30;31;32;33;34;35;36;37;38;39;40;41;42]

This body of research found a positive relationship between children's oral language facility and their reading or reading readiness test scores. This evidence suggests that unless certain levels of oral language competency are reached by children they may have difficulty in learning to read.

The degree of the positive relationship found between children's oral language proficiency and their reading ability in these 13 studies was reported in two ways. In 5 of the 13 studies, this relationship was indicated by statistically significant differences in oral language ability that were found to favor good as versus poor readers.[30;34;37;38;40]

In the remaining 8 studies of this group of 13, this positive relationship was demonstrated by coefficients of correlation (r) obtained between tests of oral language and reading ability. These r's ranged from "high,"[39;41] to moderate, e.g., $r=.45 - .51$,[32] to low, e.g., $r=.26$.[36]

Discussion

A simple count of the number of research findings that either support or contradict a certain hypothesis, as has been done here with evidence on children's oral language and reading, admittedly is not the most desirable or satisfactory way to analyze such information. Unfortunately, the published reports of the relationship of children's oral language and reading made since 1975 rarely include the statistical data necessary to conduct a more sophisticated, and therefore a more comprehensible, examination of this empirical data, such as meta-analysis.[43]

The present survey of the research since 1975 on the relationship of children's oral language proficiency and their reading ability does suggest, nonetheless, that definite conclusions about this relationship are difficult to draw today, as they were in 1941. At present, there still remain

. . . Hopkins found that only two of the ten subtests of oral language that she administered were predictive of children's reading achievement.

remarkable contrasts among the findings of individual studies on this issue. We are faced with about as much evidence that suggests a positive relationship exists between these two variables as evidence that it does not. Accordingly, the research on this relationship made since 1975 has done little to resolve the question "Is it necessary for children to demonstrate certain levels of oral language proficiency in order to learn to read most effectively?" In effect, we appear to remain in the same quandry over this matter that Groff expressed in 1977.

Compounding the difficulty of arriving at a conclusive judgment about the relationship of children's oral language and their reading ability are certain aspects of the findings of the studies of this issue. As noted, some of these studies reported they found statistically significant differences in oral language test scores that favored good as versus poor readers. These differences, while proved not to be due to chance, were relatively small, nevertheless. The accumulative evidence about $r's$ obtained over the years between oral language and reading test scores, as analyzed by Hammill and McNutt,[44] indicates, in yet another way, that the positive relationships that have been discovered between these two factors may not be very strong.

Hammill and McNutt uncovered 210 $r's$ between children's oral language and reading as reported by eight-eight studies (87 percent of which were published in the 1960s and 1970s). The average of these 210 $r's$ was .25. The explained variability of the relationship of the variables that make up this r suggests that $r=.25$ is too low to have any use for predictive purposes, however. For example, the calculation $r=.25^2$ (.25 X .25) indicates that there are only about 6 percent common factors to be found between the two variables (oral language and reading) that $r=.25$ represents.

The experts in children's language development have yet to decide among themselves what is the most valid test of children's oral language proficiency.

The fact that there was no standardized test of children's oral language proficiency used uniformly by the different investigators of the relationship between children's oral language and reading skill may explain in part why the various studies report conflicting findings about this relationship. The experts in children's language development have yet to decide among themselves what is the most valid test of children's oral language proficiency. Even if they did so, however, there would likely remain problems of reliability with such a test. The administration and scoring of even a preferred oral language test would continue to pose far more problems of human error and misinterpretation than would the application of a typical written language test.

Advice to Teachers

Considering the unsettled nature of the research findings on the relationship of children's oral language and their reading ability, probably due in large part to the inherent difficulties of testing children's oral language in valid and reliable ways, it appears unreasonable at this time to argue that the research knowledge tells us that unless children achieve some given score on an oral language test they will have difficulty in learning to read. It seems more justifiable for teachers to assume (a) that the pupil comes to school with a remarkable knowledge of how to gain meaning from oral language,[45] and (b) that this level of oral language ability normally is adequate for him or her to learn to read.

Teachers are advised, therefore, that looking to aspects of children's oral language proficiency for reasons why their pupils do not learn to read well may be unproductive. Granted that there may be some influence from children's oral language proficiency on the rate at which they learn to read. So far, this influence does not appear to be of such a magnitude, however, that it makes of this oral language a central issue in children's acquisition of reading skills.

It follows that teachers should not give up teaching phonics to children they suspect may have fewer than normal competencies in oral language. The research findings would suggest that it is far safer to maintain this instruction than to abandon or delay it under the assumption that such children cannot profit from it.

It follows that teachers should not give up teaching phonics to children they suspect may have fewer than normal competencies in oral language.

References

1. Gaines, F. P. "Interrelationships of Speech and Reading Disability." *Elementary School Journal*,41, 605-613, 1941.
2. Groff, P. "Oral Language and Reading." *Reading World,* 1977, 17, 71-78.
3. Dallmann, M., et al. *The Teaching of Reading.* New York, NY: Holt, Rinehart and Winston, 1982.
4. Stoodt, B. D. *Reading Instruction.* Boston, MA: Houghton Mifflin, 1981.
5. Miller, W. H. *Teaching Elementary Reading Today.* New York, NY: Holt, Rinehart and Winston, 1984.
6. Cheek, M. C. and Cheek, E. H. *Diagnostic-Prescriptive Reading Instruction.* Dubuque, IA: Wm. C. Brown, 1980.
7. Durkin, D. *Teaching Them to Read.* Boston, MA: Allyn and Bacon, 1983.
8. May, F. B. *Reading as Communication.* Columbus, OH: Charles E. Merrill, 1982.
9 Swaby, B. E. R. *Teaching and Learning Reading.* Boston, MA: Little, Brown, 1984.
10. Dechant, D. *Diagnosis and Remediation of Reading Disabilities.* Englewood Cliffs, NJ: Prentice-Hall, 1981.
11. Otto, W.; Rude, R.; and Spiegel, D. L. *How to Teach Reading.* Reading, MA: Addison-Wesley, 1979.
12. Ringler, L. H. and Weber, C. K. *A Language-Thinking Approach to Reading.* San Diego, CA: Harcourt Brace Jovanovich, 1984.
13. Hall, M.; Ribovich, J. K.; and Ramig, C. J. *Reading and the Elementary School Child.* New York, NY: D. Nostrand, 1979.
14. Harris, A. J. and Sipay, E. R. *How to Increase Reading Ability.* New York, NY: Longman, 1980.
15. McNeil, J. D.; Donant, L.; and Alkin, M. C. *How to Teach Reading Successfully.* Boston, MA: Little, Brown, 1980.
16. Kolker, B. "Processing Print." In J. E. Alexander (Ed.), *Teaching Reading.* Boston, MA: Little, Brown, 1983.
17. Otto, W. and Smith, R. J. *Corrective and Remedial Teaching.* Boston, MA: Houghton Mifflin, 1980.
18. Knight, L. N "Reading for the Linguistically and Culturally Different." In J. E. Alexander (Ed.), *Teaching Reading.* Boston, MA: Little, Brown, 1983.
19. Searfoss, L. W. and Readence, J. E. *Helping Children Learn to Read.* Englewood Cliffs, NJ: Prentice-Hall, 1985.
20. Brueggman, M. A. "An Analysis of First Graders' Oral Language and Receptive Vocabulary Compared with Their Reading Achievement." *Dissertation Abstracts International,* 1985, 46, 110A.
21. Buswell, J. H. "The Relationships Between Oral Language Competency and Reading Achievement of Second and Third Grade Students." *Dissertation Abstracts International,* 1980, 41, 2480A.
22. Cancroft, V.S. "Characteristics of Oral Language of Kindergarten Children as Predictors of Beginning Reading Achievement." *Dissertation Abstracts International,* 1984, 45, 795A.
23. Hopkins, C. J. H. "An Investigation of the Relationship of Selected Oral Language Measures and First-grade Reading Achievement." *Dissertation Abstracts International,* 1977, 38, 749A.
24. Lass, B. "The Relationship Between the Oral Language of Black English Speakers and Their Reading Achievement." *Dissertation Abstracts International,* 1977, 37, 6331A.

25. Mohler, L. E. Z. "The Interrelationships of Fourth Grade Students' Reading Achievement, Oral Generations and Written Productivity as Determined by Factors Found in Four Readability Formulas." *Dissertation Abstracts International,* 1983, 43, 2222A.

26. Pinzari, S. J. "An Analysis of the Syntactic Density of the Oral Language of First Grade Children: How It and Nine Other Variables Interrelate and Predict Global Reading Achievement." *Dissertation Abstracts International,* 1977, 37, 6160A.

27. Rosales, S. M. "A Study of the Relationships Between Oral Language Proficiency and Reading Readiness/Achievement of Selected Mexican-American Children in Corpus Christi, Texas." *Dissertation Abstracts International,* 1981, 41, 4668A.

28. Silva, F. S. "Relationships Between Selected Oral Language Factors and Reading Proficiency." *Dissertation Abstracts International,* 1978, 38, 5308A.

29. Sudak, D. R. "Oral Language Competency as a Predictor of Beginning Reading Achievement." *Dissertation Abstracts International,* 1979, 39, 4099-4100A.

30. Coleman, G. W. "The Relationships Between Auditory Processing, Oral Language and Reading in a Group of Third Grade Children." *Dissertation Abstracts International,* 1981, 42, 2361-2362A.

31. Dobson, S. H. "A Correlational Study on the Oral Language Development and the Reading Achievement of Beginning Second Grade Students." *Dissertation Abstracts International,* 1980, 41, 1941A.

32. Edmaiston, R. K. "Oral Language and Reading: Are They Related for Third-graders? *Remedial and Special Education,* 1984, 5, 33-37.

33. Featherly, B. M. R. "The Relationship Between the Oral Language Proficiency and Reading Achievement of First Grade Crow Indian Children." *Dissertation Abstracts International,* 1986, 46, 2903A.

34. Fechter, E. M. "The Relationship Between Bidialectal Oral Language Performance and Reading Achievement of Black Elementary School Children." *Dissertation Abstracts International,* 1978, 38, 5908A.

35. Gray, R. A. "The Relationship of Oral Language Proficiency in Five and Six Year Old Preschoolers to Readiness for School Success." *Dissertation Abstracts International,* 1979, 39, 4180A.

36. Jones, E. L. "A Study of Oral Vocabulary Scores and Reading Vocabulary Scores of Third Grade Educationally Disadvantaged Students." *Dissertation Abstracts International,* 1978, 38, 5307A.

37. Levi, G.; Musatti, L.; Piredda, L.; and Sehi, E. "Cognitive and Linguistic Strategies in Children With Reading Disabilities in an Oral Storytelling Test." *Journal of Learning Disabilities,* 1984, 17, 406-410.

38. McCartney, E. W. "Pre-reading and Reading Skills of Early Readers and Non-early Readers With Above Average Intelligence." *Dissertation Abstracts International* 1986, 47, 139A.

39. Melton, M.A. "Is a Child's Oral Language Ability at the Beginning of Kindergarten a Predictor of His/Her Performance on Reading Readiness Tests at the End of Kindergarten?" *Dissertation Abstracts International,* 1979, 39, 5928-5929A.

40. Newcomer, P. L. and Magee, P. "The Performances of Learning (Reading) Disabled Children on a Test of Spoken Language." *Reading Teacher,* 1977, 30, 896-900.

41. Scheib, V. V. "The Relationships Among the Various Language Abilities: Oral Reading, Written Language, Oral Language and Verbal Language in Grades One Through Eight." *Dissertation Abstracts International,* 1978, 39, 337A.

42. Wade, W. A. "Relationship of Elicted Oral and Written Language With Reading Comprehension Scores Among Nine-to-Twelve-Year-Old Children." *Dissertation Abstracts International,* 1982, 42, 3434A.

43. Glass, G. V. "Integrating Findings: The Meta-Analysis of Research." In L. S. Schulman (Ed.), *Review of Research in Education.* Vol. V. Itaska, IL: F. E. Peacock, 1975.

44. Hammill, D. D. and McNutt, G. "Language Abilities and Reading: A Review of the Literature on Their Relationship." *Elementary School Journal,* 80, 269-277, 1980.

45. Smith, N. B. and Robinson, H. A. *Reading Instruction for Today's Children.* Englewood Cliffs, N.J.: Prentice-Hall, 1980.

Chapter VI

Myth #6: Word Length Makes No Difference

It has been repeatedly stated by certain reading experts that in beginning reading instruction there is no need to restrict the length of the words used for this purpose, in either letter of syllable count. As is explained in this chapter, this issue is controversial, partially because it has not been extensively examined by experimental research. What limited evidence there is on this subject does not support the contention that word length makes no difference in beginning reading instruction, however. To the contrary. the available research suggests that there is a positive relationship between a word's length and its learnability for young pupils.

Setting the Stage for the Issue

Does it make a difference if one uses short, monosyllabic words to teach children who are first learning to read, as versus longer, multisyllabic words? Is it proper in the initial stages of reading instruction to teach together words of varying syllabic lengths? Should words of one-syllable length be used, rather than those of two or more syllables, to teach children the basic information of phonics?

Is it proper in the initial stages of reading instruction to teach together words of varying syllabic lengths?

To set the stage for the treatment of such questions, it is useful, first, to consider the reading tasks that face beginning readers. They view a strange set of marks, which they must learn are visual symbols. These letters are spaced along a line of print, from left to right, rather than occupying a certain part of a sequence of time, as speech sounds do. These letters in words indicate none of the rhythm and intonation (the tunes of language) the child is accustomed to using as a guide to the meaning of oral language. Then, children must learn to recognize that the spaces on the line of print signal the boundaries of words. They must learn to associate the spellings of words with the ways they are spoken (phonics). They probably will have to learn to respond to a written dialect different from the one they speak.

These letters in words indicate none of the rhythm and intonation .

For example, it has been discovered that the widely-used basal readers sometimes do not accurately reflect the dialect many children speak.[1] A final deterrent to his immediate success as a reader is the young child's short-term auditory and visual memory.

Considering all this, it is understandable why the beginning reader is little more than a "decoder" of words. That is, he uses relatively many eye fixations while reading, has a short eye-voice span, and does poorly on "cloze" tests (where he is asked to restore systematically-deleted words in a sentence). He has yet to learn about the usefulness of the "redundancy" factor of word spellings (the fact only certain letters may follow others in certain parts of a word).

These various tasks the beginner in reading faces doubtlessly account to some extent for the fact that little progress has been made in deciding what the words selected for beginning readers should be.[2] The length of words to be used in the initial stage in reading has not been clearly defined. There is the logical advice that it is clear why beginning readers need more visual information than do mature readers.

Accordingly, the teacher should begin reading instruction by carefully organizing words, so that consistent patterns of letters and rules governing their relation to sound become apparent. Beyond this, however, the determination of the syllabic length of words is often considered to be of little importance. That this problem is seldom broached in the examinations of approaches to beginning reading is readily apparent. For example, discussions of these approaches do not include the use of monosyllabic as versus multisyllabic words in beginning reading.[3]

The Conventional View on Word Length

One group of writers contends that there is no need to restrict early reading instruction, including phonics, to the use of monosyllabic words. This opinion goes back at least to the turn of the century. At this time it was noted, with approval, that for child readers word-length is but a minor factor in word-perception.[4]

More currently it is believed, for example, that most children have no difficulty with the word *grandmother*, even at the preprimer level. On the other hand, it is observed, words like *went* and *want*, and *and*, *said*, *no*, and *on*, are troublesome to many children, long after they should have been well learned.[5] The words, *grandmother* and *grandfather*, seldom cause any trouble, it is said. They supposedly are such long words that their configuration helps children to remember them.[6] To this effect, some contend that children can just as easily learn *airplane*, *monster*, or *dinosaur* as the word *cat* because the former words are relevant to them.[7]

It is clear, then, that some argue that a longer, multisyllabic word poses no additional problems to word identification for the beginning reader than does a monosyllabic word. For a beginner to learn to read *John*, for example, all he has to do is see a representative sample of words that are not *John*, so that he can find out in what respects *John* is different, it is explained.[8]

If the child learning to read, like the child learning to speak, needs the opportunity to examine a huge sample of words that have maximal spelling contrasts, then it would not be proper to begin instruction in reading

One group of writers contends that there is no need to restrict early reading instruction, including phonics, to the use of monosyllabic words.

For a beginner to learn to read John, for example, all he has to do is . . .

with monosyllabic words.[9] If nothing -- even at the very beginning of reading instruction -- should be included in the reading curriculum that is not real language, it would follow, some say, that vocabulary control should not be a criterion for basal reader content.[10]

There is some agreement with the notion that the words selected for instruction in beginning reading should not be controlled or sequenced (from the monosyllabic to the multisyllabic). Such words, it is said, must include a sampling of all kinds of complexities and contrasts, which the pupil must learn to decode.[11] For the beginning reader, who has acquired no word decoding strategies, this sampling would include words of all the syllabic lengths, if this advice were followed.

The length of a word is immaterial in your ability to learn to read it or retain it, it is contended.

About this, it is asked, "What evidence is there that the order or number of letters in a word influence a child's learning to read it?" None, it is answered: length is significant in spelling, but not in reading. The length of a word is immaterial in your ability to learn to read it or retain it, it is contended.[12] Support for such a stand might be taken from the fact that monosyllabic words normally have dozens of meanings attached to them, while such is not the case for multisyllabic words. On the basis of this, it is claimed that it is more efficacious in reading to teach longer words and words from the sciences than it is to teach little "easy" words.[13] It is obvious that the advocates of sight-word instruction (see Myth Number *3* do not believe that word length should be a factor in the choice of words given children to read.

Some advocates of individualized reading also endorse the notion that there be no restriction as to the syllabic count of words used to teach beginning readers. One such advocate describes children who were failures in reading at the end of first grade.[14] These failing children were taught in the second grade with a "key" vocabulary methodology (Each child here tells the teacher the words he wishes to learn to read.). It was found at the end of their second grade that these previous failures in reading now read significantly better than a group of second graders who had successfully completed first-grade reading instruction. Strongly implied by this evidence, of course, is the conclusion that using words of all the syllabic lengths (the "key vocabulary") with beginning readers actually improves reading instruction, rather than hindering it in any way.

Myth #6: Word Length Makes No Difference

Implications from the Research

While there is little direct evidence on this issue, it seems more reasonable to say, nonetheless, that the length of a word, in syllables, is of significant consequence in the initial teaching of reading.[15] If so, this means that the first reading material for children will consist of two-letter and three-letter words. The most suitable words with which the beginner learns to read, thus, are the monosyllabic words.[16] The use of monosyllabic words, in the beginning stages of reading instruction, will leave no uncertainty about the identifying characteristics that mark off one written word from another. This ease of identification is necessary for the automatic recognition responses that are hallmark of the initial stage of reading acquisition.

With relative beginners in phonics, one-syllable words may be used in order to simplify instruction as much as possible. One would start with a study of monosyllabic words, like *cat*, *pig*, *top*, *mud*, and *hen*.

It is best in the initial stage of reading instruction to teach the "short" (unglided) vowels within monosyllabic words.[17] The results of research suggest that a child in the first stages of reading skill typically reads in short units and as this skill develops, word recognition span increases.[18] This could be interpreted to mean that the reader at this level proceeds best from monosyllabic to multisyllabic words.

The results of research suggest that a child in the first stages of reading skill typically reads in short units and as this skill develops, word recognition span increases.

It is reasonable to contend that a child will not learn to read as he learns to speak; that is, by being given an unrestricted or uncontrolled exposure to words of all syllabic lengths. Learning to read does not normally proceed along such lines, as oral language is learned. The rich set of sound-word pairings necessary for reading do not just happen for written language at school, as they do for oral language at home.[19]

The problem a child will likely have in "blending" multisyllabic words is also pointed to by those who prefer children to start with monosyllabic words.[20] Although *umbrella*, for example, is a likely choice to illustrate the short *u* sound, it hardly is an ideal one, because by the time a child finishes saying or thinking *umbrella*, he might have forgotten the initial sound in the initial syllable.

The act of blending or synthesizing the separate speech sounds of a word, so as to pronounce a recognizable word, are put in jeopardy when multisyllabic words are involved. Many children will have forgotten the initial sounds they have pronounced before they come to the end of some of the longer words.[21]

This relationship seems not to occur to those who on the one hand believe that blending seems related to reading success[22] (which it does[23]), and yet on the other hand note that the length of a word is immaterial to the child's ability to read it or retain it.[12] So, other things being equal, the shorter the word, the fewer the potential problems it poses. Decoding of print by the beginning reader is facilitated if the shortest possible words are provided first.[24]

There is some evidence that suggests the relative difficulty beginners have in reading multisyllabic as versus monosyllabic words. This evidence supports the contention that we are justified in the statement that the shorter the word the easier it is to recognize.[25] Of leading importance here are the findings of a study that calculated the total number of spelling-to-sound correspondence rules necessary to read high-frequency, one-syllable words, as opposed to those needed to read common two-syllable words.[26] It was found there are thirty-five rules used in the former (as I count them). An additional thirty-eight rules (total of seventy-three) are required to read these two-syllable words.

Other data help confirm the argument that monosyllabic words may be easier for beginners to read than multisyllabic ones.

Other data help confirm the argument that monosyllabic words may be easier for beginners to read than multisyllabic ones. It is found for common monosyllabic words that simple phoneme-grapheme correspondences (the use of one grapheme to represent one phoneme) occurred 81 percent of the time,[27] which is higher than would be the case for multisyllabic words.

Another study showed that first-graders learned a significantly greater number of three-letter words than of five-letter words.[28] While the words learned here were all monosyllabic, this evidence suggests that multisyllabic words, most of which have five letters or more, in the main would be more difficult for beginning readers than would monosyllabic words. That the latter are shorter is obvious. Only 21 percent of the monosyllabic words (among the 200 most-used words) are over four letters in length.[29]

Myth #6: Word Length Makes No Difference

Other sources would suggest that a positive relationship exists between the syllable count of a word and its particular usefulness for teaching the beginning reader. The first of these is the percentage of multisyllabic words found in compilations of high-frequency or commonly-used words. High-frequency words are those often said to be the ones that should be first acquired by the beginning reader, since they obviously have a great service. An inspection of twelve different collections of high-frequency words indicates that only about 16 percent of such service words are multisyllabic.[30] With this statistic in mind, the argument for the use of monosyllabic words in beginning reading gains stature.

A second source of evidence to defend the use of monosyllabic words in beginning reading instruction is the vocabulary found in first-grade, standardized reading tests, and in other experimental word lists. I examined the first-grade reading sections of several of the prominent reading tests (e.g., *California Reading Test, Gates Reading Test, Diagnostic Reading Scales, Lee-Clark Reading Test,* etc.) to determine the percentage of multisyllabic words found in these sections.

For 982 words found in the initial sections of these standardized reading tests, only 190, or 20 percent, were multisyllabic. In one reading test, for example, only 23 percent of its sixty-seven easiest-to-read words are multisyllabic.[30] These data suggest that short words are easier for young pupils to read than longer ones.

For 982 words found in the initial sections of these standardized reading tests, only 190, or 20 percent, were multisyllabic.

Experimental word lists used as reading tests also show a low proportion of multisyllabic words. In one such graded word list, through grade one, only 10 percent of the words are over one syllable in length.[31] Then, in word lists devised by specialists in speech, for practice in discriminating the various phonetic elements in word combinations, none of the words provided for this are multisyllabic.[32]

Resolution of the Conflict

Answers to the questions posed at the beginning of this discussion can be gained only through a balanced evaluation of the conflicting comment on both sides of this issue. We should begin this, as is usual where there are differing opinions about some aspect of reading instruction, by ignoring the hearsay on the matter and move on to whatever objective evidence can be mustered. Keeping in mind at all times the peculiar tasks we know face the child who is beginning to read, the relative validity of the contrary evidence can be evaluated.

First, the notion that for beginning reading one should always use words that have maximal contrasts in letter-sound relationships is clearly in doubt. The evidence pointed to for this conclusion has been severely, yet fairly, criticized as to its methodology.[33] Then there is empirical evidence that supports the idea that word similarity in beginning reading results in greater word recognition skills and a lesser tendency to make false responses to other words. It is found that first grade pupils learn minimal contrast words (ones that vary in only one way, e.g., *hat*, *cat*, *mat*) better than words with maximal contrasts.[34]

Second, it has been shown that the frequency of a word positively affects its recognizability.[35] As we have seen, the standardized tests and service word lists, both of which are based essentially on a high-frequency-equals-priority-for-teaching principle, share a confidence that this holds true for children first learning to read. Until we are confronted with the evidence (not now available) that beginning readers learn as well on low-frequency as on high-frequency words, standardized tests for beginning readers that call for the learning of a relatively high percentage of monosyllabic words will continue to be used. As well, the teaching of service words, which stem from the same vocabulary stockpile as these tests, is likely to be maintained.

Third, the findings which imply that remarkable gains in reading will result from the unrestricted use of words of all syllabic counts, must be examined carefully. The above report, on the "key word" methodology, says this method caused children who were first grade reading failures to gain more reading skills in one year (their second year; the one with the key words) than normal achieving children, not using key words, could gain in two years.

This report leaves unanswered questions, however. For example, it is said that teachers using the words children give them have discovered that the child's key words are recognized instantaneously as whole words. If not, they are thrown away. Not reported, however, was the percentage of words thusly "thrown away" that were multisyllabic.[14] From what is agreed to be the kinds of tasks that face the beginning reader, coupled with the evidence that the total of rules needed to read two-syllable words is double that for one-syllable words,[26] one could

The evidence pointed to for this conclusion has been severely, yet fairly, criticized as to its methodology.

speculate that the percentage of multisyllabic key words so discarded would have to be high.

And, since children learning to read do not actually recognize words as whole words,[36] hearsay to the contrary notwithstanding, one wonders how they actually did recognize their "key" words. Then, the "key word" advice that it makes no difference if more complex word recognition skills are taught before simpler phonics skills, such as a single phoneme-grapheme correspondence, is difficult to accept, especially in the light of recent longitudinal studies of how children acquire phonics skills.[37] Finally, the "key word" belief that phonics is best taught as a spelling skill must be seen in contrast to the well-accepted fact phonics has much more applicability to reading than to the spelling of words.

Conclusions

The weight of the evidence presented here indicates that monosyllabic words are easier for beginning readers to read than are multisyllabic words. It further suggests that children learning to read should be taught phonics skills with monosyllabic rather than multisyllabic words.

One should be quick to say that no one given source for these monosyllabic words must be accepted before this principle can be adopted and put into practice. If one believes the spontaneous language of children should be the source for these monosyllabic words, they will be taken from the everyday dictations of children.

Other teachers would take monosyllabic words from the source they respect -- the printed word lists of the basal reader. On this matter, at least, the two major disputants of reading instruction -- the basal reader advocates and the proponents of individualized reading -- can agree.

Until enough empirical evidence is gathered to finally settle this problem, it seems wise to continue the use of monosyllabic words for the early stages of reading instruction. Over fifty years ago, experts concluded that the length of a word for children demonstrably influences the difficulty of their learning it.[38] As the present discussion indicates, so far these early researchers have not been proved wrong.

It should be made clear, however, that these conclusions apply only to *beginning* reading instruction. I have found[39] that by grade four the syll-

It further suggests that children learning to read should be taught phonics skills with monosyllabic rather than multisyllabic words.

If one believes the spontaneous language of children should be the source for these monosyllabic words, they will . . .

able lengths of words do not affect children's abilities to read them. For example, I found that fourth-graders read 76.2 percent of one-syllable words correctly. However, they read 74.2 percent of five-syllable words correctly. I also found a correlation of only -.004 between fourth-graders correct reading of words and the syllable count of these words. This correlation was -.023 for their correct reading of words and the letter counts of these words. It thus appears that word length in syllables or letter count does not appear to be a crucial factor in the reading performance of fourth-grade children.

Myth #6: Word Length Makes No Difference

References

1. Hatch, E. *The Syntax of Four Reading Programs Compared With Language Development of Children.* Los Alamitos, CA: SWRL for Educational Research and Development, 1971.

2. Jones, M. "Learning to Process Visually-Coded Symbolic Information." In R.E. Hodges and E. H. Rudorf (Eds.), *Language and Learning to Read.* Boston, MA: Houghton Mifflin, 1972.

3. Aukerman, R. C. *Approaches to Beginning Reading.* New York, NY: John Wiley, 1971.

4. Huey, E. B. *The Psychology and Pedagogy of Reading.* Cambridge, MA: MIT, 1968 (first published 1908).

5. Harris, A. J. *How to Increase Reading Ability.* New York, NY: Longmans, Greene, 1961.

6. Harris, A. J. and Sipay, E. R. *How to Teach Reading.* New York, NY: Longmans, 1979.

7. Aukerman, R. C. and Aukerman, L. R. *How Do I Teach Reading?* New York, NY: John Wiley, 1981.

8. Smith, F. *Understanding Reading.* New York, NY: Holt, Rinehart and Winston, 1971.

9. Smith, F. and Goodman, K. S. "On the Psycholinguistic Method of Teaching Reading." *Elementary School Journal,* 1971, 71,177-181.

10. Smith, E. B.; Goodman, K. S. and Meredith, R. *Language and Thinking in the Elementary School.* New York, NY: Holt, Rinehart and Winston, 1970.

11. Gudschinsky, S. C. "The Nature of the Writing System: Pedagogical Implications." In R. E. Hodges and E. H. Rudorf (Eds.), *Language and Learning to Read.* New York, NY: Houghton Mifflin, 1972.

12. Spache, G. D. "Reactions to Models of Perceptual Processes in Reading." In H. Singer and R. B. Ruddell (Eds.), *Theoretical Models and Processes in Reading.* Newark, DE: International Reading Association, 1970.

13. Howards, M. "How Easy are 'Easy' Words?" *Journal of Experimental Education,* 1964, 32, 377-382.

14. Duquette, R. J. "Barnette-Duquette Study; Parker Study." *Childhood Education,* 1972, 48, 438-440.

15. Carnine, D. and Silbert J. *Direct Instruction Reading.* Columbus, OH: Charles E. Merrill, 1979.

16. Scott, L. B. *Developing Phonics Skills.* New York, NY: Teachers College, Columbia University, 1982.

17. Dechant, E. V. *Improving the Teaching of Reading.* Englewood Cliffs, NJ: Prentice-Hall, 1970.

18. Gibson, E. J. "Learning to Read." *Science,* 1965, 148, 1066-1077.

19. Cazden, C. B. *Child Language and Education.* New York, NY: Holt, Rinehart and Winston, 1972.

20. Durkin, D. *Teaching Them to Read.* Boston, MA: Allyn and Bacon, 1970.

21. Bond, G. L. and Wagner, E. B. *Teaching the Child to Read.* New York, NY: Macmillan, 1960.

22. Spache, G. D. and Spache, E. B. *Reading in the Elementary School.* Boston, MA: Allyn and Bacon, 1969.

23. Chall, J. S.; Roswell, F. G. and Blumenthal, S. H. "Auditory Blending Ability: A Factor in Success in Beginning Reading." *Reading Teacher,* 1963, 17, 113-118.

24. Gough, P. B. "One Second of Reading." In J. F. Kavanagh and I. G. Mattingly (Eds.), *Language by Ear and by Eye.* Cambridge, MA: MIT, 1972.

25. Richard, G. E. "The Recognition Vocabulary of Primary Pupils." *Journal of Educational Research,* 1935, 29, 281-291.

26. Berdinansky, B.; Cronnell, B.; and Koehler, J. *Spelling-Sound Relations and Primary Form-Class Descriptions for Speech-Comprehension Vocabularies of 6-9 Year-Olds.* Los Alamitos, CA: SWRL for Educational Research and Development, 1969.

27. Hodges, R. E. "Phoneme-grapheme Correspondences in Monosyllabic Words." In J. A. Figurel (Ed.), *Forging Ahead in Reading.* Newark, DE: International Reading Association, 1968.

28. Wolpert, E. M. "Length, Imagery, Values and Word Recognition," *Reading Teacher,* 1972, 26, 180-186.

29. Kucera, H. and Francis, W. N. *Computational Analysis of Present-Day American English.* Providence, RI: Brown University, 1967.

30. Groff, P. "Long Versus Short Words in Beginning Reading." *Reading World,* 1975, 14, 277-289.

31. LaPray, M. and Ross, R. "The Grade Word List: Quick Gauge of Reading Ability." *Journal of Reading,* 1969, 12, 305-307.

32. Haspiel, G. S. and Bloomer, R. H. "Maximum Auditory Perception (MAP) Word List." *Journal of Speech and Hearing Disorders,* 1961, 26, 156-163.

33. Desberg, P. and Berdiansky, B. *Word Attack Skills: Review of Literature.* Los Alamitos, CA: SWRL for Educational Research adn Development, 1970.

34. Hartley, R. N. "Effects of List Types and Cues on the Learning of Word Lists." *Reading Research Quarterly,* 1970, 6, 97-121.

35. Postman, L. and Rosenzweig, M. R. "Practice and Transfer in the Visual and Auditory Recognition of Verbal Stimuli." *American Journal of Psychology,* 1956, 69, 209-226.

36. Groff, P. "The Topsy-Turvy World of Sight Words." *Reading Teacher,* 1974, 27, 572-578.

37. Calfee, R. C.; Lindamood, P. and Lindamood, C. "Acoustic-Phonetic Skills in Reading, Kindergarten Through Twelfth Grade." *Journal of Ecucational Psychology,* 1973, 64, 293-298.

38. Gates, A. I. and Boeker, E. "A Study of Initial Stages in Reading by Pre-School Children." *Teachers College Record,* 1923, 24, 469-477.

39. Groff, P. "The Significance of Word Length." *Visible Language,* 1983, 17, 396-398.

Chapter VII

Myth #7: Match Learning Modalities and Instruction

In this chapter, the proposal that children prefer learning to read through either a visual *or* an auditory approach is critically examined. Although there have been many testimonials to this effect, there appears to be no empirical evidence to support the proposition that pupils learn to read more effectively if their so-called "learning modalities" are matched to a method of instruction that is either visually or auditorially oriented. The finding that teachers need not be concerned with this supposed relationship is valuable in that it acts to reduce the task of teaching reading to its truly essential elements.

Many reading educators maintain that only a limited number of children can benefit from the intensive teaching of phonics.

Foundation Precepts of Learning Modalities

Many reading educators maintain that only a limited number of children can benefit from the intensive teaching of phonics. While statements of this nature are commonly found in writings on reading methods, the exact percentage of children for whom the intensive teaching of phoncs supposedly is inappropriate is never given. The lack of precision over pupil statistics in this matter does not signal any irresolution on the part of many reading experts that a significant proportion of children cannot profit from intensive phonics instruction, however.

These reading experts insist that most children learn to read best through a so-called "eclectic" approach. In this scheme for reading instruction, phonics is taught in a delayed, indirect, and incidental manner. The eclectic approach has dominated the teaching of reading for much of this century. The current widespread use of basal readers which teach phonics in this nonintensive manner demonstrates the current popularity of the eclectic concept (Beck & McCaslin, 1978).

From their loyalty to the eclectic approach to reading instruction, it appears that most reading educators have believed that the great majority of children learning to read are visually oriented. That is, they prefer to learn this skill through a visual approach. Hence, the popularity of the whole-word method in most basal readers used in beginning reading programs of the past. Other beginners in reading, of necessity a significantly smaller proportion of this group of children, are held to be auditory oriented. It is believed that they can gain in reading skill from the teaching of intensive phonics. It is well to note, however, that as a matter of practice most basal reader directions to the teacher do not advise such teaching.

These two sensory bases for the acquisition of reading abilities, the visual and the auditory, are called learning modalities.

These two sensory bases for the acquisition of reading abilities, the visual and the auditory, are called learning modalities. The idea of learning modalities involves the notion that some children are better-equipped genetically to use the auditory modality for learning to read, and thus prefer to use it for this purpose. On the other hand, it is believed that other children can be shown to demonstrate a preference for the visual learning modality, and that it suits them better for learning to read.

Myth #7: Match Learning Modalities & Instruction

The past ten years has revealed that many reading experts support the notion that children learn to read more effectively if their preferred learning modality is matched with a method of teaching that is either visual *or* auditory oriented.[1] Consequently, the teacher is advised to first determine which of these learning modalities the child favors, and second, to use a teaching methodology that complements it. Support for this supposition is one of the reasons why some reading professionals find it impossible to accept the proposition that all children should be taught phonics. They insist that because some children do not prefer the auditory learning modality they will not learn to read efficiently through the use of phonics, which teaches them the relationships between speech sounds and letters. Reading educators who oppose the teaching of intensive phonics use their beliefs about learning modalities as proof that phonics teaching is not an essential part of reading instruction for some children.

One group of reading experts has explained the purported effect of preferred learning modalities (on the acquisition of reading) by advising teachers that one important consideration, when making statements about the characterisitics of the individual child, is the child's preferred learning style -- the learning modality most likely to be effective for a given child.[2] These experts agree that some children learn best *visually*, while others learn best by *hearing* what it is they are given to learn. According to other reading authorities, the regular classroom teacher should always ask before commencing instruction: Does this student learn best visually or auditorially?[3] Then the teacher is advised to match, as nearly as is possible, different learning modalities with the different instruction styles that match the modality.[4]

These experts agree that some children learn best visually, while others learn best by hearing what it is they are given to learn.

Today's teacher constantly hears from reading experts who write for their edification that he or she, to be a capable instructor, must teach from a diagnostic point of view. Reading educators encourage teachers to accept the idea that one of the basic considerations for diagnosis of the child's learning potentials and needs is to determine whether the child has a certain strength in mode of learning.[5] It is their contention that the diagnostic teacher automatically suspects that failure in reading is related to an inappropriate matching of the teacher's instructional method and the child's preferred learning modality.[6]

Some reading experts even maintain that some children become confused if they are required to assimilate information through more than one of their sensory systems at a time.[7] This condition is exemplified by children who cannot learn phonics and thus must be taught to read whole words; or, on the other hand, by children who have visual memory problems that prevent them from remembering whole words.

The reading experts who support the idea that a child's preferred learning modality should be linked to the kind of instruction he or she receives in reading are sure that these preferred learning modalities can be determined. The most highly praised means for gaining this information is a technique whereby alternative methods of learning words are used.[4]

First, the child is taught these visually. This achievement is then compared with how well the child learns words auditorily.

The idea of matching preferred learning modalities to specific teaching methods is so attractive to some educational professionals that they have written books devoted to the idea of teaching students through their individual learning modality strengths.[8;9] Detailed instructions on the plan are given here.

Many reading educators are convinced that the research on this issue indicates that if teachers use reading materials and strategies in keeping with the preferred learning modalities of children, their reading achievement will be significantly better than could otherwise be expected.[10] These authorities in the teaching of reading are sure that the research not only indicates that there are differences within individual children, in learning modality functioning, but that the teacher's knowledge of comparative learning modality strengths among children will improve the quality of reading instruction given, and ultimately children's reading scores.[11]

Some reading experts, however, are not as confident about the implications of research done on this issue.

Some reading experts, however, are not as confident about the implications of research done on this issue. One such expert said he believed the research is ambivalent on the concept of preferred learning modalities. He is sure, nonetheless, that there does seem to be some validity for matching an instructional approach to the child's sensory strength.[12]

The positive statements from reading authorities about children's learning modalities, the need to match these to certain teaching techniques, and the reassurance that taking such steps will bring on greater reading achievement for children than is otherwise possible, obviously have had their intended effect on classroom teachers. Arter and Jenkins[13] found that 99 percent of the teachers they questioned thought that a child's learning modality strengths and weaknesses should be a major consideration when the teacher devises educational curriculum and selects methodology.

What the Research Says

In the past few years, there have been at least six competent critical reviews of the empirical research on the hypothesis that if children's preferred learning modalities are closely linked to a teaching method that reflects the nature of these sensory modalities, children as a consequence will learn to read more effectively.

In 1979, Arter and Jenkins[14] examined research on the relationship between differential diagnosis of children's learning modalities and teaching that was designed to coincide with these preferred styles of learning. They reported that "to date, there are 14 reported efforts to improve beginning reading by matching instructional materials and procedures to children's modality strengths. In none of these was reading instruction improved by modality-instructional matching" (p. 547).

Arter and Jenkins cited five reviews of the research, made prior to 1979, that come to the same conclusion about this issue as they did. Three other reviews of the research in 1979 support Arter and Jenkins' judgments about modality-instruction matching.[15;16;17] These surveys of the research agree that there is little empirical support for the notion that different reading approaches are differentially effective for children characterized as eye or ear oriented.

In 1980, Kampwirth and Bates[18] reported that there is little research to support the idea that matching children's learning modalities to teaching approaches is especially effective in reading development. Accordingly, one is hard pressed to justify the teaching of reading according to preferred learning modalities. Then, in 1981, Larrivee[19] critically analyzed the evidence on children's learning modality preference as a guide for differentiation in the kind of beginning reading instruction that should be given. As with the other reviewers of this research, she found

Accordingly, one is hard pressed to justify the teaching of reading according to preferred learning modalities.

that differentiating instruction according to children's learning modality preferences did not significantly facilitate their learning to read.

Conclusions

Keeping in mind the maxim that explanations introduced to explain reading phenomena should not be more complicated than is necessary, the finding that teachers need not be concerned with the connection, if any, between children's preferred learning modalities and the teaching techniques that should be used, comes as a relief. It is gratifying to report that there is convincing evidence to contradict and repudiate the advice often given teachers that they should be expected to match teaching methods and materials with children's preferred learning modalities. This finding helps reduce the teaching of reading to its essential elements. This reduction of tasks demanded of the reading teacher represents a part of the instructional reform that is badly needed. Taking the issue of preferred learning modalities off the list of required methodology will help teachers concentrate on the features of this teaching that are truly vital.

The evidence on children's preferred learning modalities discussed here also makes it clear than the warning often given to teachers that children who prefer the visual modality for learning will not benefit from intensive phonics teaching is a misinformed one, and therefore should be ignored. There have been many reasons given for the teaching or not teaching of intensive phonics. It is wise to note that it is not legitimate to include children's learning modalities among them. The teaching of phonics is supported by the evidence that learning to read involves *both* the visual and auditory senses, not either one or the other.

The teaching of phonics is supported by the evidence that learning to read involves both the visual and auditory senses, not either one or the other.

The confusing nature of the argument for modality-based instruction probably is well illustrated by the comments in favor of this teaching from Barbe and Swassing.[8] They begin a paragraph in their book on this subject with the statement, "Research supports the contention that modality-based instruction works" (p. 11). These authors then quote a critical review made of the research on this topic in 1978 that found the empirical evidence indicates conclusively that modality preference and method of teaching *do not* interact significantly.

Despite the explicit disavowal of modality-based teaching that this review presents, Barbe and Swassing maintain that this review, "which may be viewed as refuting the matching of teaching strategies with students' modality strengths, can be construed as indirect support for modality-based education, or at least its potential" (p.11). Barbe and Swassing base this conclusion on an analogy they find between this situation and auto racing. Imagine, they say, that after many auto races an electric-driven car finally is able to win out over a gasoline-driven car. They contend that one should anticipate from this win that there will be a significant increase, in the future, of electric car wins.

The problem of using such logic as a defense for modality-based instruction is immediately obvious. There have been many attempts made to replicate the analogue of the electric car win to which Barbe and Swassing refer. True, there have been a very few instances when teaching done in accordance with children's preferred learning modalities produced greater word recognition than was otherwise possible. Efforts to reproduce these findings have consistently failed, however. It thus is foolhardy to insist that because some isolated researcher gained a certain finding from his investigation, a finding that no one else can duplicate, that this exception to the general body of research findings substantiates the contention that modality-based teaching of reading is superior to other methodology.

In fact, it appears that only wishful thinking could lead to the conclusion that extensive observations and research verify significant improvement in both student achievement and motivation, when learning and teaching styles are matched. Dunn and Dunn's[20] comments to this effect are in violation of the procedures for evaluating scientific investigations. The crucial test of the validity of scientific data is its ability to be replicated. Accordingly, evidence that cannot be consistently duplicated is discredited. Barbe and Swassing ask us to not demand that modality-based teaching face this test.

The crucial test of the validity of scientific data is its ability to be replicated.

Enthusiasm for modality-based teaching in the face of overwhelming evidence that indicates it is not particularly successful represents a prime example of why the myths of reading instruction persist. This is reading expert bias. Bias in reading experts' judgments work in this way. These reading professionals somehow come to a self-satisfying conviction about a certain aspect of teacher behavior. Isolated, uncontrolled, or atypical bits of field experience may be the causal factor here.

In any event, this conviction in time becomes traditional to these reading experts' way of thinking about reading instruction. To give up such a conviction thus becomes painful and even humiliatingly self-critical. The reading expert in question at this point grasps at straws from the research for continued substantiation of his or her view, works up illogical arguments in its defense, refuses to accept research findings, and nitpicks about the quality of those studies whose findings refute his or her beliefs.

Paradoxically enough, these reading experts eagerly accept the results of any research that favors their bias, regardless of quality or mode of implementation. (See "Why the Myths of Reading Instruction Prevail" to follow.) The exercise of such biased thinking has resulted in some indefensible accusations being made by the defenders of modality-based instruction against those who have reviewed the research literature on this issue.

For example, while they provide no references to research reviews to buttress their support for modality-based instruction, Dunn and Dunn[9] call the conclusions drawn by those who have conducted critical surveys of the research on this teaching the result of "fallacious reasoning" (p.13). This reaction reminds one of the degree to which predetermined notions about the teaching of reading will resist to change, even from research findings.

... almost all children at school-entrance age have the auditory and visual perception powers necessary to the successful learning of phonics and reading.

The findings that modality-based reading instruction is not especially conducive to improved achievement is reinforced as well by the evidence that almost all children at school-entrance age have the auditory and visual perception powers necessary to the successful learning of phonics and reading.[21] A very high percentage of children at this age level can correctly articulate the speech sounds of their particular English dialect. The correlations that have been obtained between children's auditory discimination faculties and their beginning reading scores have been too low for predictive purposes.

Also, reviews of the research on the relationships of children's visual perception skills and their reading development reveal that scores on visual perception tests are not good predictors of reading achievement, and do not differentiate well between good and poor readers. Attempts to teach children the so-called visual discrimination tasks (copying and selecting geometric forms, eye pursuit activities, matching geometric designs or those involving concrete objects, naming the parts or details of pictures, etc.) have not proved to be productive of greater reading success than would otherwise be attainable.

Valin's[22] review of the research on these matters leads him to conclude that "the numerous American experimets with visual training programs have not proved themselves helpful in increasing reading achievement." In fact, he goes on, "when one looks at the low correlations which have to date been obtained between the [visual and auditory] functions which have been tested and the reading achievement scores, the impression arises that factors have been measured that are rather irrelevant to the reading process."

That is, there "are scarcely any relationships worth mentioning...between reading achievement and the first, second, and third school years and some variables measured at the beginning of school (visual perception, directional confusion, articulation, auditory discrimination, vocabulary, school readiness)" (p. 39).

Valtin's critical analysis of the evidence is representative of other research reviews, as well. It is apparent then, as research has shown, that children who practice discriminating and copying geometric shapes and the other activities commonly found in visual perception training programs get better at doing these activities. The research indicates, however, that learning these skills does not help improve their reading skills.[23]

It is clear that the idea of learning modality-based reading instruction arose from the ashes of the now discredited notion of reading readiness. The theory of reading readiness holds that a stage of reading readiness, something other than the child's tested ability to learn reading skills, must be reached by children before they are ready to learn to read. But as Coltheart[24] protests, "The putative maturational stage at which a child will suddenly be able to respond to reading instruction has never been identified; no method for determining whether or not a given child has reached this stage has ever been developed" (p. 16).

The view that reading readiness is brought about by appropriate instruction also is a redundant notion. That is, instead of teaching reading readiness, one must ask, why not simply teach the first elements of reading skills to children and if they progress satisfactorily in this instruc-

It is clear that the idea of learning modality-based reading instruction arose from the ashes of the now discredited notion of reading readiness.

tion, signify that they are ready for this teaching? As well, the concept of reading readiness is dangerous, since it provides a faulty explanation for a child's lack of success in reading. Saying that a child is not ready, becase he or she has failed to learn satisfactorily, does not explain what children need in order to be ready to learn. This statement also is used as an excuse to delay the teaching of reading, especially phonics, and thus helps perpetuate the myths of reading instruction.

Myth #7: Match Learning Modalities & Instruction

References

1. McNeil, J. D.; Donant, L.; and Alkin, M. C. *How to Teach Reading Successfully.* Boston, MA: Little, Brown, 1980.

2. Early, M. "Teaching Reading and Writing: The Past Ten Years." In M. M. McCulloch (Ed.), *Inchworm, Inchworm: Persistent Problems in Reading Education.* Newark, DE: International Reading Association, 1980.

3. Cheek, E. H. and Cheek, M. C. *Reading Instruction Through Content Teaching.* Columbus, OH: Charles E. Merrill, 1983.

4. Spache, G. D. *Investigating the Issues of Reading Disabilities.* Boston, MA: Allyn and Bacon, 1976.

5. Harris, L. A. and Smith, C. B. *Reading Instruction Through Diagnostic Teaching.* New York, NY: Holt, Rinehart and Winston, 1972.

6. Wilson, R. M. *Diagnostic and Remedial Reading for Classroom and Clinic.* Columbus, OH: Charles E. Merrill, 1981.

7. Johnson, D. J. "Process Deficits in Learning Disabled Children and Implications for Reading." In L. A. Resnick and P. A. Weaver (Eds.), *Theory and Practice of Early Reading,* Vol. II. Hillsdale, NJ: Lawrence Erlbaum, 1979.

8. Barbe, W. B. and Swassing, R. H. *Teaching Through Modality Strengths: Concepts and Practices.* Columbus, OH: Zaner-Bloser, 1979.

9. Dunn, R. and Dunn, K. *Teaching Students Through Their Individual Learning Styles: A Practical Approach.* Reston, VA: Reston, 1978.

10. Aukerman, R. G. and Aukerman, L. R. *How Do I Teach Reading?* New York, NY: John Wiley, 1978.

11. Robeck, M. C. and Wilson, J. A. R. *Psychology of Reading: Foundations of Instruction.* New York, NY: John Wiley, 1974.

12. Dechant, E. *Diagnosis and Remediation of Reading Disabilities.* Englewood Cliffs, NJ: Prentice-Hall, 1981.

13. Arter, J. A. and Jenkins, J. R. "Examining the Benefits and Prevelance of Modality Considerations in Special Education. *Journal of Special Education,* 1977, 11, 281-296.

14. Arter, J. A. and Jenkins, J. R. "Differential Diagnosis--Prescriptive Teaching: A Critical Appraisal." *Review of Educational Research,* 1979, 49, 517-555.

15. Bateman, B. "Teaching Reading to Learning Disabled and Other Hard-to-Teach Children." In L. B. Resnick and P. A. Weaver (Eds.), *Theory and Practice of Early Reading,* Vol. I. Hillsdale, NJ: Lawrence Erlbaum, 1979.

16. Resnick, L. B. "Toward a Usable Psychology of Reading Instruction." In L. B. Resnick and P. A. Weaver (Eds.), *Theory and Practice of Early Reading, Vol. III. Hillsdale, NJ: Lawrence Erlbaum, 1979.*

18. Kampwirth, T. J. and Bates, M. "Modality Preference and Teaching Method: A Review of the Research." *Academic Therapy,* 1980, 15, 597-605.

19. Larrivee, B. "Modality Preference as a Model for Differentiation in Beginning Reading Instruction: A Review of the Issue." *Learning Disability Quarterly,* 1981, 4, 180-188.

20. Dunn, R. and Dunn, K. "Learning Styles/Teaching Styles: Should They . . . Can They be Matched?" *Educational Leadership,* 1979, 36, 238-244.

21. Groff, P. *Phonics: Why and How.* Morristown, NJ: General Learning, 1977.

22. Valtin, R. "Dyslexia: Deficit in Reading or Deficit in Research?" In D. J. Sawyer (Ed.), *Disabled Readers: Insight, Assessment, Instruction.* Newark, DE: International Reading Association, 1980.

23. Weaver, P. *Research Within Reach.* Washington, DC: U. S. Department of Health, Education and Welfare, 1978.

24. Coltheart, M. "When Can Children Learn to Read--And When Should They be Taught?" In T. G. Waller and G. E. Mackinnon (Eds.), *Reading Research: Advances in Theory and Practice.* New York, NY: Academic, 1979.

Chapter VIII

Myth #8: Letter Names are Unimportant

The significance of letter-name knowledge by pupils learning to read has become a controversial issue. This chapter describes the research studies which have indicated that pupils taught letter names do not learn to read any better than do pupils not given this instruction. A recent critical analysis of these studies reveals, however, that each of them has conspicuous flaws that preclude one from concluding that letter-name knowledge has no positive effect on reading acquisition. Also discussed is the doubtful argument that the high statistical correlations found between letter-name knowledge and reading development are meaningless.

Present Status of the Letter Name Debate

The belief that children's knowledge of letter names is not useful to them as they learn to read was widely held by advocates of the so-called look-say or whole-word method which has dominated reading instruction during most of the present century. It is not surprising that the proponents of the look-say method, who oppose the direct and intensive teaching of phonics, also reject the idea of teaching children the names of letters. If it was unnecessary, as they claimed, for children to be taught directly the correspondences between letter shapes and speech sounds (phonics), it consequently would be a waste of time to teach them letter names.

. . . Chall concluded that a child's ability to identify letters by name, letter knowledge, is an important predictor of his or her reading achievement at various points in the first and second grades.

The look-say approach's advice to teachers (not to teach letter names) was challenged over the years by research that tested beginning readers' knowledge of letter names and their later reading achievement. An analysis of seventeen of the most highly-regarded of these studies was reported on by Chall, in 1967 (see Bibliography). From her critical review of these researches, Chall concluded that a child's ability to identify letters by name, letter knowledge, is an important predictor of his or her reading achievement at various points in the first and second grades.

With this research in mind, other reading experts advise teachers to begin reading instruction by teaching the child to associate the shape of the letter with its name.[1] They recommend that letter names be taught quite early in the beginning stage of reading instruction.[2] Contrary to the beliefs of look-say advocates, they are convinced that teaching the letter names should be started at least by the time reading instruction is begun. Some claim that this instruction is productive in developing beginning readers' abilities to discriminate.[3]

Other reading experts who insist that learning letter names contributes to a child's learning to read believe that the beginning reader is helped in this way: In saying the letter name, the child says the phoneme that he or she is later taught in phonics.[4] They see that the value to the learner of knowing letter names, even when the letter names and speech sounds are not identical, appears to be a way of labeling and separating the symbols, so that they can be discriminated more easily.[5]

Myth #8: Letter Names are Unimportant

Some reading experts refuse to make any evaluative comment whatsoever on the issue of letter-name teaching. They are content to note that educators disagree whether it is necessary for children to name letters prior to being given reading instruction.[6] These experts appear to be ducking the issue. They contend that children learn to read equally well whether the names of letters are taught before or after the child learns to read sentences or has mastered phonics.[7] (Why the learning of letter names would necessarily follow the acquisition of these other reading skills is not revealed.)

They believe that it does not matter whether systematic instruction in letter names is given before or during beginning reading instruction.[8] One authority in reading would link the teaching of letter names to the time when the pupil is required to match upper-case and lower-case pairs of letters.[9] Letter names must be taught at this time, he insists.

But since children can learn to read without experience in matching upper- and lower-case letters, it is obvious that this point in time he refers to is a highly indeterminate one. The most puzzling statements about letter-name teaching, however, come from reading experts who cite all the objections that have been made to this instruction, and then without explaining why, insist that children should be taught to associate letter forms with letter names.[10]

The most uncompromising objections to the teaching of letter names come from those who lead the movement in reading instruction called the psycholinguistic approach. One of the notable proponents of the psycholinguistic approach insists that making sure that phonics skills are learned by the child is a powerful and potential method of interfering in the process of learning to read.[11] In fact, he goes on, all the teacher can do in reading instruction is provide the raw material, the written word and its name. His view of this, he notes, endeavors to account for the identification of words without the mediation of letter identification. In like fashion, other experts argue that it obviously isn't a necessity to know the alphabet before learning to read.[12] They believe that there are many children who learn to read without knowing the alphabet.

There is opposition to the teaching of letter names for yet other reasons. One expert contends that letter names do not contain the speech sounds taught in phonics, and that there is testimony which indicates that confusions often arise when the letter name is stressed along with the letter

They are content to note that educators disagree whether it is necessary for children to name letters prior to being given reading instruction.

The most uncompromising objections to the teaching of letter names come from those who lead the movement in reading instruction called the psycholinguistic approach.

There is opposition to the teaching of letter names for yet other reasons.

sound.[13] He also argues that the high positive correlations found between letter-name knowledge and reading achievement are probably accounted for by factors such as children's cognitive development, emotional stability, ability to attend, and home backgrounds. Such an argument dismisses the statistical evidence that Chall uses for her conclusions about the positive relationships of letter-name knowledge and reading success as correlation, not causality.

Some experts refer to studies showing that teaching letter names in isolation does not have much effect on later success in reading.[14] They contend that the evidence Chall surveyed does not suggest that learning letter names will increase reading readiness.[15] They repeat the warning that a correlation does not mean causation. As to whether learning letter names helps children learn to read, or whether it and reading are the result of other factors, Weaver[31] (pp.35-36) believes "most experts think that the latter is the more likely explanation."

There are even reading experts who reject teaching children the names of letters and claim that this is an example of irrational instruction. These opponents of letter-name teaching protest that there appears to be no logic to this procedure.[16] They argue that the ability to name the letters of the alphabet in itself has no logical relationship to the task of learning to read.[17] Instead, they are persuaded that a third factor, such as intelligence or background experiences, might account for both letter-name knowledge and reading ability.[18]

It is maintained that letter-name knowledge simply reflects the child's intelligence, socioeconomic and language backgrounds, and parental aspirations.[19] Thus, the knowledge of letter names is said to be symptomatic of a certain maturation in the cognitive processes.[20] They comment that the child who knows the letter names has made progress in cognition that will enable him to cope with the first steps in reading.[21]

It appears that the knowledge of letter names is not a prerequisite in beginning reading, at least in some computer assisted instruction. Fletcher[22] describes such a program that met with substantial success, although no direct attempt was made to teach the names of letters. It was assumed in this program that teaching letter names would confuse students who were being taught to decode.

It appears that the knowledge of letter names is not a prerequisite in beginning reading, at least in some computer assisted instruction.

Myth #8: Letter Names are Unimportant

Analysis of Research on the Issue

To date there also have been at least five well-known studies that aimed to discover the effect that the direct teaching of letter names had on certain aspects of beginning reading skill. All of these investigations have been held by certain reading experts to indicate that pupils taught letter names directly do not learn to read significantly better than do pupils not taught letter names.[23;24;25;26;27]

Ehri[28] did a thorough analysis of these five studies, the ones most often cited as proof that direct instruction in letter names is not particularly helpful for children learning to read. From this analysis Ehri decided that "the negative evidence yielded by these [five] studies does not lay to rest the letter-name hypothesis" (p. 149). She argues that each of these five studies has conspicuous and serious flaws that preclude one from drawing conclusions from them as to the contributions that letter-name knowledge makes to reading acquisition.

Ehri complained that the designs of these studies did not control several important variables. That is, these studies did not determine how well letter names must be known to be useful in recognizing words, what was the relationship of letter names to the characteristics of the words used to test the relationship, the relationship of letter-name knowledge and reading ability, and what magnitude of difference letter-name knowledge might make in a child's learning to read. Especially telling was Ehri's criticism that this research isolated letter-name knowledge and tested it as if it were a separable factor in reading acquisition. She argues that if letter names are taught simultaneously with phonics, it is probable that the integration of these variables would significantly affect reading acquisition. The evidence that letter-name instruction combined with phonics facilitates reading development[24;29] appears to bear out Ehri's contentions.

The evidence that letter-name instruction combined with phonics facilitates reading development appears to bear out Ehri's contentions.

Conclusions

It is doubtful that the reading experts on either side of this issue would agree with one set of reading experts who contend that the presently available research on this matter is quite inconclusive.[30] To the contrary, it is clear that reading experts currently tend to have conclusive views about this matter, views that are highly contradictory of one another. A compromise for these opposite positions does seem possible, nonetheless.

As noted, the evidence that indicates that children's knowledge of letter names correlates highly with their later success in learning to read has been judged to be inconsequential. The acquisition of letter-name knowledge is said to be simply a reflection of the development of children's general mental abilities, and not a prerequisite for their learning to read.

However, Chall found that letter-name knowledge has a generally higher statistical association with early reading success than does mental ability.

However, Chall found that letter-name knowledge has a generally higher statistical association with early reading success than does mental ability. While it is true that high statistical correlations found between reading success and letter-name knowledge do not prove absolutely that there is a close relationship between them, Chall's finding does lead one to question the supposition, however, that reading and letter-name knowledge have no connection whatsoever. The fact that a child's letter-name knowledge correlates more highly with reading than it does with his or her intelligence thus cannot be totally dismissed.

Little confidence can be placed in the objections to letter-name teaching from the advocates of the so-called psycholinguistic approach to reading instruction, who recommend the abandonment of phonics teaching. The great mass of empirical evidence now available indicates that an early, direct, intensive, and systematic teaching of phonics brings on greater beginning reading achievement than does the approach these negative critics of phonics advocate (see Bibliography). To this effect, the claim that there are many children who read well but do not know letter names needs to be challenged. There appears to be no support in the research for such a contention.

The question remains as to whether letter-name knowledge is a prerequisite for the successful learning of phonics. There is evidence that letter-name knowledge, combined with phonics knowledge, is more productive of reading ability than is either of these aspects alone. Nonetheless, the argument that teaching letter names will confuse children who are learning phonics has been voiced. Anecdotal, testimonial evidence is offered as proof for this assumption.[13] If one accepts anecdotal evidence as confirmation one way or the other about the utility of letter-name teaching, however, then one must take the word of teachers who teach

Myth #8: Letter Names are Unimportant

phonics programs which begin with letter-name teaching -- and that their successes depend on this early letter-name instruction. It is obvious, then, that using anecdotal evidence to solve the issue of the importance of letter-name knowledge results in a standoff.

As noted, Fletcher[22] describes successful computer assisted instruction in beginning reading wherein letter names were not taught. However, he also depicts such programs that were effective in teaching reading in which letter names were an essential part.

Ehri's critical analysis of the findings that the direct teaching of letter names has proved ineffective for reading purposes deserves our special attention.[28] Her central contention, as a result of this critique, was that letter-name knowledge does have usefulness for the development of reading -- if it is combined with phonics teaching. While it is doubtful that letter-name knowledge *alone* is a prerequisite to reading acquisition, it does appear to help improve the effectiveness of the phonics teaching that is given for this purpose.

While it is doubtful that letter-name knowledge alone is a prerequisite to reading acquisition . . .

Therefore, at the present time, the following recommendation about letter-name teaching seems tenable: Letter-name teaching is appropriate if done concurrently with instruction given in phonics. Reading experts who contend that the time given letter-name teaching in the reading program is an unimportant consideration doubtless are wrong in this judgment.

Since letter-name knowledge and phonics knowledge are highly correlated, it is logical to view them as functionally related areas of information. Thus the simultaneous teaching of letter names and phonics appears to be the best way to exploit the potential for assisting children to learn to read. One of these potentials might be that letter-name knowledge is necessary for communication between the teacher and the students during reading instruction.[31]

References

1. Liberman, I. Y. and Shankweiler, D. "Speech, the Alphabet, and Teaching to Read." In L. B. Resnick and P. A. Weaver (Eds.), *Theory and Practice of Early Reading,* Vol. II. Hillsdale, NJ: Lawrence Erlbaum, 1979.

2. Carnine, D. and Silbert J. *Direct Instruction Reading.* Columbus, OH: Charles E. Merrill, 1979.

3. Durkin, D. *Teaching Them to Read.* Boston, MA: Allyn and Bacon, 1970.

4. McNeil, J. D.; Donant, L.; and Alkin, M. C. *How to Teach Reading Successfully.* Boston, MA: Little, Brown, 1980.

5. Robeck, M. C. and Wilson, J. A. R. *Psychology of Reading: Foundations of Instruction.* New York, NY: John Wiley, 1974.

6. Ollila, L. "Preparing the Child." In P. Lamb and R. Arnold (Eds.), *Teaching Reading.* Belmont, CA: Wadsworth, 1980.

7. Jones, D. M. *Teaching Children to Read.* New York, NY: Harper and Row, 1971.

8. Harris, A. J. and Sipay, E. R. *How to Teach Reading.* New York, NY: Longman, 1979.

9. Mazurkiewicz, A. J. *Teaching about Phonics.* New York, NY: St. Martin's, 1976.

10. Hall, M. *Teaching Reading as a Language Experience.* Columbus, OH: Charles E. Merrill, 1970.

11. Smith, F. *Psycholinguistics and Reading.* New York, NY: Holt, Rinehart and Winston, 1973.

12. Fry, E. B. *Elementary Reading Instruction.* New York, NY: McGraw-Hill, 1977.

13. Venexky, R. L. "The Curious Role of Letter Names in Reading Instruction." *Visible Language,* 1975, 9, 7-23.

14. Lapp, D. and Flood, J. *Teaching Reading to Every Child.* New York, NY: Macmillan, 1978.

15. Stoodt, B. D. *Reading Instruction.* Boston, MA: Houghton Mifflin, 1981.

16. Aukerman, R. C. *Approaches to Beginning Reading.* New York, NY: John Wiley, 1971.

17. Otto, W.; Rude, R.; and Spiegel, D. L. *How to Teach Reading.* Reading, MA: Addison-Wesley, 1979.

18. Karlin, R. *Teaching Elementary Reading.* New York, NY: Harcourt Brace Jovanovich, 1971.

19. Spache, G. D. and Spache, E. B. *Reading in the Elementary School.* Boston, MA: Allyn and Bacon, 1977.

20. Stauffer, R. G. *Teaching Reading as a Thinking Process.* New York, NY: Harper and Row, 1969.

21. Walcutt, C. C.; Lamport, J.; and McCracken, G. *Teaching Reading.* New York, NY: Macmillan, 1974.

22. Fletcher, J. D. "Computer-assisted Instruction in Beginning Reading: The Stanford Projects." In L. B. Resnick and P. A. Weaver (Eds.), *Theory and Practice of Early Reading,* Vol. II. Hillsdale, NJ: Lawrence Erlbaum, 1979.

23. Johnson, R. J. *The Effect of Training in Letter Names on Success in Beginning Reading for Children of Differing Abilities.* Doctoral dissertation, University of Minnesota, 1969.

24. Ohnmacht, D. C. *The Effects of Letter Knowledge on Achievement in Reading in in the First Grade.* Paper presented at American Educational Research Association annual convention, Los Angeles, 1969.

25. Jenkins, J. R.; Bausell, R. B.; and Jenkins, L. M. "Comparison of Letter Name and Letter Sound Training as Transfer Variables." *American Educational Research Journal,* 1972, 9, 75-86.

26. Samuels, S. J. "The Effect of Letter-name Knowledge on Learning to Read." *American Educational Research Journal,* 1972, 9, 65-74.

27. Silberberg, N. E.; Silberberg, M. C.; and Iversen, I. A. "The Effects of Kindergarten Instruction in Alphabet and Numbers on First Grade Reading." *Journal of Learning Disabilities,* 1972, 5, 254-261.

28. Ehri, L. C. "A Critique of Five Studies Related to Letter-name Knowledge and Learning to Read." In L. M. Gentile; M. L. Kamil; and J. S. Blanchard (Eds.), *Reading Research Revisited.* Columbus, OH: Charles E. Merrill, 1983.

29. Linehan, E. B. *Early Instruction in Letter Names and Sounds as Related to Success in Beginning Reading.* Doctoral dissertation, Boston University, 1957.

30. May, F. B; and Eliot, S. B. *To Help Children Read.* Columbus, OH: Charles E. Merrill, 1978.

31. Weaver. P. *Research Within Reach.* Washington, D.C.: Department of Health, Education and Welfare, 1978.

Chapter IX

Myth #9: Dictionary Syllabication is Needed

This chapter analyzes the claims that have been made for teaching pupils the rules of dictionary syllabication as a means of helping them acquire reading skills. The fact that research indicates that teaching pupils these dictionary rules has no particular value in regard to their development of reading skills has led some reading experts to reject the teaching of all forms of syllabication. A third proposal for the teaching of syllabication argues that this recommended procedure makes it easier for pupils to learn and apply syllabication, and above all, is a linguistically defensible approach.

Outline of the Problem

Whether instruction should be given in the syllabication of written words is a continuing controversy in modern reading programs. In the recent past, teachers have been given three distinctly different recommendations about this matter.

One group of reading experts has advised them to teach their pupils the dictionary rules of syllabication. They claim that the application of such knowledge will help pupils recognize unfamiliar multisyllabic written words. It is presumed here that this form of syllabication helps pupils break up these long words into recognizable smaller parts, which then can be pronounced in serial order, so that the names of the unknown written words can be produced by the pupil.

A second body of reading authorities argues that teaching children to syllabicate written words is not a useful or necessary procedure.

Which of these three recommendations about syllabication should teachers follow?

A third set of teacher educators believes that syllabication is a needed skill for children who are learning to read, but that dictionary syllabication should not be taught for this purpose. Which of these three recommendations about syllabication should teachers follow?

The Flaws of Dictionary Syllabication

The majority of teacher educators who have written about syllabication in the past decade advocate teaching dictionary rules for this word-breaking activity. One reading expert's comments to this effect are representative of the opinion of this group of reading professors. He reminds teachers that dictionary syllabication is a highly valuable word-attack technique.[1] Others agree that in order to divide an unknown word into smaller, pronounceable units, the student must know the dictionary rules for dividing a word.[2] Some say that children have to learn to use a number of generalizations from the dictionary in breaking words into syllables.[3] In fact, one reading authority contends that the ability to divide an unknown word into dictionary syllables is vital to phonics.[4] The application of dictionary syllabication allows children to gradually escape from an overreliance on phonics, says yet another teacher educator.[5]

Myth #9: Dictionary Syllabication is Needed

What is more, he avows, dictionary syllabication rules are fairly easy for children to learn near the end of grade two.

A smaller group of modern reading authorities is convinced that teaching children to syllabicate words is not a profitable educational practice. To this effect, they declare that the act of dividing words into syllables serves no useful purpose for reading.[6] They observe that asking children to divide words into syllables is a common teaching practice, but one which cannot possibly contribute to independent word identification. There is agreement among these experts that syllabication is probably the most misclassified and misused of the word identification skills. They are sure that teaching students to divide words into syllables is in itself nonfunctional as a decoding aid. They echo the warning that teachers should not encourage children to rely on dictionary divisions of syllables as keys to pronunciation.[7] They say they can discover no reason why syllabication activities should be included in a word-analysis program. Such activities are deemed wasteful and/or even detrimental.[8]

Part of the objection to teaching syllabication stems from the misleading and inoperable statements about rules that some advocates of dictionary syllabication have made. One can deride, rightly enough, this syllabication rule: "divide before the consonant, if the vowel is long." To follow this rule, one must know the pronunciation of the word in order to divide it correctly. But, if one knows the pronunciation of a word, why bother to syllabicate it?

Part of the objection to teaching syllabication stems from the misleading and inoperable statements about rules that some advocates of dictionary syllabication have made.

Despite this sensible criticism, some modern advocates of dictionary syllabication continue to offer unworkable rules about this activity: "If the accent is on the first syllable, the following consonant is included in the first syllable."[9] "When a consonant comes between two vowels, the consonant is part of the first syllable, if the vowel is short."[10] "When an accented syllable ends with a single vowel letter, that letter usually represents its long sound."[11] Or, "The reader should syllabicate only when he is able to apply the appropriate phonics generalizations."[12]

It is likely that the all-too-often appearance of such obviously muddled statements about dictionary syllabication (in advice given to teachers) is the basis for the criticism of the role that dictionary syllabication principles can play in identifying unfamiliar word forms. Such statements cause misunderstandings by teachers, and by authors of reading instructional materials, about the place of syllabication in reading instruction.

It is true, then, that some studies have raised serious questions about the utility of teaching children to divide words into syllables. Research evidence[13;14] indicates that teaching children dictionary syllabication rules has no particular value in the development of their reading ability. Support for the conclusion that there is little positive relationship between reading ability and knowledge of dictionary syllabication rules comes from Marzano, *et al.*[15] They obtained a correlation of only .13 between the syllabication and reading comprehension subtests scores on a standardized reading test taken by middle school remedial readers.

All Syllabication is Bad?

Thus, it is fair to say that research studies indicate that rule-oriented dictionary syllabication instruction does not improve word recognition skills or reading comprehension.[16] We must agree that these facts make formal instruction in the usual conventions of syllabication indefensible.[17] With this information in mind, some current reading experts infer that no form of syllabication has any utility in reading instruction programs. "Join us in calling for a moratorium on syllabication instruction," Cunningham, Cunningham, and Rystrom[14] urge their fellow educators.

A few reading authorities reject both the teaching of dictionary syllabication and the call for a moratorium on the teaching of all forms of this breaking down of multisyllabic words. They would argue that it is not essential to the recognition or pronunciation of a word to know exactly when some of the breaks between syllables occur, as there are given by the dictionary.[18]

For instance, a child does not have to know whether the division of syllables in the word *tumble* come before or after the *b* in order to pronounce the word correctly. Others agree with the idea that the aim of syllabication is an approximately correct pronunciation which may aid in recalling the auditory memories of the word.[19] They concur that probably the point of such instruction should be to help students approximate reasonable breaking points in multisyllabic words.[20]

We must agree that these facts make formal instruction in the usual conventions of syllabication indefensible.

Myth #9: Dictionary Syllabication is Needed

A Third Position on Syllabication

So, rather than teaching dictionary syllabication, or to the contrary, insisting that no specific syllabication procedures be taught to the child who is learning to read, they take a third position. To this effect they would substitute instruction in dictionary syllabication for having children identify phonograms or closed syllables (syllables that begin with a vowel letter and end in a consonant) in unfamiliar words. Children so instructed would then try to sound the vowel letters of these clusters using first the "short" vowel sound that is indicated by the vowel letter in question.

For example, dividing the word into units, *butt/er*, *chick/en*, will almost instantly give pupils a pronunciation they can then use to reproduce true pronunciations.[21] If this sounding does not produce a satisfactory pronunciation of the syllable, the child gives the vowel letter a "long" vowel sound.

The advice that teaching certain spelling patterns and providing practice in identifying them, until they are recognized automatically,[16] is a promising technique worthy of application and would be compatible with this new form of syllabication. The system of word identification in which children become familiar with short words, which they then compare and contrast with unfamiliar ones, could be a way to increase children's sensitivity to syllable boundaries, without teaching them dictionary syllabication.[22] Procedures for having children learn common syllables and how to combine them to make other words could also be used for this purpose.[23]

Then, from the body of empirical evidence that teaching reading by syllables is a reasonable alternative to nonsyllabic approaches,[24] one can identify studies which support the new form of syllabication described here. Children have told researchers that they recognize words by using syllables.[25;26;27] It has been found that the group of children taught to use phonograms as a decoding strategy improved significantly more in reading words in context than did a control group or a dictionary syllabication group.[13]

Children have told researchers that they recognize words by using syllables.

101

Conclusions

While the determination of the boundaries of the syllable remains a heated controversy among linguists, they do agree on one fact: Dictionary syllabication often is not a true or defensible description of the boundaries of the syllable.[28] In addition, there is no empirical evidence to support the claim that children must know how to apply the rules of dictionary syllabication in order to successfully disassemble multisyllabic words. Neither do children need to know dictionary syllabication in order to learn phonics.

In short, it is clear that today's reading experts are wrong when they defend dictionary syllabication as the knowledge needed by children in order to break up multisyllabic words into more easily pronounceable smaller units.

Equally in error, it appears, are the reading authorities who claim that teaching children to divide long words into syllables cannot possibly contribute to the identification of unknown written words. The opponents of syllabication are correct in pointing out the ineffective and unwise wordings given by certain experts about syllabication rules. However, one should not dismiss the validity of all forms of syllabication simply because some reading professors speak of it in imprecise ways.

A second major criticism of those who discourage the teaching of syllabication is that the application of this word-breaking process does not always result in the true pronunciations of words. It is contended that if the application of syllabication directs the child to say *ab-rupt* instead of *a-brupt*, then this activity is of questionable utility.[29] Such an objection appears to be inconsequential and unproductive faultfinding, however. Through either of the above pronunciations of *abrupt*, children gain an approximate pronunciation of the word; one that is close enough (in either case) to its true pronunciation for them to infer and reproduce the correct pronunciation of the word.

It is not true, then, that breaking multisyllabic words into smaller units has no utility, unless this syllabication always results in totally authentic pronunciations. I found that if children can gain the approximate pronunciation of unknown written words as a result of the application of

Dictionary syllabication often is not a true or defensible description of the boundaries of the syllable.

It is not true, then, that breaking multisyllabic words into smaller units has no utility . . .

Myth #9: Dictionary Syllabication is Needed

phonics rules, they then could correctly infer and reproduce the true pronunciation of this word (See Myth Number *2*). On the basis of this evidence, it seems reasonable to conclude that if children gain the approximate pronunciation of an unknown multisyllabic word, through the application of syllabication, they will be able to infer and reproduce its authentic pronunciation.

The best choice of what to teach children about syllabication appears to be to have them scan through the unfamiliar word, left to right, picking out letter clusters that begin with vowel letters. If these letter clusters are unfamiliar, their vowel letters first are given the "short" vowel sound. If this analysis does not result in a recognizable pronunciation, the child then gives the cluster(s) the "long" vowel sound.

It has been found that 95 percent of these letter clusters (closed syllables) can be pronounced correctly with either the "short" or "long" vowel sound, and more often with the former than the latter.[30] This form of syllabication will result in a reasonably approximate rendering of the true pronunciation of the word in question. After children can successfully make this application, they are taught to recognize affixes in words, and to realize that some words have syllables that end in a vowel letter; e.g., samp*le*. Eventually this form of syllabication will be refined when the child understands that certain consonant letter clusters are better divided into separate syllables; e.g., *ab-rupt*.

Some reading experts appear to reject this form of syllabication.[6] They believe that in teaching syllabication it is not important that the child can accurately determine where to divide a word or the difference between an open and a closed syllable. The examples that they offer as prime illustrations of their view about syllabication demonstrates the weakness of their stand on this issue, however.

For *Washington* they would teach the child the syllabication *Wash/ing/ton*; for *November*, *No/vem/ber*. Why not *Wa/shing/ton* and *Nov/em/ber*? the puzzled child, who is given no specific guidelines to follow here, must ask. In the new form of syllabication proposed as a substitute for Johnson and Pearson's[6] approach, it is held as vital that the child be able to see clearly the closed syllables in multisyllabic words: e.g., *ex-amp-le*.

Some reading experts appear to reject this form of syllabication.

An additional advantage of this new form of syllabication is that it requires no new knowledge by the teacher and a minimum number of rules for the child to learn. Previously, it was held necessary to conduct extensive studies to determine the percentages of words to which dictionary syllabication rules regularly applied.[31] But the decision as to what percentage of words so arrived at would be high enough to warrant teaching the rule in question is necessarily subjective and thus remains argumentative. No such troublesome and time-consuming efforts by researchers to gather such information, or by teachers to remember, recall, and apply it are necessary in the new form of syllabication described here.

There appears to be nothing that supposedly is gained from teaching the usually recommended rules of dictionary syllabication . . .

There appears to be nothing that supposedly is gained from teaching the usually recommended rules of dictionary syllabication that cannot be achieved by having children identify unknown letter clusters in multisyllabic words as closed syllables, and then to apply the "short" or "long" vowel sounds (in that order) to these phonograms. This new form of syllabication appears simpler to learn and to apply than is dictionary syllabication.

Moreover, one can point to empirical evidence that suggests that it works more effectively than does dictionary syllabication. Above all, there is no such evidence (or the existence of reasonable logic, for that matter) that directs us to abandon the teaching of all forms of syllabication when helping children learn to read. Teaching about syllabication should be reformed but not forsaken.

Myth #9: Dictionary Syllabication is Needed

References

1. Wilson, R. M. *Diagnostic and Remedial Reading for Classroom and Clinic.* Columbus, OH: Charles E. Merrill, 1981.
2. Otto, W.; Rude, R.; and Spiegel, D. L. *How to Teach Reading.* Reading, MA: Addison-Wesley, 1979.
3. Bush, C. L. and Huebner, M. H. *Strategies for Reading in the Elementary School.* New York, NY: Macmillan, 1979.
4. Tanner, N. B. "Phonics." In J. E. Alexander (Ed.), *Teaching Reading.* Boston, MA: Little Brown, 1979.
5. May, F. B. *Reading as Communication.* Columbus, OH: Charles E. Merrill, 1982.
6. Johnson, D. D. and Pearson, P. D. *Teaching Reading Vocabulary,* New York, NY: Holt, Rinehart and Winston, 1978.
7. McNeil, J. D.; Donant, L.; and Alkin, M. C. *How to Teach Reading Successfully.* Boston, MA: Little Brown, 1980.
8. Glass, G. G. "The Strange World of Syllabication." *Elementary School Journal,* 1967, 67, 403-405.
9 Friedman, M. I and Rowls, M. D. *Teaching Reading and Thinking Skills.* New York, NY: Longman, 1980, p. 93.
10. Otto, W., et al. *Focused Reading Instruction.* Reading, MA: Addison-Wesley, 1974. p. 140.
11. Harris, A. J. and Sipay, E. R. *How to Teach Reading.* New York, NY: Longman, 1979. p. 280.
12. Cooper, J. D., et al. *The What and How of Reading Instruction.* Columbus, OH: Charles E. Merrill, 1979. p. 103.
13. Canny, G. and Schreiner, R. "A Study of the Effectiveness of Selected Syllabication Rules and Phonogram Patterns for Word Attack." *Reading Research Quarterly,* 1976-1977, 12, 102-124.
14. Cunningham, P. M.; Cunningham, J. W., and Rystrom, R. "A New Syllabication Strategy and Reading Achievement." *Reading World,* 1981, 20, 208-214. p. 213.
15. Marzano, R.J., et al. "Are Syllabication and Reading Ability Related?" *Journal of Reading,* 1976, 19, 545-547.
16. Weaver, P. *Research Within Reach.* Washington, D.C.: U. S. Department of Health, Education and Welfare, 1978.
17. Spache, G. D. *Diagnosing and Correcting Reading Disabilities.* Boston, MA: Allyn and Bacon, 1976.
18. Dallmann, M., et al. *The Teaching of Reading.* New York, NY: Holt, Rinehart and Winston, 1974.
19. Spache, G. D. and Spache, E. B. *Reading in the Elementary School.* Boston, MA: Allyn and Bacon, 1977.
20. Arnold, R. and Miller, J. "Word Recognition Skills." In P. Lamb and R. Arnold (Eds.) *Teaching Reading.* Belmont, CA: Wadsworth, 1980.
21. Seymour, D. Z. "Word Division for Decoding." *Reading Teacher,* 1973, 27, 275-283.
22. Cunningham, P. M. "Investigating a Synthetized Theory of Mediated Word Identification." *Reading Research Quarterly,* 1975-1976, 11, 127-143.
23. Martin, J. and Sakiey, E. "Learning Sight Words by Combining Common Syllable Clusters." *Teaching Exceptional Children,* 1981, 14, 28-33.
24. Groff, P. "Teaching Reading by Syllables." *Reading Teacher,* 1981, 34, 659-664.
25. Rosinski, R. R. and Wheeler, K. E. "Children's Use of Orthographic Structure in Word Discrimination." *Psychonomic Science,* 1972, 26, 379-384.

26. Glass, G. G. and Burton, E. H. "How Do They Decode? Verbalizations and Observed Behaviors of Successful Decoders." *Education,* 1973, 94, 58-64.

27. Hardy, M.; Stennett, R. G.; and Smythe, P. C. "Word Attack: How Do They 'Figure Them Out'?" *Elementary English,* 1973, 50, 99-102.

28. Groff, P. *The Syllable: Its Nature and Pedagogical Usefulness.* Portland, OR: Northwest Regional Educational Laboratory, 1971.

29. Carnine, D. and Silbert, J. *Direct Instruction Reading.* Columbus, OH: Charles E. Merrill, 1979.

30. Wylie, R. E. and Durrell, D. D. "Teaching Vowels Through Phonograms." *Elementary English,* 1970, 47, 787-790.

31. McFeely, D. C. "Syllabication Usefulness in a Basal and Social Studies Vocabulary." *Reading Teacher,* 1974, 27, 809-814.

Chapter X

Myth #10: Discontinue Reading Tests in Favor of the ORMA

Proponents of the so-called "psycholinguistic" approach to the teaching of reading have urged that the use of standardized reading tests be discontinued. This new anti-phonics movement offers in place of these traditional measures of reading ability what it calls the *oral reading miscue analysis* (ORMA). This chapter analyzes the ORMA, and concludes that it has several disabling shortcomings. These weaknesses of the ORMA, particularly in its reliability, signify that it is unwise at this time to abandon the use of standardized reading tests in favor of the ORMA.

A Description of the ORMA

A major tenet of some reading experts who presently object to the intensive teaching of phonics rests on their assumption that standardized reading tests do not truly measure reading ability.[1] This negative criticism of reading tests obviously is necessary to discount the superior gains in reading achievement consistently found in favor of phonics teaching (see Bibliography). Opponents of phonics, when forced to concede that an overwhelming proportion of the empirical evidence indicates the relative superiority of phonics teaching, contend that the reading test scores which are used as the basis for this evidence are invalid, since they are not truly representative of children's reading abilities.

The opponents of phonics teaching accordingly claim that the research findings which indicate the superiority of phonics teaching are highly dubious. We must not use standardized test scores to compare phonics teaching and the whole-word or sentence method (they espouse), they protest. In place of standardized reading tests, some of the antagonists of phonics teaching offer what they call an *oral reading miscue analysis* (ORMA).

In place of standardized reading tests, some of the antagonists of phonics teaching offer what they call an oral reading miscue analysis (ORMA).

Since its publication in 1976, the "official" explanation of ORMA[2] has been referred to many times in the literature on the teaching of reading. These numerous citations have been of a generally favorable nature. From the approving references made to this ORMA so far, one could easily surmise that the logical and psychological framework of this particular process is virtually faultless.

The workings of this ORMA are now rather well-accepted by those who would substitute it for standardized reading tests. Children's oral readings or observed responses are coded for deviations found from the printed text that has been read aloud. Eighteen categories of miscues are so coded, followed by a comprehension rating of the child's oral reading. It is said that these miscues are arranged in a pattern or sequence of ever increasing finiteness. Each of the eighteen categories of the ORMA is said to include a scale of values; i.e., a graduated progression of steps to determine the differences between acceptable versus unacceptable miscues.

Myth #10: Discontinue Reading Tests in Favor of the ORMA

To achieve the comprehension rating of the ORMA, the child retells the story of what he or she has read orally. To properly score a child's comprehension, it is said that story and information outlines should be developed for each piece of reading material, with 100 points being distributed across the items in each outline. The child's retelling of the story is compared to each outline and points are deducted from the total of 100 for missing or confused information. Thus, the score of 100 points in the ORMA represents faultless reading comprehension.

The ORMA is not Credible

Recent research and criticism that relate to the workings of the ORMA lead one to suspect that this procedure does not qualify, however, for the perfectibility that many writers on reading instruction apparently find in it.

For example, one researcher has discovered that the linguistic competence of children, which underlies both their silent reading and oral language is not part of their reading aloud.[3] This finding obviously contradicts the major tenet of the ORMA, that oral reading miscues faithfully reflect children's language competencies.

Yet other reasons that can be used to doubt the value of the ORMA, as the best means of gaining a true understanding of the processes children use in reading. The differences in children's eye movements as they read silently and orally, the fact that silent reading gives them more time (than does oral reading) to think about what is being read, and the relatively greater psychological tension created by oral reading compared to silent reading, all are valid signs that the ORMA has shortcomings.[4] We know that readers who have recently become rapid, relatively effective silent readers are distracted and disrupted when reading aloud.[5] When silent reading becomes proficient, it becomes a very different process from oral reading, it is clear.

A Close Look at the ORMA

These indications of the fallibility of the ORMA are intensified when one closely examines the content of the monograph which, as noted, is accepted as the most authoritative description of this ORMA. Underestimated here is the degree to which subjective judgments must be made

Thus, the score of 100 points in the ORMA represents faultless reading comprehension.

We know that readers who have recently become rapid, relatively effective silent readers are distracted and disrupted when reading aloud.

by its administrators. Despite statements that the ORMA has a consistent format and an internal consistency, there is doubt that all judgments made through the ORMA are done without undue speculation.

A prime example of how highly subjective judgments of the administrator of the ORMA must be brought to bear is found in the category of miscues called "semantic change" (number ten of its eighteen-category taxonomy of reading miscues). Without guidelines, the administrator of the ORMA here is charged with deciding what the basic sense of the plot of the story is, what are major anomalies to it, what are key aspects of a story, what are deviations in a child's oral reading that seriously interfere with its subplots, what are major incidents, characters, and sequences, and which, if any, of the deviations in a child's oral reading is significant but does not create inconsistencies within the story.

The directions for administering the comprehension rating of the ORMA are also often vague, even at critical points within this process.

The directions for administering the comprehension rating of the ORMA are also often vague, even at critical points within this process. For an example, the administrator of the ORMA, without guiding criteria, must decide if a child's response to questions is unclear, if he or she knows the plot of the story, or considering the total content of the story, whether the miscue does not interfere with the story meaning.

No necessary criteria are given for determining whether or not the child comprehends unusual key words from the text read aloud. No such help is given for ascertaining how many of the characters of the story the child must name, or how they must be identified, in order to gain a total or a partial score of the points alloted this item.

The same is true for modifying statements, events, major concepts, generalizations, or specific points or examples in the passage that was read aloud.

Finally, there is no way shown in the ORMA for its administrator to resolve how much or which detail about the theme and plot of the passage the child must know, to be given any certain number of comprehension rating points. In short, decisions made about the comprehension rating points given a child in the ORMA must be subjective (in great measure) a large share of the time.

The ORMA also posits a theory of reading comprehension and the means to get at a rating of this ability that appears difficult to understand. To some experts of the ORMA, reading comprehension is more than one's deriving what an author intended his or her readers to understand. While these experts accept the idea that reading includes attempts to reconstruct the author's meaning, reading for comprehension is treated as analogy, or the relationship between a reader's idea and what the written idea represents.[2]

Does this mean that all the advocates of the ORMA view a child's reading comprehension in the traditional way, as only the similarity found between the child's judgment of the meaning of a passage and what an intelligent, mature reader would say was its author's intended meaning? Apparently not, for some defenders of the ORMA insist that comprehension is not a matching process in which something the reader does is to be matched with something the author did. Instead, it is said when a child comprehends he or she constructs his or her own knowledge of the author's thoughts.[6]

. . . it is said when a child comprehends he or she constructs his or her own knowledge of the author's thoughts.

The goal here for the reader is the construction of personal knowledge. Thus, it appears that some experts of the ORMA consider it proper for a child to form his or her own individual, eccentric representations of what is meant by a passage of print -- and that this kind of inference should be respected as ideal reading comprehension.

Nonetheless, the advocates of the ORMA defend the comprehension rating they make with it (from the child's retelling of the "story" he or she reads aloud) as the best means to obtain evidence of reading comprehension. To this effect they do not believe that existing standardized reading tests can be used for accurate individual assessment of this skill. They see standardized reading tests to grossly underestimate reading competence, since these tests to not measure reading competence. Because of this, one defender of the ORMA would put a five-year moratorium on the use of all standardized tests in schools.[1]

It follows, of course, that if unguided subjective speculation is needed to decide about the acceptability of a child's miscues, then other miscue factors that are said to be easily compared to this miscue cannot actually be handled with such precision. Thus, it is likely that the claim, for example, that the degree of children's corrections of their miscues can be accurately compared to their semantic miscue scores remains unconfirmed.

It is easy to say that the comprehension of a passage is the sum of the miscues a child makes, that are semantically acceptable, plus those that are corrected to make them acceptable. This formula falls apart, however, if there is no standard way to determine if a miscue is semantically acceptable. It appears efficient to say that a child is an ineffective reader if he or she is wasting a lot of time trying to achieve accuracy that is unnecessary. It appears that the administrator of the ORMA is given no precise criteria as to what is necessary accuracy, however.

It appears that the administrator of the ORMA is given no precise criteria as to what is necessary accuracy, however.

To suppose, as do the originators of the ORMA, that evaluations of miscues are reliable from one administrator to another, obviously taxes one's credulity. We have ample evidence, for example, that judgments of the quality of written compositions are not reliable unless the separate judges involved in a given evaluation are provided special, communal training to make such evaluations. There is a strong likelihood, therefore, that certain codings made of children's miscues, through ORMA, suffer a lack of reliability. If this is so, the usefulness of such codings as research data is badly damaged.

There is a strong likelihood, therefore, that certain codings made of children's miscues, through ORMA, suffer a lack of reliability.

The supposed hierarchical or taxonomical nature of the ORMA must be brought into question, as well. One critic says that the category levels of miscues in the ORMA are not strictly hierarchically ordered. This "taxonomy" is really nothing more than a simple inventory, he claims.[3]

It is true, of course, that if one can correctly criticize the taxonomy of the ORMA, in a negative manner, this faultfinding would seriously damage its validity. Of the particular interest to this critical processing is the position that the defenders of the ORMA take toward hierarchy, vis-a-vis reading behavior. Leaders of the ORMA movement are well known for their consistent opposition to the idea that there is a hierarchy of reading skills, or that this sequence can or should be taught in reading programs.

To the contrary, they insist that there is not any sequence of skills in learning to read; it has to be altogether from the very beginning.[1] This distrust for a hierarchy of reading skills curiously enough does not carry over for them into the area of oral reading miscues children are said to make, as represented by the ORMA.

A scale of values supposedly has been constructed for each of the categories of the taxonomy of reading miscues used by the ORMA, without any foreboding as to the need to defend the order of these sequences, either theoretically or empirically.

Thus we find, for example, this taxonomy to fearlessly assert that if an original word in a passage and the oral reading miscue of it has a key letter or letters in common (e.g., *for* read as *of*) then this miscue must be coded lower in this category scale of values than if the words in question have middle portions that are similar (e.g., *took* read as *look*). The proliferation of such unexplained and therefore unjustified distinctions in the ORMA taxonomy make it clear that it doubtless is correct to judge that it is questionable whether the ORMA has developed a taxonomy in the strictest sense of the word.

The ORMA and Reading Instruction

In the light of the criticisms made so far of the ORMA, one must also consider the implications of the findings of the ORMA for the classroom teaching of beginning reading that its advocates recommend. We learn from the description of the ORMA that these findings indicate that children learning to read are quite proficient at relating their complex and highly developed speech system to the graphic cues within the total context of language. But then we are expected to believe that growth in reading is retarded when phonics drills which isolate the phonemic and graphic systems are used.

The research on this matter indicates no such settled state of affairs, however. In fact, there is no empirical data available at present to compare the relative efficiency of teaching phoneme-grapheme correspondences within words, as against teaching them as isolated items. Thus, the writers of the ORMA mislead teachers into believing that this issue has been finally determined.

Thus, the writers of the ORMA mislead teachers into believing that this issue has been finally determined.

Confusing statements over the importance that phonics has in reading, given by individual advocates of the ORMA, are also apparent. Some proponents make it clear that phonics is necessary, for without its use none of the three cue systems to reading (graphophonic, syntactic, and semantic) could function properly.[2] But at the same time, others insist that phonics problems are not the cause of pupils' inability to read a piece of written material.[2] The contradictory nature of these two positions goes without saying, of course, since to follow the prior reasoning any problem that readers have in controlling any of the three cue systems would doubtless result in a negative effect on their general reading ability.

Other advocates of the ORMA simply find phonics to be an out side, external, superficial or nonessential aspect of reading. The best-known spokesman of this position concludes that phonics, in any form of reading instruction, is at best a peripheral concern.[7] Obviously an aspect of reading that is superficial at best could not serve the very important functions that other ORMA advocates say it does.

Other writers on the ORMA emphasize that if an intensive and systematic teaching of phonics or word attack skills is undertaken, reading teachers will inevitably become so preoccupied with this instruction that they will ignore the other cue systems completely and overlook opportunities for children to read connected discourse.[2] No evidence is given to support this demeaning accusation, significantly enough.

The reviews of the pertinent empirical evidence on this matter indicate that quite the opposite situation exists; that is, that the intensive and systematic teaching of phonics brings on greater gains in both comprehension and word reading than does the incidental and unsystematic approach to reading instruction that advocates of the ORMA endorse (see Bibliography). There is no empirical evidence to support the notion that too early or too much emphasis on the code interferes with later comprehension. (See Chapter 1)

Conclusions

This discussion has revealed that there are several outstanding uncertainties that remain in regard to the usefulness of the ORMA.

This discussion has revealed that there are several outstanding uncertainties that remain in regard to the usefulness of the ORMA. Notwithstanding the overall favorable comments that have been given this ORMA of late, it has been demonstrated that various problems of interpretation still surround the theory and workings of this process. It is recommended that the claims of the ORMA be approached with caution until the matters raised in this discussion are satisfactorily resolved. It would be unwise to abandon the use of standardized tests for a use of the ORMA.

References

1. Goodman, K. S. "Manifesto for a Reading Revolution." In M. Douglass (Ed.), *Claremont Reading Conference Fortieth Yearbook*. Claremont, CA: Claremont Graduate School, 1976.

2. Allen, P. D. and Watson, D. J. *Findings of Research in Miscue Analysis: Classroom Implications.* Champaign, IL: National Council of Teachers of English, 1976.

3. Mosenthal, P. "Psycholinguistic Properties of Aural and Visual Comprehension as Determined by Children's Abilities to Comprehend Syllogisms." *Reading Research Quarterly,* 1976-1977, 12, 586-603.

4. Newman, H. "Oral Reading Miscue Analysis is Good But Not Complete." *Reading Teacher,* 1978, 31, 883-886.

5. Goodman, K. S. and Niles, O. *Reading: Process and Program.* Urbana, IL: National Council of Teachers of English, 1970.

6. Goodman, Y. M. "Reading Strategy Lessons: Expanding Reading Effectiveness." In W. D. Page (Ed.), *Help for the Reading Teacher.* Urbana, IL: ERIC Clearinghouse on Reading and Communication Skills, 1975.

7. Goodman, K. S. "Do You Have to be Smart to Read? Do You Have to Read to be Smart?" *Reading Teacher,* 1975, 28, 625-632.

116

Chapter XI

Myth #11: Subvocalization is Bad

Over the years many reading experts have warned reading teachers of the necessity to take action to repress the subvocalization they observe in their pupils during silent reading. Subvocalization was said to hinder the development of reading speed and thus reduce the amount of comprehension in reading gained over a period of time. Mechanistic therapies have been recommended for use to stop the so-called undesirable habit of subvocalization. The research on this issue does not agree with these suppositions. To the contrary, it discloses that subvocalization is a normal behavior; indeed, one that aids, not interferes, with the reading process.

The Supposed Bad Effects of Subvocalization

Subvocalization is the movement of the lips, tongue, or vocal chords as one reads silently.

Subvocalization is the movement of the lips, tongue, or vocal chords as one reads silently. This phenomenon sometimes is characterized by whispering sounds. The activity also is called silent speech, implicit speech, or inner speech.

Many of the writers of reading methods texts are convinced that subvocalization by the child as he or she reads silently is a decided hindrance to the development of good silent reading habits. In the views of 100 nationally recognized authorities in reading, queried about subvocalization, there was noted a definite trend, however, to consider silent speech a natural developmental reinforcement to the development of reading abilities.[1] The authorities in reading who comment on subvocalization in the texts teachers use when learning how to teach reading obviously do not tend to approve of subvocalization, however. They believe they have observed that readers who are poor comprehenders continue to use the auditory symbol, subvocal speech, as a bridge between the written symbol and the semantic meaning of what they read silently.[2]

It is said that the child comes to the stage when he applies linguistic principles in silent reading only after he has moved beyond the stage of subvocalization.[3] Other experts add that subvocalization is a distraction, a crutch to help the very immature readers who have a better speaking than reading knowledge of the language.[4]

Others agree that the child's lip movements during silent reading prevents the growth of adequate speed in reading.[5;5a;5b;5c] Unless subvocalization is suppressed, teachers are warned, speed of silent reading is frequently restricted to the rate of oral reading.[6]

Children will read three or four times faster silently than orally, if there is no vocalizing, some say.[7] Vocalization blocks the way to speed up silent reading, they caution. Subvocalization can be the stumbling block to the mastering of silent reading. It is a common cause of slow reading, it is insisted.[8] For rapid reading, all forms of vocalization must be either greatly reduced or eliminated, it is claimed.[9]

Myth #11: Subvocalization is Bad

In sum, then, these writers reflect the judgment that the best silent reading is devoid of subvocalization. That is, with ordinary reading tasks, it should approach nonexistence. In general, these writers also affirm the notion that the time taken in the articulation of the speech organs involved when subvocalization is practiced is of such magnitude that this time accounts for the difference found between the reading rates of normal and retarded silent readers.

The Purported Causes of Subvocalization

The causes of subvocalization and its supposedly dreadful consequences usually are said (by the above writers) to be rooted in the earlier stages of reading, when children read orally a great deal. It is normal, they attest, that in the early stages of learning to read silently, in the primary grades, many children tend to articulate words rather precisely and fully.

Thus, closely related to the habit of vocalization is the feeling some readers have that they must read aloud every word in order to comprehend. However, at this level, vocalization does not slow down speed of silent reading, for the child can read no faster than he can talk. But, silent reading should be a process of association between perceptual stimulation and meaning, without a mediating subvocalization, these experts insist.[10]

It follows, they deduce, that too much emphasis on oral reading as a means of teaching silent reading could well make for vocalization cases, who would be in difficulty in about the fourth, fifth, or sixth grade.[11] To this effect, they see subvocalization in reading largely as a byproduct of teaching methods in use. It is maintained that subvocalization is nothing more than a regression to classroom-induced behavior, and therefore something that can be suppressed without the slightest detriment to comprehension.[12]

Phonics is tabbed as the second major cause of the purportedly undesirable habits of subvocalization noticed in young readers. Phonics teaching in the initial stages of reading tends to cause lip movements and possibly excessive subvocalization in later stages, it is claimed.[6] A third cause of subvocalization is said to be materials assigned children that are excessively difficult for them to read.

It is normal, they attest, that in the early stages of learning to read silently, in the primary grades, many children tend to articulate words rather precisely and fully.

Therapy for Subvocalization

The therapy suggested for this "problem," (that is, actions to restrict the child from the lip movement of subvocalization) sometimes is of a mechanistic nature. An effective technique, some prescribe, is to use some device so that the jaws of the child are held apart and the tongue pressed down. A large eraser, a clean teaspoon, a tongue depressor, or a piece of wood of suitable size may be used to bite upon. Or the child may be allowed to chew vigorously on a large wad of gum during silent reading.[9]

The therapy suggested for this "problem," (that is, actions to restrict the child from the lip movement of subvocalization) sometimes is of a mechanistic nature.

It is judged that when the habit of subvocalization persists in spite of efforts to overcome it, one can prevent lip movements by having the child hold the tip of a pencil between his teeth. For subvocalization, some experts[5a] advise having the child hum a familiar tune when reading silently.

Finally, it is held that the provision of very easy and extremely interesting and unimportant reading materials for the subvocalizing child will help cure his or her difficulties here. This action is said to be effective for this purpose because easy materials can be read rapidly, a rapid reader cannot vocalize, and when vocalization has been reduced to a minimum, better comprehension will return.

It is agreed that having children do a great deal of timely easy reading is one helpful procedure to use; and it has the advantage of not requiring fancy gadgets or machines.[8] Others contend, however, that rather than avoid the use of speed reading drills involving the use of the tachistoscope and other controlled speed reading devices, these devices ar essential to a well-balanced program for the elimination of subvocalization.[5]

There is some sharp disagreement among the reading experts who fear what, nonetheless, they see as the negative effects of subvocalization of children's silent reading abilities. Some suggest that usually the students can be made aware of this by teachers' warnings.[4] It is said that in most cases reminding the child that he is not supposed to move his lips, or that he should try to read the way grownups do, is all that is needed to eliminate unwanted subvocalization.[5] Some experts vehemently disagree that such admonitions should be made. One sternly warns teachers not to discuss subvocalization with the children.[8]

Some experts vehemently disagree that such admonitions should be made.

Myth #11: Subvocalization is Bad

What the Research Says

One would have expected that such strongly-worded opinions about sub-vocalization and silent reading, as given above, would have been carefully documented. It is surprising to note, therefore, that none of the writers of the reading methods texts, referred to above, point to the research on subvocalization they consider as verification for their views on this matter. Accordingly, it is pertinent to ask, what, in fact, has the research on subvocalization and silent reading concluded about this phenomenon and its relationship to silent reading?

First of all, it is important to remember that adequate research on this problem had only been done at a late date. This work was not realized until 1960. At that point the relationship of subvocalization and silent reading (through the use of electrodes that picked up contractions of the vocal muscles of children while they read silently) had been conducted.[13]

The findings of the study led to the inevitable conclusion that while better silent readers engaged in less subvocalization than did poorer readers, silent speech or subvocalization occurs in the reading of all people. It was found that even very good readers engage in increased amounts of silent speech if the texts read are very demanding from the standpoint of reading ability.

It is then impossible to view silent speech as a habit detrimental to reading. In short, silent speech cannot have a detrimental effect on reading performance. And since subvocalization is a symptom of a reader not being able to grasp the content of a text without difficulties, it follows that the advisability of any direct attempt to eliminate silent speech is highly dubious. It is certain that all kinds of training aimed at removing silent speech should be discarded since it appears likely that silent speech actually constitutes an aid toward better reading, this study concluded.

Other researchers, after 1960, who used the electromyographic method of investigating this issue, have uncovered essentially the same findings, to wit: If the material one attempts to read is conceptually complex, then the degree of subvocalization one uses will increase. This later research also attests to the fact that young or relatively uneducated readers

First of all, it is important to remember that adequate research on this problem had only been done at a late date.

It is then impossible to view silent speech as a habit detrimental to reading.

If the material one attempts to read is conceptually complex, then the degree of subvocalization one uses will increase.

will exhibit more subvocalization when reading silently than will mature readers.

The two remaining questions are, of course, "Will the elimination of subvocalization act to improve the quality of one's comprehension of reading material?" and "Will this elimination significantly accelerate one's speed of reading?" The research of late has also provided some seemingly definitive answers to these questions.

It has been found that subvocalization can be repressed by means of a mechanical form of feedback, whereby the reader's subvocalization is converted into a sound which he or she concurrently hears as he or she subvocalizes. The subjects whose subvocalizing was so eliminated did not read significantly faster than did a control group of subjects whose subvocalizations had not been so suppressed. But most importantly, it was found that the group whose subvocalization was not suppressed exhibited significantly superior comprehension of the material the two groups read silently.[14] It was clear that the subvocalization used by this group of subjects had aided them in their comprehension of reading material.

But most importantly, it was found that the group whose subvocalization was not suppressed exhibited significantly superior comprehension of the material the two groups read silently.

In addition to this, other research studies have indicated that there is a positive relationship between the rate of reading one can attain and the amount of subvocalization one engages in. It has been found that mature readers not only read faster after they had completed a course designed to increase their reading rates, but that they also used more subvocalization as a result of their increase in reading speed.[15]

Increases in reading rate in mature readers are accompanied by increases in their use of subvocalization.

Increases in reading rate in mature readers are accompanied by increases in their use of subvocalization.[16] So, whatever the cause of subvocalization, its effect does not seem to be to decelerate reading. Rather than subvocalization, familiarity and interest to the reader of the reading act and other personal variables are the true determiners of silent reading rate.

In short, in reading the rate of information flow is determined by the complexity of the message and not by the physical limitations of the speech organs. Since subvocalization waxes and wanes in the silent reading act as needed to support the reconstruction of the message the silent reader is examining, it appears that the practicing reader has few tools more useful than subvocalization.

Myth #11: Subvocalization is Bad

Then, the relationship of visual perception, auditory discrimination, auditory comprehension, and reading speed with the subvocalizations of pupils classified as having either "high" or "low" visual perception abilities was studied.[17] The effects of these factors on subvocalization in silent reading were not found to differ significantly between the high and low group. The view that subvocalization is only a behavior associated with children who exhibit low levels of the above four abilities was not supported by this study. The theory that children who have good visual perception do not need to use subvocalization when reading silently was invalidated by this study.

Conclusions

It is readily apparent that the views of writers of reading methods textbooks on subvocalization, and its effect on silent reading, are at odds with the findings of the experimental researchers on this question. If we are to put our confidence in the empirical studies on this issue, conducted so far, then we can say with some confidence that the convictions about subvocalization and its effects on silent reading held among many writers of reading methods texts generally are wrong.

Their notion that silent reading is best done without subvocalization is in error. The reader does not comprehend better if he eliminates his subvocalization. The reverse appears to be the case. Subvocalization helps the reader comprehend. Thus, the application of linguistic principles to silent reading is not interfered with by subvocalization.

The reader does not comprehend better if he eliminates his subvocalization.

Subvocalization is not a crutch for silent reading, used only by immature readers. The cause of subvocalization is not an arrested or immature reaction to written material. It is not simply a symptom of a primitive stage of growth in the overall development of silent reading abilities. Subvocalization is done by all readers. It therefore is not true, as some claim,[18] that in silent reading there is no need to subvocalize.

Subvocalization is not a classroom induced phenomenon. It is not the result of too much of the wrong kind of instruction in oral reading or in phonics. Opponents of phonics have claimed that intensive phonics teaching causes subvocalization, which interferes with good reading.[12] This attack on phonics obviously fails, since subvocalization is neither a cause of retarded reading skill nor caused by intensive phonics teaching.

This attack on phonics obviously fails, since subvocalization is neither a cause of retarded reading skill nor caused by intensive phonics teaching.

Subvocalization does not prevent the growth of an adequate rate of silent reading speed.

Subvocalization does not prevent the growth of an adequate rate of silent reading speed. Instead, increases in subvocalization are shown to accompany increases in the rate of reading. It is highly likely, however, that subvocalization neither prevents nor causes speed of reading. Instead, it is merely a manifestation of the reader's attempt to comprehend what he reads.

Therefore, the notion that an exclusive use of easy-to-read material by the reader will eliminate his need to subvocalize with difficult-to-read material is highly doubtful. The difference in time it takes a fast reader and a slow reader to read silently a piece of written material cannot be accounted for, then, by the different amounts of subvocalization exhibited by slow and fast readers. The slow reader's difficulty in mentally comprehending material is the true cause of his retarded rate of reading. Thus, the elimination of his or her subvocalization would not help him or her comprehend material he or she finds difficult to comprehend.

It is time-wasting and foolhardy to attempt to suppress subvocalization, by whatever means.

It is time-wasting and foolhardy to attempt to suppress subvocalization, by whatever means. And, while the suppression of subvocalization apparently can be accomplished in mature readers, efforts with children in this direction have proved to be a failure.

Accordingly, we can agree that attempts at suppressing subvocalization in children on the part of supervisors and reading experts causes more retardation in reading than any moving of the lips has ever done.[19] It follows, of course, that it is unnecessary for teachers to be concerned to any degree about children's subvocalizations. No attempt should be made, therefore, to bring the fact that they subvocalize to children's attention, despite some reading experts' advice[20] to do so.

Myth #11: Subvocalization is Bad

References

1. Cleland, D. L. and Davies, W. C. "Silent Speech--History and Current Status." *Reading Teacher,* 1963, 16, 224-228.

2. Robeck, M. C. and Wilson, J. A. R. *Psychology of Reading: Foundations of Instruction.* New York, NY: John Wiley, 1974.

3. Jones, D. M. *Teaching Children to Read.* New York, NY: Harper and Row, 1971.

4. Fry, E. *Reading Instruction for Classroom and Clinic.* New York: McGraw-Hill, 1972.

5. Harris, A. J. *How to Increase Reading Ability.* New York, NY: David McKay, 1970.

5a. Ekwall, E. E. *Locating and Correcting Reading Difficulties.* Columbus, OH: Charles E. Merrill, 1981.

5b. Gilliland, H. *A Practical Guide to Remedial Reading.* Columbus, OH: Charles E. Merrill, 1978.

5c. Bond, G. L., et al. *Reading Difficulties: Their Diagnosis and Correction.* Englewood Cliffs, NJ: Prentice-Hall, 1984.

6. Dallmann, M., el al. *The Teaching of Reading.* New York, NY: Holt, Rinehart and Winston, 1974.

7. Tinker, M. A. and McCullough, C. M. *Teaching Elementary Reading.* New York, NY: Appleton-Century-Crofts, 1962.

8. Durkin, D. *Teaching Them to Read.* Boston, MA: Allyn and Bacon, 1970.

9. Bond, G. L. and Tinker, M. A. *Reading Difficulties: Their Diagnosis and Correction.* New York, NY: Appleton-Century-Crofts, 1967.

10. Smith, H.P. and Dechant, E. V. *Psychology in Teaching Reading.* Englewood Cliffs, NJ: Prentice-Hall, 1961.

11. Bond, G. L. and Wagner, E. B. *Teaching the Child to Read.* New York, NY: Macmillan, 1960.

12. Smith F. *Psycholinguistics and Reading.* New York, NY: Holt, Rinehart and Winston, 1973.

13. Edfeldt, A. W. *Silent Speech and Silent Reading.* Chicago, IL: University of Chicago, 1960.

14. Hardyck, C. D. and Petrinovich, L. R. "Subvocal Speech and Comprehension Levels as a Function of the Difficulty Level of Reading Material." *Journal of Verbal Learning and Verbal Behavior,* 1970, 9, 647-652.

15. McGuigan, F. J. and Pinkney, K. B. "Effects of Increased Reading Rate on Covert Processes." *Interamerican Journal of Psychology,* 1973, 7, 223-231.

16. Feldman, J. M. "Why I Move My Lips When I Read." In M. P. Douglass (Ed.), *Claremont Reading Conference Fortieth Yearbook.* Claremont, CA: Claremont Graduate School, 1976.

17. Anderson, G. W. "An Investigation of the Effects of Two Levels of Visual Perception, Auditory Discrimination, Auditory Comprehension and Reading Speed on Implicit Speech During Silent Reading." *Dissertation Abstracts International,* 1971, 31, 5021A-5022A.

18. Dauzat, J. A. and Dauzat, S. V. *Reading: The Teacher and the Learner.* New York, NY: John Wiley, 1981.

19. Zintz, M. V. *The Reading Process.* Dubuque, IA: Wm. C. Brown, 1970.

20. Spache, G. D. *Diagnosing and Correcting Reading Disabilities.* Boston, MA: Allyn and Bacon, 1976.

126

Chapter XII

Myth #12: Oral Reading is Dangerous

This chapter describes how oral reading, once a major element of reading programs, has fallen into disfavor. The major reasons given by its opponents (since 1900) as to why oral reading should be deemphasized, if not abandoned, are cited. None of these reasons are found to be convincing, however. Therefore, there appears to be no legitimate justification for discontinuing oral reading with pupils who are learning to read. Insights into the underlying causes for the seemingly illogical opposition to oral reading are offered.

Why Oral Reading has been Criticized

The preceding discussion of the myth that "Subvocalization is Bad" dealt with the misinformation that has circulated over the years regarding this form of vocalization while reading. The more obvious form of reading vocalization, *oral reading*, is also plagued with many faulty notions about its nature and usefulness.

To understand why reading experts today consider oral reading dangerous requires a review of the history of this opposition.

To understand why reading experts today consider oral reading dangerous requires a review of the history of this opposition. Oral reading was taught extensively in American schools up until about the turn of the century.[39;61] It is highly unlikely, however, as Rubin claims,[56] that oral reading was so dominant then that silent reading was ignored by reading teachers. Neither is it probable that before the 1920s all reading instruction was done orally.[50] Fry's[23] tale that teachers of this time were discharged if their pupils were not good oral readers is also presumably apocryphal.

It is correct to say, however, that by 1915 strong objections to the continued teaching of oral reading had been voiced by many reading experts.[39] The 1921 yearbook of the prestigious National Society for the Study of Education notes this growing dissatisfaction with oral reading.[73] There was nothing to justify the amount of oral reading commonly found in schools of the time, this yearbook protested.

This "widespread protest"[29] against oral reading was fueled at the time by the advent of the standardized silent reading test. The scores on such tests by WW1 servicemen revealed that about 25 percent of these recruits were functionally illiterate.[47] These military personnel had received instruction that stressed oral reading. It follows, said the negative critics of oral reading, that this stress on oral reading was a prime cause of this functional illiteracy.[39]

It had become clear that a deemphasis on oral reading would result in greatly increased sales of these learning-to-read textbooks.

Especially enthusiastic at this time about the proposed deemphasis on oral reading were the authors of basal readers and standardized silent reading tests. It had become clear that a deemphasis on oral reading would result in greatly increased sales of these learning-to-read textbooks.

Myth #12: Oral Reading is Dangerous

The authors of basal readers claimed now that a host of silent reading abilities had been discovered and should be taught.[39]   Later evidence taken from analyses of standardized silent reading tests would reveal that no such large number of silent reading skills actually existed.[17]

Despite the fact that the opponents of oral reading advised teachers to spend class time (to be taken away from oral reading), on the instruction of nonexistent skills, they were successful in selling many workbooks and teachers' manuals for this purpose. The eagerness on the part of many authors to replace oral reading with the silent reading of such materials (These authors doubled as reading experts of the day) is understandable. It is not surprising that these reading experts' evaluations of school reading programs after 1915 negatively criticized them for using oral reading.[36] The gross conflict of interest involved in this situation should not pass unnoticed, however.

The gross conflict of interest involved in this situation should not pass unnoticed, however.

Since the teacher who deemphasized oral reading could gain far less explicit information about a pupil's progress in word recognition, the use of standardized silent reading tests now became mandatory. It was decided at this time, as well, that the standardized silent reading test was to be an invaluable and necessary aid to the experimental investigation of reading. As research into reading instruction became increasingly "scientific," those who carried out such studies were required to report statistical data, if their reports were to be acceptable for publication. It is clear that the widespread use of such tests worked to the disadvantage of oral reading.

A historian of oral reading practices has observed that by 1925 the anti-oral reading movement had "swept the country."[39] Oral reading by this time was almost universally condemned. Some schools had abandoned entirely the teaching of oral reading. For the next five years, attention to oral reading in educational journals was almost completely absent. The 1925 yearbook of the NSSE, while not so radical in its rejection of oral reading, did advise teachers that much less time be given to it.[74] There is no evidence, therefore, to support the belief that the deemphasis of oral reading did not begin until 1930,[79] or until 1938, as Hildreth would have it.[35]

A historian of oral reading practices has observed that by 1925 the anti-oral reading movement had "swept the country."

Apparently in recognition of the remarkable rejection of oral reading by reading experts of the preceding fifteen years, the NSSE in 1937 called for some return to oral reading.[75] Oral reading cannot be taught effectively in an incidental manner, its yearbook for this year noted. This plea obviously was ignored by the advocates of a non-oral method of reading instruction, which aimed to prohibit all kinds of oral reading. The proponents of this method theorized that children could go straight from a printed word to its meaning, without any involvement in the pronunciation of a word.

It was found that there were no statistically significant differences between the reading growth of children in the sixth grade who had been taught with the non-oral approach and those who had been taught to read orally.

The supposed successes of this type of reading instruction were reported as early as 1937.[48] Negative reviews[55] of the methodology and design of non-oral reading instruction research led to a critical evaluation of the superior achievement it purported to produce. It was found that there were no statistically significant differences between the reading growth of children in the sixth grade who had been taught with the non-oral approach and those who had been taught to read orally.[7] Most significantly, no significant differences in the amount of lip movement (subvocalization) was found between these two groups of children.

When it was discovered that children for whom oral reading had been prohibited used almost as much subvocalization (which the non-oral method claimed to eliminate) as did children taught to read orally, the non-oral method lost much of its attraction for reading experts.

This setback to the opponents of oral reading did not lessen their resentments toward this form of reading, however.

This setback to the opponents of oral reading did not lessen their resentments toward this form of reading, however.[44] By 1949, the NSSE yearbook estimated that there still were marked differences of opinion among reading experts regarding the place of oral reading.[33] There were teacher educators who maintained that oral reading was expanding rapidly,[29] that there was a renewed emphasis on oral reading,[60] even that teachers were turning to it with great frequency and enthusiasm.[76] These statements appear to be wishful thinking, however. The available evidence on this issue suggests that teachers in the 1960s were unsure about the values or usefulness of oral reading.[57] It is fair to say that many teachers today still evidence little interest in oral reading.[79]

This uncertainty about oral reading was abetted in the 1960s by the NSSE which felt it best at this time to ignore the argument that surrounded oral reading. In its 1961 and 1968 yearbooks on reading instruction, no references are made to oral reading in either of their tables of content or indexes. Avoidance of the oral reading issue was also the position taken by editions of the *Encyclopedia of Educational Research* published after 1960. Nor is there any mention of oral reading as an instructional technique in its latest volumes, 1969 and 1982.

Textbooks versus Teachers on Oral Reading

It is not surprising, therefore, that most methods textbooks for reading teachers, written in the past twenty years, have dealt with oral reading in one of two ways. In general, they either warn against its extensive use,[18;23] or display their displeasure with oral reading by ignoring it altogether. One seldom hears a call for an increase in oral reading instruction in these texts, Hoffman[36] correctly observes. Recent texts on the methods of teaching reading, to the contrary, remind today's teachers that oral reading remains a highly controversial subject,[79] or that it continues to be a point of argument,[14] with some reading experts saying it should be repressed entirely.[12]

Textbooks on the methods of teaching reading sometimes depict oral reading as a crutch that children must discard when they are ready to read silently.[6] Others claim that research findings suggest the inferiority of oral reading.[11] The "utter uselessness" of having children take turns reading orally is denounced.[41] This so-called "meaningless procedure"[50] is said to be a "misused practice"[46] that is "counterproductive and actually harmful to students."[53] It is claimed that oral reading often reinforces children's bad habits and develops patterns of reading failure.[68] Worse yet, it is decried, the development of both oral reading and silent reading may be impeded if oral reading is practiced often, even in the primary grades.[67] The only justifiable reason for oral reading, according to Jones,[40] is to communicate thoughts to a listener. This excludes its usefulness in phonics, as a diagnostic tool of reading skill, etc.

Despite the fact that many reading authorities decry the use of oral reading, there is evidence that some teachers continue to favor its practice. Spache and Spache found that up through grade four 30 percent of teachers gave most of their instructional time in reading to oral reading.[66] There is serious doubt about the belief that until just a few years ago all teachers gave over most of their pupils' reading time to oral reading.[4] There are findings, however, that teacher guided oral reading today is a commonly used part of reading instruction in the primary grades.[37]

There are findings, however, that teacher guided oral reading today is a commonly used part of reading instruction in the primary grades.

It is apparent, however, that whatever prompts teachers to emphasize oral reading does not come from advice given in the teachers' manuals of the fifteen major basal reader series.

It is apparent, however, that whatever prompts teachers to emphasize oral reading does not come from advice given in the teachers' manuals of the fifteen major basal reader series. In his analysis of these readers, Aukerman[2] observed that there were twenty-two features common to most of them. Oral reading was not one of these features.

In Aukerman's detailed description of the modes of instruction of these fifteen basal reader series, there is no mention, at all, of oral reading in five of them. There is no published evidence to substantiate the observation that today's basal reader manuals usually advise teachers to have pupils read each story aloud that they have just finished reading silently.[69]

The major thrust of this discussion about oral reading so far is that reading experts over the years have downgraded its value and usefulness, while at the same time teachers, to varying degrees, have resisted the derogations against this form of reading. It is readily noticeable, that since 1900, there have been many reasons given as to why oral reading in schools should be greatly deemphasized, if not eliminated. These refutations of oral reading not only have been frequent; they also are usually voiced in a confident and authoritative-sounding manner. The tone of this disapproval of oral reading would lead its reader to believe that it was solidly based in empirical research findings.

Countermanding the Objections to Oral Reading

A careful inspection of the pertinent research on oral reading reveals that this is a presumptuous attitude to take toward this subject. As Danks and Hill[15] correctly conclude, "We know very little of the processing requirements of oral reading or how it relates to silent reading." For example, the question of whether the slower, more deliberate eye movements used by oral readers will permanently transfer to the silent reading of those who listen to such oral reading, while following along in the text silently, has been bypassed by researchers.[18] Despite the lack of evidence as to whether such a transfer takes place when children follow along in silent reading while listening to an oral reader, teachers who allow this practice have been sharply rebuked.

This caution against making easy generalizations about he place of oral reading in schools must be kept in mind, if one is to properly examine the validity of the reasons given since 1900 why the use of oral reading should be deemphasized. Chief among the reasons given for this proposed reduction in oral reading are those to follow. Presented after each of the protests against oral reading are critical examinations of these challenges to its usefulness and value.

> 1. *Almost all reading in real-life situations is done silently.* Schools should prepare their graduates for the true conditions of life. Since little oral reading in done in actual life experiences, only a small amount should be done in school.[16] The large increase in available reading material in the society since 1915 is proof of the need for silent reading to become dominant. The oral reading that is carried out in schools is not conducted in true-to-life situations.[79]

This argument against oral reading begs the question as to whether oral reading facilitates children's *development* of phonics and word recognition skills, improves upon their vocabulary knowledge and their ability to comprehend written material, and satisfies their need to socialize, to share, and to enjoy literature.[36] Most teachers agree that school experiences should be a preparation for life, as well as life itself. The weakness of the contention that only those things done in everyday life should be taught about in school is readily apparent. The application of this principle would eliminate the large majority of the curriculum matter that the schools now expound.

> 2. *Subvocalization, the movement of the lips or other speech organs when one reads silently, interferes with silent reading ability.* (See Myth Number 11.) Oral reading promotes subvocalization.[20] Therefore, oral reading should be abandoned.

The misconceptions about subvocalization have been dealt with in the preceding chapter. The charge[19] that subvocalization impedes silent reading effectiveness is one of these discredited notions. There is no evidence that an emphasis on oral reading will cause subvocalization. Equally at fault is the claim that subvocalization is caused by children being taught to read silently before they can read well orally.[52] This is a phantom statement, since children must always first read silently what they read orally.

Presented after each of the protests against oral reading are critical examinations of these challenges to its usefulness and value.

3. *Oral reading interferes with the development of reading comprehension.*[8;13;23;38;66]   Oral reading creates "word callers," readers who can read aloud with very acceptable pitch, stress, and juncture, but who do not understand what they have so read.[9;19;28;32;39;46;54;61;65;67]   There are children who read aloud poorly but who have excellent comprehension of what they read. Teachers who emphasize oral reading lose sight of the chief goal of reading instruction; i.e., to develop reading comprehension.[39]

The contention that oral reading impedes comprehension has been dealt with (in part) in the above discussion of Myth Number 1, "Phonics Hinders Comprehension." It appears that, to dismiss the value of phonics, its opponents also find it necessary to condemn oral reading. The facts of the matter to not support this rejection, however.

Generally speaking, poor oral readers are poor silent readers, while good oral readers are good silent readers.

There is a substantial correlation found between children's comprehension of matter read aloud and read silently.[1;25]   Generally speaking, poor oral readers are poor silent readers, while good oral readers are good silent readers. Some believe that young or poor readers can comprehend reading material better if this is read orally, rather than silently.[63;72]

It is clear that the best known history of oral reading practices up to 1943 can offer no findings of empirical research for its conclusion that pupils trained in oral reading cannot grasp the meaning of what they read silently, and that proficiency in oral reading does not imply an understanding of what is read aloud.[39]   Not that the writer of this history did not cite empirical studies as proof for these beliefs. A close inspection of such studies reveal, however, that their findings do not support these contentions.

Oral reading thus makes for a natural learning environment for the beginning stages of reading instruction.

It also appears reasonable to contend that since children at school-entering age depend almost wholly on oral language for communication, their reading instruction should emphasize oral language. Oral reading thus makes for a natural learning environment for the beginning stages of reading instruction.[53]   Young children are observed to have a need to have their reading heard, to get a feedback as to its accuracy, if they are to acquire silent reading skills most effectively. It is not convincing to argue that the lack of perfect matchup between spoken and written language precludes children from the realization that written material is derived from oral language.[66]

This hypothesis cannot mean, however, that one can teach children to read orally before they can read silently. This mistaken view is proffered,[64] nonetheless. For example, it is explained that one reason poor readers have difficulty reading silently is that they have never learned to read well orally. The error of this statement is obvious. Children must read well silently before they can become proficient oral readers. Fluent oral reading of a sentence cannot take place until the child can effectively read the sentence silently. Reading orally first and then silently is a physiological impossibility. The reader mentally processes words before reading aloud. It does seem possible, however, that oral reading can reinforce the pupil's recognition of words in his or her later silent reading.[36]

> *The reader mentally processes words before reading aloud.*

4. *The practice of oral reading will impede the development of desirable speed in silent reading.*[8;23;30] Oral reading will result in the loss of children's ability to scan or skim reading materials. Oral reading will cause subvocalization, which in turn reduces silent reading speed.[31]

These appear to be unsubstantiated assumptions about oral reading. That is, there is little evidence to show that the rate at which children read orally has a transfer effect on the rate that they read silently.[79] Of course, children cannot read aloud faster than they can speak. Assuming that 150 words-per-minute is the average rate of speaking of which children are capable,[8] this appears to be the optimum rate for their oral reading. Children's rate of silent reading, with which they comprehend 70 percent of grade-level material, does not reach 150 wpm until the end of the fourth grade, on the average.[8]

> *Children's rate of silent reading, with which they comprehend 70 percent of grade-level material, does not reach 150 wpm until the end of the fourth grade, on the average.*

Thus, at the end of grade four, children's rates of oral reading and silent reading are approximately equal. The average sixth-grader reads silently, with 70 percent comprehension, at about 185 wpm.[8] There is an advance, then, of only about 15 percent in silent reading rate from grade four to grade six. It is not likely that this 15 percent difference in rate between oral reading and silent reading will result in the negative effect on the silent reading rate that the opponents of oral reading suggest. Not much opportunity exists for this transfer to take place, even if it actually did, since teachers in grade five onward conduct a minimum amount of oral reading.

> 5. *Oral reading is a more difficult kind of reading than is silent reading.*[6;14;24;33;45;46;49;59;78] Oral reading thus is not to be recommended because of its relative complexity. It is too time-consuming, for the value gained, to teach this complicated reading ability.

It is wrong, however, to say that oral reading is a more difficult task than is silent reading.

It is wrong, however, to say that oral reading is a more difficult task than is silent reading. Silent reading is the recognition of individual words and the gaining of the meaning of sentences and longer pieces of written material. Silent reading is more difficult than is oral reading, because the latter involves only the overt vocalization of word names and the meanings of sentences and passages that silent reading has previously generated. It obviously is more arduous for a child to recognize the name of a written word and/or to grasp the meaning of a sentence through silent reading than it is to overtly vocalize this word or sentence, giving it the degrees of pitch, stress, and juncture that indicates that its oral reader understands what its author intended.

Only if we could say that children can recognize a word or gain the meaning of a sentence in silent reading, after they first had read it aloud, could we say that oral reading is a more difficult procedure than is silent reading.

It is clear, then, that oral reading begins where the silent reading processes end.

It is clear, then, that oral reading begins where the silent reading processes end. Some reading experts persist, however, in maintaining that proficient oral reading is the gaining of the author's meaning, as well as passing it on to the listener.[29;77]

It is not difficult to find reading experts who make erroneous comparisons of oral and silent reading. For example, it is said that in silent reading the reader can skip words, theorize about possible meanings of the passage, and/or get only a general idea of it. Oral reading is more difficult than silent reading, it then is claimed, since in oral reading one cannot do these things.[40]

This is a faulty comparison, however, since it is between imprecise silent reading and precise oral reading. The argument that silent reading is simpler than oral reading because it is done faster[38] also lacks merit.

Myth #12: Oral Reading is Dangerous

Oral reading is slower than silent reading because of the physiological limits of the rate of speech that are put upon oral reading. The most specious argument however, is that if children read a sentence aloud, in a slow and halting fashion, the imprecise application of proper rate, pitch, stress, and juncture has been caused by having children read orally.[14]

6. *Oral reading in school is the cause of much personal embarrassment to children.*[43] Oral reading creates so much emotional tension for them that it inhibits their development of reading skills and destroys their interest in reading. Numerous anecdotes are told of children so embarrassed while oral reading that they have broken down and cried.[51;77] It is common for children who are poor oral readers in reading groups to be ridiculed by good oral readers.[66] Oral reading thus often serves as a direct instrument in the lowering of the self-esteem of children.[5;13;24;40;62;79]

To prove their point that oral reading often causes emotional trauma for children, the opponents of oral reading usually construct a worst-case scenario for this practice.[65] Modern teachers are described as teaching oral reading or having children read orally in groups, where the differences in ability to read orally are very great. Excellent oral readers are commonly grouped with very poor oral readers, it is claimed. In these implausible groups, there has been no preparation given for oral reading. That is, children here have not first read the material on hand silently, asking for help with unknown words. The good readers in such groups, it is vouched, are urged by teachers to make negative criticisms of the slightest imperfections in the oral reading of their less capable classmates.

None of these conditions likely prevail in modern classrooms, however. Children are grouped for reading instruction in schools, so that differences in oral reading ability can be minimized. Capable teachers are aware of the fact that unless children can read a passage silently well, they cannot do this effectively when reading aloud. By describing the worst possible situations under which oral reading could be conducted, the opponents of oral reading are able to demolish a strawman of their own creation. It is important to report, on the other hand, that no evidence of an empirical nature has been forwarded as support for the

Capable teachers are aware of the fact that unless children can read a passage silently well, they cannot do this effectively when reading aloud.

137

hypothesis that children who read aloud extensively in school exhibit more emotional problems than do those who do not.

> 7. *Oral reading is so time-consuming that it grossly reduces children's opportunities to read silently.* Oral reading thus inhibits the establishment of extensive, independent reading habits. It is an inefficient use of the time available to teach reading, and thus takes time needed for the more important aspects of reading.[13;23] Worst, yet, the teaching of oral reading tends to eliminate in teachers' minds the value of extensive silent reading. Teachers who emphasize oral reading no longer perceive that the chief function of reading instruction is to develop reading comprehension.[39]

This charge against oral reading rests on the presumption that if oral reading is allowed to be practiced, it inevitably will be "overemphasized." While the overemphasis of oral reading is said to interfere with reading comprehension, as noted above, such "overemphasis" is never defined. Even those who protest this overemphasis find it impossible to determine what constitutes a proper balance in the amount of instruction given to oral as versus silent reading.[27;32] It remains convenient, nonetheless, to charge that oral reading instruction will lead to an overemphasis of this teaching, since it is common for teachers to recoil from educational practices so designated. While fallacious, this charge seems to have had some of its intended effect. Some teachers have been anxious about teaching oral reading, although there is no credible evidence that children who read orally intensively dislike to read.

...there is nothing in research to support the notion that children who have done little oral reading are those who develop broad reading interests and read expansively.

To the contrary, there is nothing in research to support the notion that children who have done little oral reading are those who develop broad reading interests and read expansively. It appears safer to predict that children whose instruction in literature involves oral reading, like readers' theatre, choral verse, and the sharing of favorite stories, will demonstrate longer-lasting appreciation and affection for literature than will children denied oral reading experiences.

> 8. *Oral reading detracts from the development of good listening skills.*[16;58] Children who are required to follow along

silently in a passage, while another child reads aloud, are likely to become habitually careless listeners.

This charge against oral reading is a critical one, if true. It is doubtless true that children who came to maturity listening to radio, as versus viewing television, developed better listening habits than do modern children. The very nature of verbal radio forces the listener to pay close attention to the organization, word choice, and author's intention in the stories and documentation that is projected. Present-day children do not receive such a rigorous training in becoming good listeners.

Would not the requirement that children pay close attention to a passage being read aloud help in this matter? Modern teachers find good listening habits in children so troublesome and arduous to develop that it appears reasonable to assume that any listening action which demands cognizant mindfulness during a spoken activity would be helpful here. Following the oral reader along silently, as he/she reads dull, uninspiring, irrelevant, or abstract material will cause any pupil's attention to wander, of course. On the other hand, following oral reading along silently, as poetry or drama is vocalized, can add to the attraction of this performance.

There is no empirical evidence that good listeners in school are the result of reading programs free of oral reading. Hoffman and Segal's comprehensive review of the research on this matter suggests the opposite.[37] They found that guided oral reading practice has the potential to contribute significantly to growth in reading ability. The evidence from research says that teacher guided practice in oral reading can develop reading fluency, as it causes the reader to focus on units of language larger than the word, and reading comprehension, as it requires effective interpretation of the author's intended meaning. The notion that such reading growth in children would cause them to suffer the side effect of poor listening ability seems unsupported.

9. *As opposed to silent reading, oral reading cannot be measured accurately or objectively.* Unless a school activity can be measured effectively, it should not be conducted intensively. Moreover, the usual measurement made of oral reading is irrelevant.[65] It means nothing if a child can correctly read a word aloud a dozen consecutive times. This

The very nature of verbal radio forces the listener to pay close attention to the organization, word choice, and author's intention in the stories and documentation that is projected.

There is no empirical evidence that good listeners in school are the result of reading programs free of oral reading.

does not prove anything about the child's comprehension of the word. It is improper to think that oral reading gives the teacher an opportunity to diagnose children's word recognition abilities, plan corrective steps to improve them, or teach children how to read with proper pitch, stress, and juncture. Teachers do not make this use of oral reading systematically enough for it to be of any value.

These appear to be especially unreasonable criticisms of oral reading. The argument that the diagnosis of oral reading should be abandoned because teachers to not carry it out systematically enough is much like concluding that the evidence that smoking is injurious to one's health is invalid because people continue to smoke. Oral readings have been used effectively for many years as a means of diagnosing children's silent reading abilities.[3] This diagnosis can be used to discover words children do not recognize in silent reading, words they pronounce incorrectly (do not know the meaning of), and how much they use the context of sentences as a way to gain their meanings.

Oral readings have been used effectively for many years as a means of diagnosing children's silent reading abilities.

This does not mean that all diagnoses of oral reading can be defended. Some reading experts wrongly insist that analyses of oral reading errors should be carried out without first allowing the child to practice silent reading of the passage to be read aloud.[19;42;46;53;56] Reading authorities also unfortunately advise teachers that all the different kinds of mistakes in oral reading should be judged to have the same significance. Thus, the omission of a word while oral reading, which greatly disturbs the meaning of the passage read aloud, is given the same weight in the oral reading test as is an addition or substitution of a word which has little such effect.

> 10. *The use of oral reading in schools creates lazy teachers.* Oral reading is an activity that can be carried out with no time or effort spent on its preplanning. Consequently, reading teachers who emphasize oral reading become lackadaisical and unenterprising. They become unconcerned as to whether or not their pupils comprehend what they read aloud.[39]

The best response to this unfair criticism of oral reading is to simply deny that good teachers approach oral reading, or any other aspects of reading for that matter, in this deplorable manner. There is potential in oral reading, as in any other aspect of reading, of course, for negligent or indolent teachers to avoid their responsibilities for careful planning. This kind of teacher undoubtedly carries out silent reading instruction in the same disgraceful way as he or she does oral reading, however.

It is important to say, therefore, that careful planning is necessary for effective oral reading to occur. The falsity of the assumptions that effective oral reading can take place prior to silent reading, or that children's oral reading should be tested before they have silently read a passage in question, have been noted above. It is such misbegotten notions that lead teachers to neglect planning for oral reading activities.

> 11. *The eye movements used by children to read silently and orally are different.* Oral reading eye movements are characterized by longer and more frequent eye fixations and regressions. This slower and more deliberate pattern of eye movements will transfer to silent reading if oral reading is practiced.[18] Having children follow along, reading silently, while another child reads orally is especially harmful in this respect.

This argument against the use of oral reading is much like saying that slower, more deliberate physical movements made when walking will transfer to and detract from one's ability to run, if much walking is done. The basic fault of the contention that the kind of eye movements done when reading orally will transfer to silent reading lies in the assumption that certain eye movements are a cause of reading disability. This is a mistaken view of the nature of eye movements. They are symptoms, not causes of reading ability. Ineffective reading and undesirable eye movements when reading orally or silently are thus caused by factors common to them both. The inability to decode words in an automatic way is a factor that will cause both ineffective reading and faulty eye movements.

As for the research on this issue, even the 1949 yearbook on reading in the elementary school,[33] published by the NSSE, which is no friend of the intensive teaching of decoding or phonics application (it argues that beginning readers should not be encouraged to associate print with

It is important to say, therefore, that careful planning is necessary for effective oral reading to occur.

Ineffective reading and undesirable eye movements when reading orally or silently are thus caused by factors common to them both.

spoken symbols), disputes the notion that eye movements in oral reading will transfer to silent reading.

It is true that the eye movements of children who follow along, reading silently as another child reads aloud, tend to approximate the eye movements of the oral reader.[26] It would not be possible to follow along reading silently unless this happened. The eye movements of the silent reader who follows along in the text being read aloud naturally are governed by the rate and quality of the vocal delivery of the oral reader.

It has not been demonstrated, however, that this procedure makes for inefficient eye movements which transfer into silent reading. The argument that this procedure is highly dangerous to children's silent reading rate and comprehension has never been proved.[71]

But is having children follow along, reading silently, while a child reads orally, useless, as it is commonly held by today's reading experts? Not at all, the evidence on this issue suggests.[37]

As the oral reader emphasizes the author's intended meaning of a passage, he or she helps reinforce the comprehension of this for the silent reader who follows along. This relationship is particularly fruitful with poetry. The best way to share poetry is with an oral reading, while the audience follows along, reading it silently. The pitch, stress, and juncture used by the poetry reader here can reveal unsuspected aspects of meaning for the silent reader. The oral reader can relate to the silent reader who follows along his or her enthusiasm for the passage, an emotion that can be contagious.

The well-prepared oral reader presents an appropriate model for silent readers -- for their turns at reading aloud. The rehearsals necessary for effective oral reading give opportunities for the meaning of a passage to be confirmed. Teachers can require high standards for oral reading which makes it necessary for the oral reader to have full knowledge of the meaning of the passage so interpreted. And, finally, much of oral reading can be a theatrical event, an entertainment to silent readers who follow along.

12. *Oral reading will narrow the child's eye-voice span and thus reduce silent reading efficiency.* When one reads orally, one's eyes usually fixate on a word farther along the line

---

It is true that the eye movements of children who follow along, reading silently as another child reads aloud, tend to approximate the eye movements of the oral reader.

The well-prepared oral reader presents an appropriate model for silent readers -- for their turns at reading aloud.

of writing than the word that is read aloud. One's eye fixation when reading aloud is not at the same place as one's voice. When reading aloud, one's eyes and voice normally are not on the same written word. The eye-voice span thus is the distance at any given point in oral reading between a fixation of the eyes on a line of written material and the word from this line that is said aloud. Wide eye-voice spans are indications of good silent reading ability. There is no evidence, however, as Jones[40] claims, that the eye-voice span means that whole groups of words are seen in single eye fixations. The data about eye-voice span do not support this look-say notion.

The refutation, previously made, of the charge that slower, more deliberate eye movements in oral reading will transfer to silent reading, if much oral reading is done, can justifiably be repeated here. The eye-voice span is a symptom of reading ability, or the lack of it, not its causation. A wide eye-voice span thus is the result of children's abilities to quickly recognize words when reading silently, plus the establishment of the habit of using the context of a sentence as an aid to its comprehension. There is no empirical evidence that extended practice with oral reading will reduce the size of one's eye-voice span. A wide eye-voice span means that children have developed quick word recognition and can use context cues, and not that they have done little oral reading.

The eye-voice span is a symptom of reading ability, or the lack of it, not its causation.

13. *Those who support the use of oral reading advocate a wrong theory about reading; viz., that good silent reading is the quick and accurate recognition of individual words.* The skills involved in proficient oral reading will interfere with silent reading facility because attention to each word in a written passage, as is done in oral reading, will hinder the reader's comprehension of the passage.[16] When pupils are taught to read words aloud they inevitably lose sight of the fact that the true purpose of reading is to get meaning.[21] Teachers who emphasize oral reading wrongfully stress the importance of word recognition.[74] Their pupils gain the false notion that reading is the ability to recognize words.[41] That oral reading does not aid in the acquisition of meaning,

since it merely expresses previously acquired meaning, is further reason why it should be abandoned.

The theory that reading is best taught in sentences and that the recognition of words in reading is relatively unimportant has been carefully examined in a preceding chapter of this book. (See Myth Number 4: Reading is Best Taught in Sentences.) Since it is clear that the argument used to disparage the value of oral reading, that it stresses individual word recognition, is the same one used to defend the teaching of reading in sentences, the statements from Myth Number 4 pertain here.

Despite the wishful thinking of some reading experts to the contrary, the evidence is clear that quick and accurate word recognition is essential for efficient silent reading.[9] The research up through the 1970s gives continued support, as well, to the importance of accuracy in oral reading.[10] The advice proffered by certain reading authorities to teachers (to believe otherwise) accordingly must be viewed as dangerous misinformation.

Despite the wishful thinking of some reading experts to the contrary, the evidence is clear that quick and accurate word recognition is essential for efficient silent reading.

14. *Good oral reading comes naturally as a consequence of learning to read silently.*[22] When the habit of oral reading is acquired, oral reading needs little attention. In the course of learning to read silently, children become conscious of the need to use appropriate stress, pitch, and juncture in their oral reading. Since silent reading must, by the nature of the reading act, precede oral reading, little or no attention need be given children as to how to read orally.

This criticism of the intensive teaching of oral reading appears to be the least offensive of any of those discussed so far. It is true that silent reading must precede oral reading. Nonetheless, there are certain aspects of oral reading that make necessary the requirement of explicit instruction in this skill.

Principally, these conditions arise when oral reading must be more faithful to the written text than does silent reading. For example, when oral reading is used to provide precise answers to questions, to read poetry or plays, to give announcements or directions, to explain scientific and mathematical processes, or to cite unacceptable as versus more accept-

Myth #12: Oral Reading is Dangerous

able sentence structures taken from pupils' compositions, it is necessary that the oral reader not wander from the text. Upon occasion in silent reading, word substitution and addition do not greatly disturb the overall meaning of a sentence. The uses of oral reading, on the other hand, often call for precise, if not faultless, rendering of the written text. These distinctions between oral and silent reading may not occur to children simply as a consequence of learning to read silently.

The "language experience" approach to beginning reading development[30] uses children's oral language, as dictated to their teacher, as its main body of instructional material. The reading aloud by children of these dictated sentences immediately follows their transcription. These oral readings are expected to be faithful to the actual oral language, as it was dictated. This is an oral reading procedure that children must be expressly taught to follow.

Teachers also must deal with the phenomenon of the occasional child who reads well silently but who reads poorly aloud. Although teachers have been reminded that certain highly-skilled silent readers to not like oral reading, and will never be good oral readers,[19] this advice seems unnecessarily defeatist.

Unless children have gross physiological defects, there is no reason they cannot be taught to read aloud effectively and share in the enjoyment that such an attainment can bring. The problem of the good silent reader/poor oral reader is usually emotional, not linguistic, in nature. While complicated, this is a condition that does lend itself to resourceful teacher intervention, nonetheless.

It is likely that neither good oral reading habits by children, nor their desirable school behavior in general, is learned naturally; that is, without direct teacher guidance. It is pertinent to note that during the development of children's oral reading skills, the teacher holds them accountable for specific patterns of reading behavior. Such a requirement is a key aspect of the successful learning of any educational skill. The direct management of pupils that is necessary for them to develop oral reading ability thus provides a useful model for teachers to follow in other school activities.

The uses of oral reading, on the other hand, often call for precise, if not faultless, rendering of the written text.

Unless children have gross physiological defects, there is no reason they cannot be taught to read aloud effectively and share in the enjoyment that such an attainment can bring.

Conclusions

The fourteen reasons cited above that have been given by the opponents of oral reading as to why it should be deemphasized, if not abandoned, have all been shown to be unconvincing. There appears to be no legitimate justification, therefore, for this position against the use of oral reading in schools.

The underlying causes for such seemingly illogical stands against oral reading have been alluded to in the course of this discussion. None of these more hidden causes appear to have any more merit than does the open opposition to oral reading. These hidden causes include the fact that oral reading obviously is a traditional school practice. Educators who see change as the only means of making progress in school practices would deny a place in reading programs for oral reading on this ground alone.

Oral reading also is closely allied to phonics teaching.

Oral reading also is closely allied to phonics teaching. The strong sentiment in force among many teacher educators against phonics teaching (since 1915) undoubtedly is of consequence in the movement to deemphasize oral reading.

In addition, there were great financial benefits to leading reading experts -- the ones who authored basal reader textbooks over the years -- from the demise of oral reading. Teachers who were convinced by them that reading comprehension would be handicapped if time was spent in class on oral reading were quick to demand that their school district purchase the many-volumed, costly basal readers plus their consumable workbooks, etc.

Oral readings in school presented a practical time for the intensive inculcation of such a set of beliefs.

The financial royalties from such materials to their reading-expert authors have been notorious. Even the philosophy, increasingly defended by reading experts since 1915, that there must not be an explicit set of ethical, moral, artistic, historical, sociological, or legal precepts that all children should learn to defend, worked against oral reading. Oral readings in school presented a practical time for the intensive inculcation of such a set of beliefs.

Myth #12: Oral Reading is Dangerous

It became more and more accepted in the course of this century, however, that pupils should not be help accountable for understanding a predetermined group of trustworthy certainties about personal and social life. Accordingly, it was deemed correct that oral reading sessions be curtailed so the reading time could be given to pupils to pursue silent reading aimed at a gratification of egoistic, even eccentric interests and proclivities.

The permissive attitude of teachers toward non-conforming pupil behavior in school also has tended to make unnecessary the use of oral reading as a means of pupil management. Oral reading demands pupil adherence to a prescribed standard of performance. This standard-setting runs counter to the view of some teachers that, unless they indulge unorthodox pupil behavior, reading attainment by pupils will be handicapped. This perception of pupil responsibility fits well into the popular theory among teacher educators that the direct teaching of any academic skill is to be avoided.

Oral reading demands pupil adherence to a prescribed standard of performance.

References

1. Allington, R. L. "Oral Reading." In P. D. Pearson (Ed.), *Handbook of Reading Research.* New York, NY: Longman, 1984.

1. Anderson, I. H. and Dearborn, W. F. *The Psychology of Teaching Reading.* New York, NY: Ronald, 1952.

2. Aukerman, R. C. *The Basal Reader Approach to Reaing.* New York, NY: John Wiley, 1981.

3. Beldin, H. O. "Informal Reading Testing: Historical Review and Review of the Research." In W. K. Durr (Ed.), *Reading Difficulties: Diagnosis, Correction, and Remediation.* Newark, DE: International Reading Association, 1970.

4. Bond, G. L.; Tinker, M. A.; Wasson, B. b.; and Wasson, J. B. *Reading Difficulties: Their Diagnosis and Correction.* Englewood Cliffs, NJ: Prentice-Hall, 1984.

5. Burmeister, L. E. *Foundations and Strategies for Teaching Children to Read.* Reading, MA: Addison-Wesley, 1983.

6. Bush, C. L. and Huebner, M. H. *Strategies for Reading in the Elementary School.* New York, NY: Macmillan, 1979.

7. Buswell, G. T. *Non-Oral Reading: A Study of Its Use in the Chicago Public Schools.* Supplementary Educational Monograph No. 60. Chicago, IL: University of Chicago, 1945.

8. Carnine, D. and Silbert, J. *Direct Instruction Reading.* Columbus, OH: Charles E. Merrill, 1979.

9. Carver, R. P. *Reading Comprehension and Reading Theory.* Springfield, IL: Charles C. Thomas, 1981.

10. Chall, J. S. *Learning to Read: The Great Debate.* New York, NY: McGraw-Hill, 1983.

11. Cheek, M. C. and Cheek, E. H. *Diagnostic-Prescriptive Reading Instruction.* Dubuque, IA: Wm. C. Brown, 1980.

12. Cooper, J. D., et al. *The What and How of Reading Instruction.* Columbus, OH: Charles E. Merrill, 1979.

13. Cunningham, J. W.; Cunningham, P. M.; and Arthur, S. V. *Middle and Secondary School Reading.* New York, NY: Longman, 1981.

14. Dallmann, M., et al. *The Teaching of Reading.* New York, NY: Holt, Rinehart and Winston, 1974.

15. Danks, J. H. and Hill, G. O. "An Interactive Analysis of Oral Reading." In A. M. Lesgold and C. A. Perfetti (Eds.), *Interactive Processes in Reading.* Hillsdale, NJ: Lawrence Erlbaum, 1981.

16. Dauzat, J. A. and Dauzat, S. V. *Reading: The Teacher and the Learner.* New York, NY: John Wiley, 1981.

17. Davis, F. B. "Research in Comprehension in Reading." *Reading Research Quarterly,* 1968, 3, 499-545.

18. Durkin, D. *Teaching Young Children to Read.* Boston, MA: Allyn and Bacon, 1972.

19. Durkin, D. *Teaching Them to Read.* Boston, MA: Allyn and Bacon, 1983.

20. Edward, T. "Teaching Reading: A Critique." In J. Money (Ed.), *The Disabled Reader.* Baltimore, MD: Johns Hopkins University, 1966.

21. Farr, R. and Roser, N. *Teaching a Child to Read.* New York, NY: Harcourt Brace Jovanovish, 1979.

22. Fries, C. C. *Linguistics and Reading.* New York, NY: Holt, Rinehart and Winston, 1963.

23. Fry, E. B. *Elementary Reading Instruction.* New York, NY: McGraw-Hill, 1977.

24. Gates, A. I. *The Improvement of Reading.* New York, NY: Macmillan, 1947.

25. Gibson, E. J. and Levin, H. *The Psychology of Reading.* Cambridge, MA: MIT, 1975.

26. Gilbert, L. C. "Effect on Silent Reading of Attempting to Follow Oral Reading." *Elementary School Journal,* 1940, 40, 614-621.

27. Gilliland, H. *A Practical Guide to Remedial Reading.* Columbus, OH: Charles E. Merrill, 1978.

28. Gray, L. *Teaching Children to Read.* New York, NY: Ronald, 1963.

29. Gray, W. S. "Characteristics of Effective Oral Reading." In A. J. Harris (Ed.), *Readings on Reading Instruction.* New York, NY: David McKay, 1963.

30. Hall, M. *Teaching Reading as a Language Experience.* Columbus, OH: Charles E. Merrill, 1981.

31. Harris, A. J. and Sipay, E. R. *How to Teach Reading.* New York, NY: Longman, 1979.

32. Heilman, A. W. *Principles and Practices of Teaching Reading.* Columbus: Charles E. Merrill, 1977.

33. Henry, N. B. (Ed.). *Reading in the Elementary School.* 48th Yearbook, National Society for the Study of Education, Chicago, IL: University of Chicago, 1949.

34. Henry, N. B. (Ed.). *Development in and Through Reading.* 60th Yearbook, National Society for the Study of Education. Chicago, IL: University of Chicago, 1961.

35. Hildreth, G. *Teaching Reading.* New York, NY: Henry Holt, 1958.

36. Hoffman, J. V. "Is There a Legitimate Place for Oral Reading Instruction in a Developmental Reading Program?" *Elementary School Journal,* 1981, 81, 305-310.

37. Hoffman, J. V. and Segal, K. "Oral Reading Instruction: A Century of Controversy (1880-1980). Washington, DC: National Institute of Education, U.S. Department of Education, 1982.

38. Huey, E. B. *The Psychology and Pedagogy of Reading.* Cambridge, MA: M.I.T., 1968 (first published in 1908).

39. Hyatt, A. V. *The Place of Oral Reading in the School Program: Its History and Development from 1880-1941.* New York, NY: Teachers College, Columbia University, 1943.

40. Jones, D. M. *Teaching Children to Read.* New York, NY: Harper and Row, 1971.

41. Karlin, R. *Teaching Elementary Reading.* New York, NY: Harcourt Brace Jovanovich, 1971.

42. Kennedy, E. C. *Methods in Teaching Developmental Reading.* Itaska, IL: F. E. Peacock, 1981.

43. Lamb, P. and Arnold, R. *Teaching Reading.* Belmont, CA: Wadsworth, 1980.

44. Layton, J. R. *The Psychology of Learning to Read.* New York, NY: Academic, 1979.

45. Lee, D. M. and Allen, R. V. *Learning to Read Through Experience.* New York, NY: Appleton-Century-Crofts, 1963.

46. Mangieri, J. N.; Bader, L. A.; and Walker, J. E. *Elementary Reading: A Comprehensive Approach.* New York, NY: McGraw-Hill, 1982.

47. Mathews, M. M. *Teaching to Read: Historyically Considered.* Chicago, IL: University of Chicago, 1966.

48. McDale, J.E. "A Hypothesis for Non-Oral Reading: Argument, Experiment, and Results." *Journal of Educational Research,* 1937, 30, 489-503.

49. McKee, P. *Reading.* New York, NY: Houghton Mifflin, 1966.

50. Miller, W. H. *The First R: Elementary Reading Today.* New York, NY: Holt, Rinehart and Winston, 1972.

51. Morrow, A. E. "Moral: Go Oral--Some of the Time." In A. J. Harris (Ed.), *Readings on Reading Instruction.* New York, NY: David McKay, 1963.

52. Otto, W. and Smith, R. J. *Corrective and Remedial Teaching.* Boston, MA: Houghton Mifflin, 1980.

53. Quandt, I. J. *Teaching Reading: A Human Process.* Chicago, IL: Rand McNally, 1977.

54. Robeck, M. C. and Wilson, J. A. R. *Psychology of Reading: Foundations of Instruction.* New York, NY: John Wiley, 1974.

55. Rohrer, J. J. "An Analysis and Evaluation of the Non-Oral Method of Reading Instruction." *Elementary School Journal,* 1943, 43, 415-421.

56. Rubin, D. *Diagnosis and Correction in Reading Instruction.* New York, NY: Holt, Rinehart and Winston, 1982.

57. Russell, D. H. *Children Learn to Read.* Boston, MA: Ginn, 1961.

58. Schubert, D. and Torgerson, T. *Improving the Reading Program.* Dubuque, IA: Wm. C. Brown, 1981.

59. Smith, F. *Understanding Reading.* New York, NY: Holt, Rinehart and Winston, 1982.

60. Smith, H. P. and Dechant, E. V. *Psychology in Teaching Reading.* Englewood Cliffs, NJ: Prentice-Hall, 1961.

61. Smith, N. B. *American Reading Instruction.* Newark, DE: International Reading Association, 1965.

62. Smith, N. B. and Robinson, H. A. *Reading Instruction for Today's Children.* Englewood Cliffs, NJ: Prentice-Hall, 1980.

63. Smith, R.J. and Barrett, T. C. *Teaching Reading in the Middle Grades.* Reading, MA: Addison-Wesley, 1979.

64. Smith, R. J. and Johnson, D. D. *Teaching Children to Read.* Reading, MA: Addison-Wesley, 1980.

65. Spache, G. D. *Diagnosing and Correcting Reading Disabilities.* Boston, MA: Allyn and Bacon, 1976.

66. Spache, G. D. and Spache, E. B. *Reading in the Elementary School.* Boston, MA: Allyn and Bacon, 1977.

67. Stoodt, B. D. *Reading Instruction.* Boston, MA: Houghton Mifflin, 1981.

68. Swaby, B. E. R. *Teaching and Learning Reading.* Boston, MA: Little, Brown, 1984.

69. Wallen, C. J. *Competency in Teaching Reading.* Chicago, IL: Science Research Associates, 1972.

70. Wardhaugh, R. *Reading: A Linguistic Perspective.* New York, NY: Harcourt, Brace and World, 1969.

71. Weaver, P. *Research Within Reach.* St. Louis, MO: CEMREL, 1978.

72. Weber, R. "The Relation Between Oral and Silent Reading." In A. Berry; T. C. Barrett and W. R. Powell (Eds.), *Elementary Reading Instruction: Selected Materials.* Boston, MA: Allyn and Bacon, 1974.

73. Whipple, G.M. (Ed.). *Second Report of the Society's Committee on New Materials of Instruction.* 20th Yearbook, part 1, of the National Society for the Study of Education. Bloomington, IL: Public School, 1921.

74. Whipple, G. M. (Ed.). *Report of the National Committee on Reading.* 24th Yearbook, part 1, of the National Society for the Study of Education. Bloomington, IL: Public School, 1925.

75. Whipple, G. M. (Ed.). *The Teaching of Reading: A Second Report.* 36th Yearbook, part 1, of the National Society for the Study of Education. Chicago, IL: University of Chicago, 1937.

76. Witty, P. A.: Freeland, A. M.; and Grotberg, E.H. *The Teaching of Reading..* Boston, MA: D. C. Heath, 1966.

77. Worthington, L. W. "Oral Reading? Certainly!" In A. J. Harris (Ed.), *Readings on Reading Instruction.* New York, NY: David McKay, 1963.

78. Zintz, M. V. *Corrective Reading.* Dubuque, IA: Wm. C. Brown, 1972.

79. Zintz, M. V. and Maggart, Z. R. *The Reading Process: The Teacher and the Learner.* Dubuque, IA: Wm. C. Brown, 1984.

Chapter XIII

Why the Myths of Reading Instruction Prevail

This chapter describes why support continues to be given to suppositions about reading instruction that have been discredited by research findings. It is demonstrated that there is no single reason for this untenable position. Instead, there appear to be several causes for the resistance to disestablishment of the myths related to reading instruction. This reluctance to acknowledge these myths is due to the forces of tradition, the interlocking relationships between basal reader publishers and reading experts, the refusal of reading experts to accept outside criticism, their lack of knowledge about phonics teaching, their negative biases toward this instruction, their fear that phonics advocacy equals political conservatism, the negative attitudes toward phonics by teachers' organizations, unsubstantiated information in educational publications, the expectancy that research will not affect teaching practices, the refusal to admit that there is a literacy crisis, the lack of legal redress for malpractice in reading instruction, and the establishment of public schools and teacher education as a monopoly.

It is obvious that the myths of reading instruction described so far have had a remarkable staying power.

It is obvious that the myths of reading instruction described so far have had a remarkable staying power. In spite of the impressive statistical evidence which indicates the weaknesses of their point of view, these conceptions of how reading should be taught still present a strong attraction for many reading educators. Unfortunately, there is no single reason why these erroneous practices in reading instruction persist. However, there are several prevailing conditions that create this undesirable and unseemly situation.

Traditional Beliefs and Practices

A major cause of the myths of reading instruction is tradition.

A major cause of the myths of reading instruction is tradition. Erroneous practices in reading instruction often continue simply because it is customary for reading professors to recommend them and for reading teachers to utilize them. It undoubtedly is easier and more comfortable for reading teachers to continue use of the same methodology year after year, than it is to critically examine these practices for their potential shortcomings. The professors of education who write the texts and articles on reading instruction are guilty of perpetuating this condition. Usually, the writing of such material involves the reproduction of aspects of reading instruction that were included in a high percentage of texts on this subject. In short, if a large number of existing texts on the teaching of reading include certain erroneous notions about this instruction, it is highly likely that this faulty information will then find its way into future publications of a similar nature.

It is probably true that the longer professors advocate (and teachers use) certain parts of methodology in reading, the more loyal they become to them.

A part of the traditional reluctance to give up malpractice in reading instruction is the embarrassment that would be engendered by a public announcement that one's previous views about these bits of inappropriate teaching behavior were false. It is probably true that the longer professors advocate (and teachers use) certain parts of methodology in reading, the more loyal they become to them. For the textbook-writing professors of education, the giving up of positions that they had strongly defended in the past in previous writings about reading instruction is even more painful. It is apparent that such reading experts often will go to great lengths to try to maintain credibility for previously held (although indefensible) views concerning the teaching of reading. In spite of overwhelming research evidence that discredits such views, these professors will maintain a brave face as to their virtues. Here, then, is an example, of which there are many in the history of the advancement of technology, of supposedly scientific-minded professionals who must be forced into an acceptance of the ascertained realities of their life's work.

Publishers and Writers of Basal Readers

The publishers of basal readers are also often responsible in great measure for encouraging the perpetuation of certain unsound practices in the teaching of reading. The directors of these publishing companies are extremely loath to invest the tens of millions of dollars it presently takes to launch a new basal reading series, for basal readers that are different in any significant respect from the previous sets of these books that have had successful sales records.

The result of this conservative financial reaction to what the research says about reading instruction, as versus what existing sales records say, is the appearance of dozens of highly similar basal reader series on the market, each published by a different company. It is clear that communication between publishers of beginning reader series and the researchers investigating the process of learning to read is clearly inadequate. Accordingly, decisions by publishers about basal readers are largely based on their intuitions or other arbitrary decisions or on marketing considerations.[1]

The interlocking nature of basal reader publishers, university reading experts who write these books and profit from their sales (while advising teachers to use them), public school reading specialists, and teachers' organizations has been aptly described by Yarington.[2] It is his thesis, which he argues compellingly, that the current literacy problem in our schools is based on a series of unethical financial interrelationships between and among members of the federal government, state education departments, local school boards and administrators, professional organizations, and professors of education. At the root of this pecuniary wheeling and dealing, Yarington says, are professors of education. It doubtlessly is true that the establishment of vested and entrenched interests that results from the network of basal reader publishers and reading experts who double as writers of these books and as high-ranking officers in teachers' organizations, creates a status quo condition in school reading programs in schools that stubbornly resists change.

The publishers of basal readers are also often responsible in great measure for encouraging the perpetuation of certain unsound practices in the teaching of reading.

At the root of this pecuniary wheeling and dealing, Yarington says, are professors of education.

This connection is part of what Yarington calls the "Great American Reading Machine":

> "The best graphic description of the Machine I can provide is the drawing below illustrating the flow of both money and influence. The Great American Reading Machine is a stable social institution in which leadership is controlled and limited to proven followers of the creed for the protection of the organization. As an institution, it determines the quality of the teaching of reading to children. It is an institution that is so established that it has withstood continued criticism from within and without for 200 years" (p. 18).

THE GREAT AMERICAN READING MACHINE

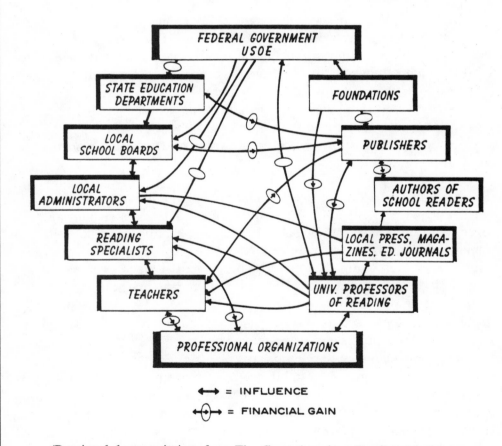

(Reprinted, by permission, from The Great American Reading Machine by David J. Yarington, Hayden Book Company, Rochelle Park, NJ 1978.)

Negative Attitude Toward Outside Criticism

An additional reason why myths of reading instruction prevail is the unwillingness of reading professionals to accept, or in any way respond favorably, to negative analyses of their work made by critics who are not members of the reading establishment "in" group. The history of the reform of professions of various kinds clearly has indicated, however, that judgmental observations made by outsiders are helpful in the progressive reform of these special vocations. The stimulus of constructive evaluations, by critics whose lack of emotional attachment to the customary workings of a profession gives them an unbiased vision, often can be used to help improve the behavior of professional workers. It is apparent, however, that reading professionals often reject this truism.

One of the earliest attempts to persuade the advocates of the look-say, whole-word method to reconcile their viewpoint about reading with research findings came from Orton in 1929. In his classic text, *Reading, Writing and Speech problems in Children* (1937)[3] Orton presented in even greater detail the undesirable effects of the look-say method. Orton explained that not only was repeated flash exposure of the whole word not an effective teaching techniques. It tended to even increase the tendency of confusion and failures of word recognition, he observed in his practice with children who had difficulty in learning to read.

Orton presented in even greater detail the undesirable effects of the look-say method.

Orton's suggestions for needed changes in reading instruction had virtually no effect upon the attitudes of reading professionals of the period towards this teaching, however. Nor did they respond any more favorably to the next well-argued plea for the teaching of intensive phonics, that by Bloomfield, a linguist, in 1942.[4] These two plans for improving the teaching of reading suffered the most ignoble of all forms of rejection: They were simply ignored by reading educators and basal reader publishers.

Orton's suggestions for needed changes in reading instruction had virtually no effect upon the attitudes of reading professionals of the period towards this teaching, however.

It was not until 1955 that the advocates of the look-say teaching method felt compelled to defend their beliefs. In that year, *Why Johnny Can't Read,*[5] by Flesch, was the occasion for a change in the response to outside criticism by reading professionals.

Flesch's call for the rejection of the look-say method, in favor of intensive phonics teaching, was denounced . . .

The efforts of the Reading Reform Foundation appear to be less than successful in this respect.

While the disagreements with the look-say method by Orton and Bloomfield had been gentle, indirect, and nonpersonal, those by Flesch were highly caustic and attacked professors of education by name for their mistaken views about reading instruction. Flesch's call for the rejection of the look-say method, in favor of intensive phonics teaching, was denounced in turn by reading professionals as misinformed and irresponsible, at best, and as demagogic, hysterical, scare tactics, at worst. In any event, the publication of Flesch's best-selling book had little if any ascertainable effect on reading professionals' views of reading, beyond their renewed dedication to the rejection of intensive phonics teaching.

The efforts of the Reading Reform Foundation appear to be less than successful in this respect. This organization was founded over twenty years ago to restore the intensive teaching of phonics to reading instruction throughout the nation's schools. For several years its official organ, *The Reading Informer*, has reported regularly on the statistics of illiteracy, on the research as to the relative superiority of phonics teaching, and on news concerning the advancement or depression of phonics teaching.

The RRF, through its numerous phonics workshops and its national conventions, presents information about phonics teaching from reading experts who are convinced of the merit of this instruction. The RRF, a nonprofit body, takes no official position as to the relative excellence of the various intensive phonics programs now published. Instead, it distributes literature in which phonics programs are listed and only briefly described.

While it is clear that the RRF has and is making a significant impact on the way information about phonics teaching is disseminated, notice of its existence has been effectively suppressed. Never has the organization been acknowledged in any way by the International Reading Association or the National Council of Teachers of English. Its name has never appeared in any well-known text on the teaching of reading.

The intervening years from the advent of Flesch's 1955 book and his update of his topic in 1981, *Why Johnny Still Can't Read*,[5] witnessed the publication of several other books that offered negative criticisms of the popular look-say method. These included those by Terman and Walcutt (1958),[6] McCracken (1959),[7] Diack (1960 and 1965),[8] Walcutt (1961),[9] Mayer (1961),[10] Spaulding and Spaulding (1962),[11] Fries (1963),[12]

Trace (1965),[13] Walton (1965),[14] Mathews (1966),[15] Johnson (1970),[16] and Blumenfeld (1974).[17] These books accurately predicted that the United States would suffer illiteracy on a grand scale in the future, if its schools failed to teach systematic phonics in an intensive manner. The 1983 report of the National Commission on Excellence in Education, *A Nation at Risk*,[18] indicates that these predictions truly have come to pass.

Despite the accuracy of the warnings of these books of the 1950s, '60s, and '70s, that the look-say methodology results in diminished reading achievement, they went unheeded by the general community of reading professionals. Austin and others in 1961[19] found that only three of the 638 reading professors across the country who were questioned believed that there was a need for more emphasis on "phonetic" methods of teaching. All of the seventy-four reading professors whom they interviewed in depth were unalterably opposed to the intensive teaching of phonics. Each of these professors expressed a firm commitment to an indirect, delayed, and incidental approach to the teaching of word analysis, the type found in the popular basal readers of that day.

Then, in 1963, Austin and Morrison[20] found that fifty-nine of the sixty-five school systems that they studied depended heavily upon basal readers which advised teachers to instruct phonics in an indirect, delayed, and incidental manner.

The latest critical analysis of popular basal readers, made by Beck and McCaslin[21] in 1978, finds that there has not been enough emphasis in these books on the intensive teaching of phonics to actually teach this information effectively. These researchers found that the phonics taught through these modern readers is not explicit enough for children to acquire mastery of the speech sound-letter correspondences that are taught. These critics note that to profit from the phonics instruction in these modern basal readers the child must have sophisticated phonemic analysis abilities -- abilities which are expected by these texts but not taught by them.

The Lack of Knowledge about Phonics

Yet another reason why myths of reading instruction have continued to find favor among some reading professionals is their lack of knowledge about phonics. It is not correct to assume that all professors of reading have had equal access to the information about phonics that is needed to

Despite the accuracy of the warnings of these books of the 1950s, '60s, and '70s, that the look-say methodology results in diminished reading achievement, they went unheeded by the general community of reading professionals.

make reasonable judgments about its teaching. Unfortunately, advanced academic degrees in education do not necessarily ensure that their holders are cognizant enough about phonics to make informed decisions about its instruction, as Mazurkiewicz[22] found out.

This researcher reported on what is perhaps the only set of empirical findings gained so far of reading professors' understanding of phonics information. He sent a questionnaire to a random sample of members of the College Reading Association, a prestigious body of reading professors. These professors of reading were asked what they taught about phonics in their university classes. Their answers obviously reflect the state of their knowledge about this subject.

Mazurkiewicz concluded from his findings that college professors who teach teachers to teach reading do not agree on the generalizations that are used in phonic analysis. He found that his "evidence also indicates that only a small percentage of the sample had a satisfactory knowledge of those decoding elements he deems it important for teachers to know, that gross misinformation characterizes his instruction to teachers, that contradictory information is supplied teachers, and that college professors, as reflected in this sample, are generally poorly instructed about or meagerly conversant as a result of self-study with those elements [of phonics] which are basic to reading instruction" (p. 128).

Examples of these reading professors' misinformation about phonics underscores this conclusion.

Examples of these reading professors' misinformation about phonics underscores this conclusion. Some of these professors believe that there are fifty or more speech sounds in any given dialect of English, or to the other extreme, that there are only ten vowel sounds and only twenty-one consonant sounds; that the word, *chill*, contains a diphthong; that *now* has a "long" vowel sound; that *know* has a "short" vowel sound; or that the final *e* in *home* is not a signal for the speech sound to be given by the reader to the *o* in this word.

It is difficult to assume that professors of reading who have such grossly inadequate knowledge about the technical nature of phonics would be ones, on the other hand, who are familiar with the results of research as to the relative effectiveness of the teaching of phonics. To the contrary, it appears more likely that their ignorance about the technological aspects of phonics strongly implies their lack of interest in this subject and thus their unfamiliarity as to its experimentally determined usefulness. It is pertinent to note that scholars in psychology and linguistics (see Bibliography), as well as teacher education, who have carefully studied the issue of phonics in reading almost invariably conclude that phonics and reading acquisition are closely related. It seems clear, then, that the more knowledge commentators on phonics have about this subject the more likely they are to endorse its utility.

Prejudice and Intolerance of Phonics

While unenlightenment about phonics undoubtedly helps perpetuate malpractice in reading instruction, it is equally clear that the judgments about phonics by certain professors of education are handicapped by an apparent bias toward this matter. These are professors whose writings indicate that they do keep abreast of reading research in general. For example, one eminent reading educator, otherwise renowned for his dependence on research findings for the conclusions that he draws about reading practices, contended in 1977 that phonics "helps *beginning readers only*."[22a]

It is impossible to believe that this reading educator is ignorant of the 1973 findings that phonics skills are significantly and substantially related to reading and spelling performance through high school.[23] Turning a blind eye to such impressive documentation concerning phonics obviously does not indicate impartiality about this issue.

In 1965, Gurren and Hughes[24] completed the most comprehensive survey of the experimental investigations in the effectiveness of intensive phonics teaching as versus gradual, incidental, or delayed phonics instruction to that date. They found this research to say that gradual phonics teaching was significantly less effective for the development of reading skills. Several attempts have been made to discredit the soundness of this review. Claims have been made that Gurren and Hughes were prejudiced in favor of phonics and that their criteria for selecting the studies they critiqued were flawed.

The latest of these protests about the Gurren and Hughes review concluded that it at best offers very limited insight into the teaching of reading.[25] This critic of Gurren and Hughes offers no body of evidence nor any review of the reading research, however, supporting the position that the gradual teaching of phonics should be the preferred approach, however. In fact, the only reviewers of research he cites in his objec-

It seems clear, then, that the more knowledge commentators on phonics have about this subject the more likely they are to endorse its utility.

It is impossible to believe that this reading educator is ignorant of the 1973 findings that phonics skills are significantly and substantially related to reading and spelling performance through high school.

tion to Gurren and Hughes are those who have come to the same general conclusions about phonics as did these two reviewers.

It is difficult, then, to interpret the rationale about phonics leading to the conclusion he made, that while one can cite no evidence to support one's displeasure with intensive phonics teaching, one still should not favor it. A predisposed negative attitude toward phonics surely must be operative in this situation.

Pflaum and her fellow reading experts[26] determined whether, of the methods in use in reading instruction, the intensive phonics method is the superior one. For this purpose they examined a representative sample of studies reflecting the relative merit of different teaching methods that were reported on in the *Reading Research Quarterly* from 1965 to 1978.

Pflaum concluded that one specific treatment -- sound-symbol blending -- made a significantly greater impact on reading than the other experimental treatments did.

After this systematic statistical analysis of data on the relative effectiveness of different reading methods, Pflaum concluded that one specific treatment -- sound-symbol blending -- made a significantly greater impact on reading than the other experimental treatments did. As she correctly indicates, this finding supports the earlier evidence as to the superiority of regular, systematic, phonics instruction. Thus, the support for systematic phonics appears to be a strong one, she concludes.

Were Pflaum and her associates convinced from this evidence that the phonics method should be the one used by teachers? Not at all, it turns out. What else, other than a distaste for phonics, could account for a positive conclusion regarding the superiority of phonics, followed by a rejection of it as the preferred method in reading instruction? Only a predetermined dislike for phonics conceivably could generate the logic leading to the conclusion that, *yes*, phonics is the superior method, but, *no*, it should not be designated as the preferred method for teaching reading.

One more example of the negative attitude of present-day professors of education toward phonics teaching comes from a survey made by Froese.[27]

He asked 371 of today's professors of reading to cite the books on their subject to which they would give the highest rank -- ones that have the most lasting significance or recognizable worth. Frank Smith, a leader of the anti-phonics psycholinguistic approach to the teaching reading was cited 154 times by these professors. Smith states in his book, *Psycholinguistics and Reading,*[28] that phonics teaching is a potential and powerful method of interfering in the process of children's learning to read. To ensure that phonics skills are learned and used by children, he warns teachers, is one of the easy ways to make learning to read difficult.

These same professors of reading cited Jeanne Chall 52 times. Her survey of research on the relative effectiveness of intensive phonics teaching over the look-say method (the one Smith advocates) appeared in *Learning to Read: The Great Debate.* Chall interpreted the research to say that phonics teaching brings on significantly higher reading achievement. It is clear from Froese's survey, then, that three times as many of today's reading professors place greater confidence in, and award more esteem to, Smith's defense of the look-say method, than they do to Chall's comprehensive survey of the experimental research. In this instance, it is apparent that bias won out over empirical research findings as the means to be used in evaluating the merit of phonics teaching.

Chall interpreted the research to say that phonics teaching brings on significantly higher reading achievement.

Chall (1983) found that less than one-third of the methods of reading instruction textbooks for teachers that she examined, published between 1972 and 1978, endorsed an intensive phonics approach to this instruction. In short, more than two out of three of the reading expert-authors here were unwilling to accept the research evidence on phonics.

Examples of this kind of failure in objective reasoning for other scientific investigations has been described in detail by Broad and Wade.[28a] These critics demonstrate convincingly that while "the essence of the scientific attitude is objectivity," it is equally true that "with some scientists, however, objectivity is only skin deep." It is not uncommon for scientists to "become the prisoners of their own dogma," it can be seen (p. 193).

It is not uncommon for scientists to "become the prisoners of their own dogma," it can be seen.

Broad and Wade's denunciation of scientists in this regard applies well to the reading experts who espouse the scientific method and yet at present defend the myths of reading instruction: "Many scientific communities do not behave in the way they are supposed to. Science is not self-policing. Scholars do not always read the scientific literature carefully. Science is not a perfectly objective process. Dogma and prejudice, when suitably garbed, creep into science just as easily as into any other human enterprise" (p. 210).

Myths about reading instruction also prevail because it has been easy for the perpetrators of biased thinking to escape the consequences of their flawed opinions.

Myths about reading instruction also prevail because it has been easy for the perpetrators of biased thinking to escape the consequences of their flawed opinions. The information about reading instruction is not what is called a "hard" science. In medical science, for example, it is relatively easy to determine the effects on the human body of given dosages of different drugs; but this cause and effect relationship is far less possible to ascertain in reading instruction.

In this teaching, it is difficult to account for the effects of the numerous factors that have a potential influence upon a child's acquisition of reading skills. It is relatively difficult to control the effect of all these factors when children are learning to read, or to delineate the proportional effect of each factor. Thus, when the advocates of reading myths are challenged with empirical evidence which disputes one of their beliefs, they often claim that other factors than the one in contention have been at work.

For example, they will argue that it is not the unsystematic, nonintensive teaching of phonics which causes children's reading disabilities. When it is readily observable that children become relatively disabled in reading under such teaching, other factors than incidental phonics teaching are said to be the culprit.

The large number of factors that truly can have some potential effect on a child's learning to read thus provide a means by which a given myth of reading instruction can continue to be defended.

The children who fail under such teaching were not "ready" to learn to read, it is said. Or, they had "special" learning handicaps, were the products of broken homes, the victims of too much television viewing, culturally disadvantaged, speak a nonstandard dialect, etc., etc. The large number of factors that truly can have some potential effect on a child's learning to read thus provide a means by which a given myth of reading instruction can continue to be defended.

Phonics and Conservatism are Linked

Adding to the disposition of some reading professors to accept all and any discrediting of phonics (and by so doing, helping to perpetuate some myths of reading instruction) is the apparent need of these reading educators to feel that they are progressive, ultramodern, or even futuristic in their beliefs about reading instruction.

Why the Myths of Reading Instruction Prevail

It is true that junior professors of education, seeking academic advancement and tenure, usually are required to produce research findings that help to advance the "state of the art" in their intellectual discipline. It is hardly surprising, therefore, that few of these aspiring academics in reading education choose to study phonics, a subject that is hundreds of years old.

It is obvious that true scholars are those who thoroughly familiarize themselves with the results of past efforts at experimental research in their respective fields. Few such scholastics elect to investigate phonics, however, because of their perceptions of it as a dated, unfashionable, or even obsolete subject. As a consequence, many professors of reading are unprepared to make valid critical responses to those colleagues who choose to denigrate phonics teaching. Being unprepared to make such challenges, they tend to accept these denunciations at face value.

Few such scholastics elect to investigate phonics, however, because of their perceptions of it as a dated, unfashionable, or even obsolete subject.

A vicious cycle that works to the detriment of the dissemination of accurate information about phonics thus ensues: Young reading educators are persuaded that phonics is not worthy of further study. They accordingly do not spend time studying the relevant research concerning its effectiveness. They in turn become highly suggestible to beliefs in unfounded claims that the intensive teaching of phonics is not the preferred approach in beginning reading instruction.

It is also highly probable that some opponents of phonics teaching take this negative position as a result of political and sociological considerations, rather than from purely psychological and pedagogical ones. Reading professionals who judge themselves to be political and social liberals note that many of the defenses of intensive phonics teaching emanate from sources that are identified as having conservative or right-wing political and social beliefs. This is not an altogether inaccurate conclusion to make. Strong advocacy for phonics teaching has come from groups or individuals who otherwise defend traditional morality, harsh punishment for crime, extensive military preparedness, open displays of patriotism, vigorous anti-communism, strict meritocracy in the workplace and school, the work ethic, states rights, laissez-faire economics, and even ethnocentrism.

It is also highly probable that some opponents of phonics teaching take this negative position as a result of political and sociological considerations . . .

Liberal-minded reading professors who associate support of phonics teaching with the acceptance of these conservative political and sociological axioms frequently are convinced that the advocacy of phonics must be tainted by political or social motives of a reactionary nature. One reading professor tells how this operates on campus among her professional colleagues: "Even though we might agree with a part of what they [phonics advocates] say, the association of phonics instruction and conservatism suppresses our saying so. In some circles, mentioning that you think a code-breading approach to beginning reading might be appropriate for some children is tantamount to supporting John Birch" (p. 909).[29]

It is true in an absolute sense that attempts at the preservation of phonics teaching are conservative acts.

It is true in an absolute sense that attempts at the preservation of phonics teaching are conservative acts. Any behavior that works to maintain or safeguard the existence of a confirmed ideal surely is conservative. In this manner of thinking, those who presently strive to preserve the environment in its pristine form are conservative in their efforts.

It is wrong, therefore, to judge the advocates of phonics (as a whole) to be uncompromising, political reactionaries, who have fixed upon the defense of phonics as a devious means of attacking progressive educational practices. No doubt there are promoters of phonics who fit this description. There is nothing inherent in giving encouragement to phonics, however, that makes it necessary for the giver to take sides in any political or social issue. Phonics has no legitimate relationship to these matters.

It is obvious that the NEA has continuously and methodically endorsed all the varied aspects of left-wing political thought that might impact on school in any way.

Nonetheless, there are anti-phonics groups and individuals who wish to make up such an association, even where it does not exist. By doing so, they abet the perpetuation of reading instruction myths.

Blumenfeld[29a] convincingly documents, however, that the National Education Association, the world's largest teachers' union, has over the years forthrightly and consistently promoted a progressive, if not a socialistic, political ideology. It is obvious that the NEA has continuously and methodically endorsed all the varied aspects of left-wing political thought that might impact on school in any way.

At the same time, the NEA has remained a dedicated foe of intensive phonics instruction.

At the same time, the NEA has remained a dedicated foe of intensive phonics instruction. In 1983, the NEA denounced this teaching as a practice "ready for the scrap heap." This set of circumstances has led Blumenfeld to argue that since (a) literacy creates individual judgment and authority, and (b) that such individualism is a threat to socialism, that (c) it follows that those who favor socialism (in this case, the NEA) foster illiteracy.

Whether one agrees or not with Blumenfeld's rationale, the question that he raises about the NEA does remain: "Why has this organization persistently chosen to reject phonics teaching, the instruction that research has shown is the best method to prevent illiteracy?" It does seem apparent that the NEA, because of its extremely liberal political orientations, is leery of giving support to phonics for fear that such action will tarnish the organization's highly liberal image. In the case of the NEA, there thus appears to be a definite connection between a position about political ideology and an attitude toward phonics.

The influence of ideology on beliefs about reading instruction has also been examined by Mosenthal.[29b] He reasons that to adequately understand why beliefs ("discourses") about reading are held to be either legitimate or meaningless "one must examine the ideologies, or sociopolitical implications the various discourses have for society" (p. 17).

Whether a certain myth in reading instruction, as described above, would be defended or rejected by reading professionals thus will depend, Mosenthal maintains, on their loyalty to one of five different ideologies about this matter. These doctrines are: (1) the *Academic*, which says that effective reading is the ability to reproduce written material -- for example, to decode words rapidly and accurately; (2) the *Utilitarian*, which stresses the reader's resourcefulness in meeting the reading requirements set by society; (3) the *Romantic*, which emphasizes that meaning for individuals, as they read, is created through their prior knowledge -- it does not simply reside in the material being read; (4) the *Cognitive-developmental*, which directs the use of reading material in line with, or that will develop, cognitive mechanisms; and (5) the *Emancipatory*, which holds that the goal of reading instruction is to help create a more egalitarian society through the destruction of socioeconomic class distinctions.

There is no experimental evidence at present, however, to serve as a basis for making a sound choice between these reading ideologies, Mosenthal insists. Why reading educators choose one of them, as their favorite, thus remains a mystery. This confused state of affairs doubt-

In the case of the NEA, there thus appears to be a definite connection between a position about political ideology and an attitude toward phonics.

less provides a fertile ground for the nurturing of myths about reading instruction.

Opposition of Phonics from Teachers' Organizations

There are two teachers' organizations whose basic reason for being rests exclusively in their alleged commitment to the effective teaching of reading and language.

There are two teachers' organizations whose basic reason for being rests exclusively in their alleged commitment to the effective teaching of reading and language. These are the International Reading Association and the National Council of Teachers of English.

An inspection of the official journals of these organizations for elementary school teachers, *Reading Teacher* and *Language Arts*, reveals, however, that these publications do not provide equal opportunity for the appearance of views favorable to the intensive teaching of phonics.

During a recent five-year period of publication of the *Reading Teacher*, I found in the journal at least twenty-eight articles that were unstintingly complimentary to the so-called psycholinguistic approach to the teaching of reading. (This is the approach which has denounced phonics teaching as a powerful method of interfering with children's learning to read.) During this five-year period, not a single article appeared in *Reading Teacher* that was negatively critical of the psycholinguistic approach.

The record of the NCTE in this respect is just as bad.

The record of the NCTE in this respect is just as bad. During a five-year period of late, *Language Arts* published thirty-four articles that dealt in some degree with the intensive teaching of phonics. Only two of these articles were supportive of this form of instruction. The remaining thirty-two denounced it. This prima facie evidence of the negative position of the NCTE toward phonics teaching suggests that there is little chance for any manuscript that compliments the teaching of phonics to be accepted for publication by its journal.

The November-December 1982 issue of *Language Arts* presented (with considerable satisfaction) the list of recommendations set in 1925 that were then thought to be essential to a satisfactory program for the teaching of reading. It is apparent that the NCTE, if it could, would move the teaching of reading back to the time when the discredited look-say method reigned supreme. That the NCTE's committees on reading are filled with those on record as being opposed to intensive phonics teaching, is also of note. The reaction to the numerous national reports of the decline of reading skills in today's students by the immediate past president of the NCTE reveals his antagonism toward phonics. "Many of these descriptions of the faults of the school appear to be calling for more phonics instruction," he rightly observed (*Education Week*, September 28, 1984). "That I see as a distraction," he complained.

Over the years, the national presidents of the IRA have often been the authors of popular basal readers which teach phonics in a non-intensive manner. A leader of the anti-phonics, psycholinguistic approach to reading, Kenneth Goodman, was one of its recent presidents. Then, during its recent national conventions, in 1982, 1983, and 1985, the IRA has had only one session, among the many hundreds it schedules at these events, that was devoted to phonics.

Over the years, the national presidents of the IRA have often been the authors of popular basal readers which teach phonics in a non-intensive manner.

In 1985 the president of the IRA insisted that research on the efficacy of phonics is inconclusive. To say otherwise, this leader of the IRA maintained, is simply to display an unwarranted favoritism toward phonics. Accordingly, he rejected on these grounds the report on phonics by the National Academy of Education's Commission on Reading (Anderson, et al., 1985) which concluded that phonics teaching is an important part of beginning reading instruction (*Education Week*, May 15, 1985). This rejection by the IRA of a report by such a highly prestigious, scientific-minded body as the NAE suggests that the IRA could not be convinced about the merit of phonics by any academic analysis, regardless of the quality of such a critique.

It is normal to assume that the IRA would reflect, as it does, the beliefs of its many reading professor members, that a nonintensive manner of teaching phonics is to be preferred. Nonetheless, when an organization, which claims to be an open forum for all legitimate ideas about reading, openly suppresses the dissemination of information about phonics that teachers need in order to make reasoned choices or decisions about its use, it does the teaching of reading a disservice. The myths of reading instruction flourish in such a climate.

. . . the highly permissive attitudes of reading professionals toward each other's opinions regarding reading instruction also partly accounts for the persistence of certain myths of reading instruction.

The Popularity of Eclecticism

On the other hand, the highly permissive attitudes of reading professionals toward each other's opinions regarding reading instruction also partly accounts for the persistence of certain myths of reading instruction. There appears to be a prevailing attitude among reading professionals that every type of comment about the teaching of reading should be perceived to have some kind of merit. This belief, that all proposals about the teaching of reading have some usefulness, and on the other hand, that there is no possibility of deciding upon a preferred methodology, is called the "eclectic" approach to reading instruction. Under this rubric, almost any conceivable sort of advice to teachers about reading instruction, much of it contradictory of other views, has been published in the texts on reading methodology.

Reviews of these texts in educational journals often celebrate the fact that different authors of these books often give teachers diametrically opposed recommendations for their classroom practices. This the-more-the-better viewpoint toward such advice is the prevalent attitude taken by critics of these volumes. In circumstances where almost any conviction or opinion about the teaching of reading is permissible, or even expected, it is understandable that the myths of reading instruction would abound.

The Dismal Utilization of Research Findings

This overly complimentary or conciliatory criticism of educational writing has handicapped the degree to which research findings have affected instructional practices in reading.

This overly complimentary or conciliatory criticism of educational writing has handicapped the degree to which research findings have affected instructional practices in reading. The result of this condition has been a general lack of any practical effects of research on this instruction over the years.

Barton and Wilder,[30] for example, noted the inability of research reports to ameliorate the ills, the myths as they are called here, of reading instruction. After a careful study of changes made in basal readers, changes that reflected the findings of empirical investigations, these writers concluded that research in reading had had no effect on basal readers for the thirty years from 1933 to 1963.

It is fair to say, however, that the research favoring

This finding suggests that over 3000 studies on reading, as reviewed in the *Journal of Educational Research* during this period, were ignored by those in the strongest position to influence reading instruction -- the reading experts who write the basal readers and the publishers of these books. No recent survey of the kind is available. The continuing nature of the myths of reading instruction, suggests, nonetheless, that today's research findings are not readily adopted by reading professors into their practice.

Why the Myths of Reading Instruction Prevail

There is some evidence that following Chall's review of the research in 1967, which found that intensive phonics teaching was superior to the traditional nonintensive phonics approach, more phonics activities have appeared in basal readers. It is fair to say, however, that the research favoring phonics has had limited effect on the phonics content of the material that always has had the greatest influence on reading instruction: the basal reader.

Beck and McCaslin,[21] in 1978, critically reviewed the reading programs offered by the popular basal readers of that time. They found them inadequate in that they did not teach phonics as explicitly as it should be. Even Flesch[5] concedes that since he wrote *Why Johnny Can't Read*, in 1955, the popular basal readers began to offer more phonics instruction. He is correct in protesting, however, that this added amount of phonics teaching does not meet the standard for intensive teaching of phonics which research findings suggest are needed if children are to use phonics in an automatic fashion. The examples Flesch offers of predictably spelled words that the modern basal readers do not expect children to be able to decode until grade three, seem proof that these readers indeed are not intensive phonics textbooks.

Aukerman's extensive analysis of the content of the basal readers up to 1981[31] confirms that most of these textbooks still commence their instruction with the whole-word, look-say method. Some phonics elements are taught in these volumes, it is true, but generally in a delayed manner. This procedure, called the "eclectic" approach, is one that Austin and Morrison[20] found reading professors firmly committed to, twenty years earlier. That many of the research findings on phonics are not reflected in most of the basal readers currently in use thus can be said without fear of contradiction.

The Claim there is No Reading Problem

Pleas for the abandonment of support (by reading educators) for the myths of reading instruction have been hindered, as well, by some professors of reading who claim that the statistics on the alarming degree of illiteracy in the United States, such as those reported by the 1983 National Commission on Excellence in Education,[18] are false. These reading experts attempt to soothe any potential anxiety among their colleagues and reading teachers about this matter by telling them

phonics has had limited effect on the phonics content of the material that always has had the greatest influence on reading instruction: the basal reader.

Aukerman's extensive analysis of the content of the basal readers up to 1981 confirms that most of these textbooks still commence their instruction with the whole-word, look-say method.

that the reports on declining achievement scores in reading, that they repeatedly see and hear in the mass media and elsewhere, are inaccurate representations of actual conditions.

Fay's remarks to this effect are typical of these attempts to reassure reading educators that reports such as those of the National Commission on Excellence in Education are merely scare tactics intended to alarm teachers and lay citizens unnecessarily. Fay insists that "in regard to reading achievement, the picture is anything but bleak. Basic fundamental literacy has increased, particularly among our younger people" (p. 21).[32] Stoodt agrees that the research data "make it difficult to support the notion that reading skills are indeed declining" (p. 12).[33]

Within each profession there are members who have strong protectionistic impulses toward the general welfare of the group.

It is not difficult to fathom the motives for such statements. Within each profession there are members who have strong protectionistic impulses toward the general welfare of the group. They deem it their self-appointed responsibility to turn aside all forms of negative criticism; to act, in effect, as a shield against its perceived enemies by denying that there is any valid basis for such criticism.

There is nothing wrong, of course, for members of professions to harbor impulses of self-preservation or loyalty to their group. Medical doctors must be provided the civil rights to defend themselves when necessary against charges of malpractice that are ill-founded. Professions have a predilection to convince the public of the destructive nature of outrageous criticisms.

It is not a sign of appropriate professional guardianship to protect unscientific or irrational behavior simply by alleging that the consequences of dangerous medical conduct do not exist.

On the other hand, it little behooves medical practitioners, as an example, to defend septic medical conditions which experimentally can be shown to cause discomfort or even death among their patients. It is not a sign of appropriate professional guardianship to protect unscientific or irrational behavior simply by alleging that the consequences of dangerous medical conduct do not exist.

In like fashion, it is unfortunate that certain reading professors are unwilling to accept the fact that, in truth, there is a reading problem in our society, and as a consequence, the teaching of reading desperately needs to be reformed and improved. It is not surprising that those who contend that there are no dangerous deficiencies in reading achievement largely come from reading professors who work on the side as writers of popular basal readers. The vested financial interests that they have in this matter virtually demand that they proclaim the successes of their basal reader products and deny their failings. It is necessary, therefore, to examine carefully the sources of information as to the extent of reading difficulties in our society. It is to be recommended, for obvious reasons, that only the evaluations and judgments of disinterested parties be accepted as legitimate.

Lack of Legal Redress

The myths of reading instruction are perpetuated also by the inability of the victims of educational malpractice in reading instruction to gain redress from the courts for its consequences. Students who have been graduated from high school with only elementary reading skills have alleged that their schools legally were wrong to award them diplomas. These students asked the courts to require the school districts involved to pay for reading instruction that would bring their reading abilities up to a specified level of competency. In such lawsuits,[34] the courts in general have ruled against these students. An exception has been the Karen Morse case in Henniker, NH, in 1987. She was awarded $27,000 for reading instruction to overcome her illiteracy.

The courts have judged that it is impossible to resolve the extent to which the practices of reading teachers are the cause of a student's failure to read. First, the courts noted that the science of reading instruction is fraught with many different and contradictory theories as to how a child should be taught. In effect, the courts asked how reading teachers can be held responsible for their practices when the reading experts who educate them cannot agree as to how reading should be taught.

Second, the courts judged that there are factors beyond the control of teachers; namely, the physical, neurological, and emotional status of illiterate students and the cultural and environmental influences on them, which are determinants, to a degree, of the reading failure these students have suffered. Since the causes of a student's reading failure are not to be found entirely in the instruction given in schools, the courts have ruled that schools cannot be held legally responsible for a student's failure to learn. Apparently the courts in their deliberations on this issue did not take into consideration the fact that phonics-intensive reading instruction can overcome out-of-school influences that normally are found

The myths of reading instruction are perpetuated also by the inability of the victims of educational malpractice in reading instruction to gain redress from the courts for its consequences.

to work against reading acquisition (see especially Wallach and Wallach, 1976).

It is clear that the courts' findings in the case of illiterate students provide no impetus for the schools to resolve what is the best way to teach reading. On the contrary, if this question was settled, and it was determined that certain schools did not use the preferred instruction, these schools would be open to a new round of lawsuits from their illiterate students.

With the courts' rulings in mind, it also behooves the schools not to find out precisely what effect its instruction has on students' acquisition of reading skills. To do otherwise, a school might have to admit in court that its reading program was the major cause of reading failure. The implication from the courts to the schools, that it pays them to remain ignorant about reading instruction, obviously creates an atmosphere in which myths of reading instruction prevail.

The Monopoly of the Public Schools and Departments of Education

A final reason why the myths of reading instruction have found favor among reading professionals rests in the nature of the financial makeup of the public school system. First, the public schools of the nation obviously dominate the educational scene. They have achieved this position of eminence and authority because they receive most of the tax monies that are allocated for education. None of these funds can be directly spent for the support of nonpublic schools.

As a consequence, the public school has become an educational monopoly. As such, it faces no serious competition from any other system of education in our society. It is normal for monopolies to stifle competition. Monopolies which face no competition, also do not have to be accountable for the quality of their product. These conditions are reflected in the present public school system.

There is little incentive here to reject the myths of reading instruction, since the public school as a monopoly knows full well that it will be supported from tax funds regardless of the level of academic attainment gained by its graduates. In fact, the public school recently has discovered a unique bounty in such fundings. It has discovered that the less successful it becomes in its mission to develop basic skills in its

It is clear that the courts' findings in the case of illiterate students provide no impetus for the school to resolve what is the best way to teach reading.

As a consequence, the public school has become an educational monopoly.

There is little incentive here to reject the myths of reading instruction, since the public school as a monopoly knows full well that it will be supported from tax funds regardless of the level of academic attainment gained by its graduates.

graduates, the more money it can expect from tax sources for its educational programs.

Thus, the workings of the "great American reading machine," as Yarington[2] calls it, have resulted in an attempt to establish a monopoly in the dispensation of instruction in reading pedagogy by departments of education in colleges and universities. College students ordinarily are not allowed to enroll in these reading pedagogy courses unless they agree beforehand to officially enter the teacher education programs at these institutions. Courses in reading instruction offered by private sector commercial enterprises cannot be substituted for these college department of education courses. State departments of education ordinarily refuse to honor the private sector courses in fulfillment of the requirements for teaching credentials. Neither will local school districts normally accept this private sector coursework as evidence that their teachers have made the improvement in proficiency that is used by school districts to award teachers increases in pay or promotion in job status.

These monopolistic practices bring with them other disadvantageous side effects. As evidence from the field of economics would attest, production in monopolies tends to become sluggish and inefficient. Product quality inevitably suffers. Costs accelerate. The almost exclusive control of how the training of reading teachers shall be conducted by colleges and universities has proved to be no exception to this rule.

The present monopoly in the training of reading teachers by college and university departments of education thus has had a greater effect on such training than merely making it difficult to obtain.

The present monopoly in the training of reading teachers by college and university departments of education thus has had a greater effect on such training than merely making it difficult to obtain. This seemingly impregnable authority over teacher education has led to the perpetuation of practices in reading instruction that have been discredited by experimental research findings. A consequence of the heretofore invulnerable power over the education of reading teachers by departments of education has been a group of serious mistakes in the way teachers have been trained to carry out reading instruction. These mistakes are what has been described as the myths of reading instruction.

References

1. Willows, D. M.; Borwick, D. and Hayvren, M. "The Content of School Readers." In G.E. MacKinnon and T. G. Waller (Eds.), *Reading Research: Advances in Theory and Practice,* Vol. II. New York, NY: Academic, 1981.

2. Yarington, D. J. *The Great American Reading Machine.* Rochelle Park, NY: Hayden, 1978. p. 18.

3. Orton, S. T. *Reading, Writing and Speech Problems in Children.* New York, NY: W. W. Norton, 1937.

4. Bloomfield, L. "Linguistics and Reading." *Elementary English Review,* 1942, 19, 125-130; 183-186. See Also: Soffietti, J. B. "Why Children Fail to Read: A Linguistic Analysis," *Harvard Educational Review,* 1955, 25, 63-84.

5. Flesch, R. *Why Johnny Can't Read,* and *Why Johnny Still Can't Read.* New York, NY: Harper and Row, 1955 and 1981.

6. Terman, S. and Walcutt, C. C. *Reading: Chaos and Cure.* New York, NY: McGraw-Hill, 1958.

7. McCracken, G. *The Right to Learn.* Chicago, IL: Henry Regnery, 1959.

8. Diack, H. *Reading and the Psychology of Perception,* and *The Teaching of Reading in Spite of the Alphabet.* New York, NY: Philosophical Library, 1960 and 1965.

9. Walcutt, C. C. (Ed.), *Tomorrow's Illiterates.* Boston, MA: Little, Brown, 1961.

10. Mayer, M. *The Schools.* New York, NY: Harper, 1961.

11. Spaulding, R. B. and Spaulding, W. T. *The Writing Road to Reading.* New York, NY: Whiteside, 1962.

12. Fries, C. C. *Linguistics and Reading.* New York, NY: Holt nd Rinehart, 1963.

13. Trace, A. S. *Reading Without Dick and Jane.* Chicago, IL: Henry Regnery, 1965.

14. Walton, G. *The Wasted Generation.* Philadelphia, PA: Chilton, 1965.

15. Mathews, M. M. *Teaching to Read.* Chicago, IL: University of Chicago, 1966.

16. Johnson, M. *Programmed Illiteracy in Our Schools.* Winnipeg, Canada: Clarity, 1970.

17. Blumenfeld, S. L. *The New Illiterates.* New Rochelle, NY: Arlington House, 1974.

18. National Commission on Excellence in Education. *A Nation at Risk.* Washington, DC: U. S. Department of Education, 1983.

19. Austin, Mary C., et al. *The Torch Lighters: Tomorrow's Teachers of Reading.* Cambridge, MA: Harvard University, 1961.

20. Austin, M. C. and Morrison, C. *The First R: The Harvard Report on Reading in Elementary Schools.* New York, NY: Macmillan, 1963

21. Beck, I. L. and McCaslin, E. S. *An Analysis of Dimensions That Affect the Development of Code-Breaking Ability in Eight Beginning Reading Programs.* Pittsburgh, PA: University of Pittsburgh Learning Research and Development Center, 1978.

22. Mazurkiewicz, A. J. "What the Professor Doesn't Know About Phonics Can Hurt!" In W. B. Barbe; A. S. Francis and L. A. Braun (Eds.), *Spelling: Basic Skills for Effective Communication.* Columbus, OH: Zaner-Bloser, 1982.

22a. Spache, G. D. and Spache, E. B. *Reading in the Elementary School.* Boston, MA: Allyn and Bacon, 1977. p. 389.

23. Calfee, R. C.; Lindamood, P., and Lindamood, C. "Acoustic-Phonetic Skills and Reading–Kindergarten Through Twelfth Grade." *Journal of Educational Psychology,* 1973, 64, 293-298.

24. Gurren, L. and Hughes, A. "Intensive Phonics vs. Gradual Phonics in Beginning Reading: A Review." *Journal of Educational Research,* 1965, 58, 339-346.

25. Johns, J. J. "A Critique of Louise Gurren and Ann Hughes's Study: Intensive Phonics vs. Gradual Phonics in Beginning Reading: A Review." In L. C. Gentile: M. L. Kamil and J. S. Blanchard (Eds.), *Reading Research Revisited.* Columbus, OH: Charles E. Merrill, 1983.

26. Pflaum, S. W., et al. "Reading Instruction: A Qualitative Analysis." *Educational Researcher,* 1980, 9, 12-18.

27. Froese, V. "Classics in Reading: A Survey." *Reading Teacher,* 1982, 36, 303-306.

28. Smith, F. *Psycholinguistics and Reading.* New York, NY: Holt, Rinehart and Winston, 1973.

28a. Broad, W. and Wade, N. *Betrayers of the Truth.* New York, NY: Simon and Schuster, 1982.

29. Eeds-Kniep, M. "The Frenetic, Fanatic Phonic Backlash." *Language Arts,* 1979, 56, 909-917.

29a. Blumenfeld, S. L. *NEA: Trojan Horse in American Education.* Boise, ID: Paradigm, 1984.

29b. Mosenthal, P. "The Problem of Partial Specification in Translating Reading Research into Practice." *Elementary School Journal,* 1984, 85, 1-29.

30. Barton, A. H. and Wilder, D. C. "Research and Practice in the Teaching of Reading: A Progress Report." In M. B. Miles (Ed.), *Innovation in Education.* New York, NY: Teachers College, Columbia University, 1964.

31. Aukerman, R. C. *The Basal Reader Approach to Reading.* New York, NY: John Wiley, 1981.

32. Fay, L. "The Status of Reading Achievement: Is There a Halo Around the Past?" In C. M. McCulloch (Ed.), *Inchworm, Inchworm: Persistent Problems in Reading Education.* Newark, DE: International Reading Association, 1980.

33. Stoodt, B. D. *Reading Instruction.* Boston, MA: Houghton Mifflin, 1981.

34. McCarthy, M. M. "Court Cases With an Impact on the Teaching of Reading." Journal *of Reading,* 1979, 23, 205-212.

176

Chapter XIV

Can the Myths of Reading Instruction be Dispelled?

It is clear that the forces that act to perpetuate the myths of reading instruction are numerous and varied. Over the years, these pressures upon reading experts' outlook about the myths have grown in strength. As a consequence, it appears obvious that influences, more powerful than those presently at work which perpetuate these myths, are necessary, if an abandonment of the myths is to take place. This chapter argues that such a compulsion for change must come from forces the reading establishment opposes: A National Commission on Literacy, merit pay for teachers, an educational voucher system, and private sector training of teachers.

The fact that there are at least twelve different reasons why the myths of reading instruction continue as strong influences on teaching practices obviously poses a significant handicap to the solution of this problem. Is it possible to remove or reform the prime causes of these myths? These are: the forces of tradition, the interlocking relationships between basal reader publishers and reading experts, the refusal of reading professionals to accept outside criticism, their lack of knowledge about phonics teaching, their negative biases toward this instruction, their fear that phonics advocacy equals political conservatism, the negative attitudes toward phonics by highly influential teachers' organizations, the circulation of much unsubstantiated information in educational journals, the expectancy that research findings will have no effect on teaching practices, the refusal of reading professionals to admit that illiteracy has become a national calamity, the lack of legal redress for malpractice in reading instruction, and the evolution of the public school as a monopoly that now faces no significant competition.

Considering the number of dominant reasons why the myths of reading instruction persist, it is apparent that dispelling these myths is a task that seemingly has little chance of success -- unless some significantly different approach to its solution is taken.

The Need for Outside Intervention

The general public, which pays for the conduct of reading instruction, has the right to expect that today's teachers will be given validated information from reading experts . . .

The general public, which pays for the conduct of reading instruction, has the right to expect that today's teachers will be given validated information from reading experts, as to how to conduct this instruction. Critics outside the reading establishment have the responsibility to insist that today's teachers not be given radically divergent advice as to how to develop children's reading skills. It is to be expected that concerned citizens are shocked to find that the opinions of reading experts as to the efficacy of intensive phonics teaching are polarized over this issue. They must view this spectacle of professional bickering as a grave weakness in the intellect and the scholarship of the educational establishment. The public at large would not condone an engineering profession so split among its members, regarding facts about physics and mathematics, that they proposed radically opposed plans for the building of dams and bridges. In this event, the public would demand that for the sake of safety and efficiency these basic differences be resolved before the construction of the public works was commenced.

Can the Myths of Reading Instruction be Dispelled?

The public must take this same kind of attitude toward the myths of reading instruction. It must take actions to create forces stronger than those that presently work to perpetuate these myths. It is clear that most reading professionals today are comfortable living under the domination of the myths of reading instruction. They therefore have little incentive to shake off the power of this influence on their professional practices. There are reading experts who currently do fight against the forces that tend to perpetuate the myths of reading instruction. References to their writings on this matter can be found in the Bibliography of Reviews of Research on Phonics at the end of this book.

It is clear, however, that reading experts who favor intensive phonics teaching are given little space for the expression of these beliefs in the journals of the national teachers' organizations. There also is a noticeable lack of invitation to these phonics advocates from these teacher organizations to speak about the merit of phonics instruction at their state and national conventions. The reading expert who vigorously defends phonics does not find himself or herself appointed to the committees of reading instruction of these organizations. Finding a forum for the advocacy of the intensive teaching of phonics appears to have become more difficult today than ever before.

This condition demands that solutions outside the purview of the reading establishment be found to resolve the problems caused by the myths of reading instruction. Most of the books written over the years by critics who were not members of the established body of reading educators have urged that citizens march en masse to their local school boards to demand that needed changes be made in school reading programs. There is little chance, however, that the attitudes of the public can be galvanized in this way.

There also seems little possibility that parents can teach phonics at home, or can identify a school that teaches phonics intensively and transfer their child. This inference does not intend to imply that society is insensitive to the deficiencies in the development of children's basic skills by our schools. To the contrary, current public opinion polls indicate its awareness of this condition.

At the time of this writing, a reputable poll of California citizens found that great majority of them would even be willing to place additional taxes on themselves as a means of improving their schools' records in

It is clear, however, that reading experts who favor intensive phonics teaching are given little space for the expression of these beliefs in the journals of the national teachers' organizations.

developing children's basic skills. It is clear that the public not only sees the need for reform in the teaching of reading. It is willing to pay for it.

Four Needed Forces for Change

There are at least four methods to channel public opinion in ways which would help to overthrow the myths of reading instruction.

There are at least four methods to channel public opinion in ways which would help to overthrow the myths of reading instruction. The success of each of these actions would require the active support and lobbying efforts of the general public. These plans are all opposed by most reading professionals. But since some reading experts appear to have chosen to become part of the problem rather than agents for its solution, their opposition need not be considered as legitimate.

First, a proposal for a National Commission on Literacy makes great sense.

First, a proposal for a National Commission on Literacy makes great sense. The previous initiative for this Commission, sponsored by Senator Robert Dole and ex-Senator George McGovern, died from lack of interest. The idea should be revived, it is clear. This Commission would be made up of lay persons who have a critical, yet disinterested, view of the problems of teaching children to read.

The Commission would meet periodically to make recommendations to the nation as a whole regarding the best way to teach reading after hearing from educational professionals and any other interested parties. Advice as to how to properly teach reading would not be sought by the Commission, however, from any reading expert who has vested financial interests in the sales of reading materials used in schools. It has become abundantly clear that the ideas of reading educators who profit from the sale of reading materials may not be impartial. The Commission thus would rule out these potential conflicts of interest from all its proceedings.

The reports of this Commission doubtless would be given wide publicity and dissemination through the mass media, as well as by educational publications. Its findings and recommendations thus would become familiar not just to reading professionals and school board members but to the public as a whole. Parents and other patrons of the schools could use reports of the Commission as measures with which to evaluate reading practices in their local schools. When these local practices involved teaching procedures in violation of Commission recommendations, local groups of concerned citizens could lobby their school boards for redress.

Can the Myths of Reading Instruction be Dispelled?

The Commission could not legally dictate to local school boards the ways they should conduct reading instruction. However, it could give them useful guidelines with which they could make better use of public tax monies. How this plan could benefit local schools can be easily demonstrated.

For years San Diego school boards have approved of basal readers for its elementary schools which do not teach phonics in an intensive manner. As a result of this mistake, the school boards have had to spend millions of dollars to write and produce special reading materials that do emphasize the teaching of phonics. These materials are used with children who do not learn to read well with the nonintensive phonics basal readers previous boards have adopted. Recommendations from the Commission as to what is a preferred method of teaching reading could have prevented such wasteful, ineffective, and unsatisfactory school board decisions.

The alternative to the formation of such a high-level recommendation-generating mechanism as the National Commission on Literacy unfortunately is to perpetuate the seemingly endless debate among professors of reading over the issues presented by the myths of reading instruction. These reading professionals have made little advance toward a sound resolution of these critical problems over the years. Therefore, to expect that they will reform their behavior in this respect (at least in the near future) appears to be foolish optimism.

Since both sides in the current contention over the myths of reading instruction cannot give true advice on this matter to classroom teachers, one of these parties has to be misinformed.

Since both sides in the current contention over the myths of reading instruction cannot give true advice on this matter to classroom teachers, one of these parties has to be misinformed. If the proposed National Commission on Literacy could speed up the decision as to which of the opposing views about these myths is accurate and which is irresponsible, surely the arrival of this solution is to be welcomed.

The advocates of phonics teaching should have no apprehension about use of the Commission as an arbitrator in this issue. The mass of documented evidence that supports the teaching of intensive phonics would not be dismissed by a body of concerned citizens who were willing to take a disinterested view of this research.

Second, the proposal to introduce the quality of their instructional practice into teachers' pay schedules, if adopted, would have a salutary ef-

Second, the proposal to introduce the quality of their instructional practice into teachers' pay schedules . . .

fect on dispelling the myths of reading instruction. The merit pay plan for teachers provides extra salary for those instructors who can demonstrate superior teaching performance. Among the aspects of exceptional teaching behavior that would be evaluated is the raising of children's reading achievement beyond that ordinarily attained.

In the merit pay for teachers system, there would be increased incentives for teachers to seek out and use the type of reading instruction that research has shown to produce the highest test scores. Through this process, teachers would soon learn that the intensive teaching of phonics is a necessary component of the superior reading program. In the present school circumstances, in which there is no additional pay for superior teaching, there is no inducement for teachers to identify and employ the most productive instructional procedures. To the contrary, it is clear that teachers who currently produce the least successful achievement records in reading are those who receive the same financial rewards as do teachers who are the most successful. There is no disadvantage (in a monetary sense) for failing in the teaching of reading.

There is no disadvantage (in a monetary sense) for failing in the teaching of reading.

The merit pay plan exemplifies a diametrically opposite principle. It provides monetary rewards for successful teaching. With this tenet in mind, teachers would become more critical of the support given by reading experts to the myths of reading instruction; and they almost certainly would be more sensitive to the implication of research findings, as a consequence. Moreover, they would place more confidence in the recommendations given by research and less to the advice found in the popular basal readers teachers' manuals. The merit pay plan therefore is one way to overcome the inertia of traditional practices and to lessen the acceptance of the "eclectic" approach to reading instruction.

The administration of any merit pay plan is said by teachers' organizations to be impossible to conduct fairly. This argument ignores the safeguards that can be built into the plan to ensure that it is carried out in a just manner.

For example, teachers' efforts in high-income schools would not be judged against those in low-income schools. The socioeconomic status of students would be a key element in the plan. Teachers would gain merit pay after a review by their peers and administrators from outside the school district in question. The National Commission on Excellence in Education[1] believes that problems in the administration of the merit pay plan can be resolved. The Commission recommends that it be instituted.

A *third* change in schooling that would help eliminate the myths of reading instruction would be a restructuring of the way education for our children is financed. Today the nonpublic school system does not have access to tax monies for its operation. Only the public schools receive such financial aid. This fiscal arrangement for educating the nation's children has created a monopoly on educational opportunity for the public schools. After being taxed for the support of the public schools, few parents have the additional means to purchase education for their children from the nonpublic school system.

As with other enterprises that face no significant competition, the public school has not believed itself accountable for the quality of the educational product it produces, especially the development of reading. If a given public school provides its students with ineffective reading instruction, it nonetheless receives the same yearly financial aid (and sometimes more) from the federal, state, and local governments as does the public school that teaches reading in an efficient manner. On the other hand, if a nonpublic school is found by its patrons to have a poor record in the teaching of reading, it usually goes out of business.

Because of the fiscal support that the public schools have enjoyed, they have developed little incentive to seek out and to eliminate inefficient practices in reading instruction. They thus are prone to teach reading in traditional ways, to ignore research findings that could help them improve reading instruction, and to be unresponsive to negative criticism by lay citizens who find fault with their practices. As noted, the lack of competition the public school must face from the nonpublic school system is yet another reason why the myths of reading instruction prevail.

The means to provide this needed competition to the public schools has been devised: the voucher system. In the voucher system all parents of children of school age would be provided monetary warrants, which they in turn would cash for their children's education at schools of their choice. Now, if low-income parents believed that the nonpublic school system better served the educational needs of their children, they would be provided the financial means needed to enroll their children in these schools. Now, as never before, children from low-income families would have equal opportunity to attend nonpublic schools. Under the

A third change in schooling that would help eliminate the myths of reading instruction would be a restructuring of the way education for our children is financed.

As noted, the lack of competition the public school must face from the nonpublic school system is yet another reason why the myths of reading instruction prevail.

voucher system, public schools would be required to convince parents as to the quality of the education that they offer, rather than basing their enrollment on the simple expedient of *compelling* parents to send their children to them.

This plan to give parents of low income an equal opportunity to choose the education of their children, and not restrict this privilege to affluent families, unfortunately has had vigorous opposition from teacher organizations. It is not surprising that the public school, as a monopolistic enterprise, will not voluntarily give up the special status it has gained through the exclusive educational controls that it employs.

It is not surprising that the public school, as a monopolistic enterprise, will not voluntarily give up the special status it has gained through the exclusive educational controls that it employs.

As might be expected, however, in efforts to dismiss the worthiness of the voucher plan, the defenders of the public schools' right to exercise exclusive domain in education have come up with arguments that can be easily refuted.

They believe that the voucher system violates that part of Amendment 1 of the Constitution that reads, "Congress shall make no law respecting an establishment of religion." The warrants in the voucher system would be paid out of state monies. The opponents of the voucher system have never explained how this plan would bring into effect the establishment of a national religion, to which all citizens would have to belong. The federal government contributes very little to this fund, in any event.

It is charged further that only the public school system graduates students who are vigorous defenders of democratic principles. There is no evidence that can be cited, however, that nonpublic school graduates are any less committed to the protection of the Constitution than are their public school counterparts. Then it is said that the voucher plan would create schools that were racially imbalanced. The facts are that at present the nonpublic school system is more balanced racially than are the public schools.

"Parents, in general, are too stupid and indifferent about their children's futures to choose a proper education for them," the opponents of the voucher plan also contend.

Parents, in general, are too stupid and indifferent about their children's futures to choose a proper education for them, the opponents of the voucher plan also contend. This is an egregiously elitist slur of the capabilities of citizens in a democratic society. Indeed, this aspersion is so outrageous that it falls of its own weight.

Can the Myths of Reading Instruction be Dispelled?

Opponents of the voucher system warn society that the implementation of this plan would result in public schools filled with children who have been rejected by the nonpublic schools. Supposedly these would be minority children, or those with learning and behavioral handicaps. The voucher plan provides for racially balanced schools, and substantial extra payment for the education of children who are educational handicapped in any way. It acknowledges that it takes significantly more money to educate students who have physical and psychological problems than children who are normal.

Accordingly, the voucher plan would bring considerably more money into the entire educational system than it now receives. Thus, if by any chance handicapped children were dumped into the public school system, as a result of the voucher system, the public schools would be amply recompensed for their attendance. Since special education would be granted superior funding under the voucher plan, it is more likely, however, that adequate numbers of qualified nonpublic schools would come into being to better serve the needs of educationally handicapped children. The reserve of qualified yet unemployed teachers in our nation at present would doubtlessly rush in to staff these special schools.

The main objections to the voucher plan suggest that they are based on concerns about education that are self-serving. In fact, it is the fear of the public schools that they would be forced to compete for students and to make the special efforts that meeting such competition would entail, that is at the heart of their opposition. The public schools denounce this as an unjust intrusion on their traditional rights to dominate educational opportunity in the nation. The proponents of the voucher plan, on the other hand, insist that only through this challenge to the public schools will American education as a whole be reformed and improved.

The *fourth* change in educational practices that would impact favorably upon the quality of instruction in reading would be private sector training of reading teachers. Historically, training in the teaching of reading has become the monopoly of college and university departments of education. The ills usually attendant on monopolistic practices unfortunately have accompanied this control by departments of education over teachers. It is common knowledge that departments of education do not graduate reading teachers who are prepared fully to carry out this instruction.[2]

Accordingly, the voucher plan would bring considerably more money into the entire educational system than it now receives.

The fourth change in educational practices that would impact favorably upon the quality of instruction in reading would be private sector training of reading teachers.

The domination over the training of reading teachers by departments of education has led to a tendency among members of these departments to develop arrogant attitudes toward outside criticism of their work.

There is a readily apparent need, therefore, for the utilization of an alternative approach to the training of reading teachers.

The domination over the training of reading teachers by departments of education has led to a tendency among members of these departments to develop arrogant attitudes toward outside criticism of their work. As has been explained, this rejection of criticism from those outside the reading establishment is one of the reasons the myths of reading instruction prevail. The monopoly held by departments of education over the training of reading teachers thus has become, and is now, a significant contributor to the crisis in literacy development that now engulfs the nation.

There is a readily apparent need, therefore, for the utilization of an alternative approach to the training of reading teachers. Private sector organizations who offer this training have several inherent advantages over departments of education in this respect.

To stay in business these organizations must deliver successfully what they promise their clients. No such requirement is made of departments of education. Departments of education are restricted by a myriad of largely self-imposed rules and regulations as to what they can teach and to whom. Private sector organizations face no such conditions. It thus is far more likely that they can make the changes in the instruction of reading teachers, called for by the research, than can departments of education.

The use of private sector organizations for the training of reading teachers offers an opportunity to eliminate one of the systematic structural problems in teacher education that currently hinders the implementation of reforms in this system. This problem is the typical requirements people must meet in order to receive teaching certification. The difficulties that beset teacher education could be remedied, in part at least, if the teacher education delivery system would follow Finn's[3] advice that "the ranks of the education profession be opened to permit the entry of more and different people than have typically been welcomed in public schools. State licensing of teachers should rely on a person's demonstrated knowledge, skill, and character, not on accumulated credits and paper credentials." The fact that critics of this issue find that the present teacher certification system is a catastrophe,[2] obviously strengthens Finn's position.

If schools followed Assistant Secretary of the U. S. Department of Education Finn's wise counsel, they would not concern themselves with whether prospective teachers had passed university department of education courses in reading instruction. Instead, they would determine whether these teacher candidates' demonstrated knowledges and skills about this teaching, and accept a positive finding in this regard, irrespective of where, when, or how this competence was obtained. This proposal seems to match one made by the Carnegie Forum on Education,[4] calling for the establishment of a National Board for Professional Teacher Standards that would test teachers' competencies and certify teachers who met its standards.

There is reason to believe that private sector training in reading instruction could be competitive with that from departments of education, under these conditions.

There is reason to believe that private sector training in reading instruction could be competitive with that from departments of education, under these conditions.

Conclusions

The establishment and implementation of any of these four proposals -- a National Commission of Literacy, merit pay for superior teaching; the voucher plan for financing children's education, in which parents would have free choice of schools; and private sector training of teachers -- all would help dissipate the myths of reading instruction. Working together, these four reforms could not only effectively dispose of the myths that have long plagued the teaching of reading, they would help prevent future myths from developing and exerting influence and control on the teaching of reading.

The final questions to ask should include the following: Are these four reforms feasible? Are they workable and just? Would their creation and execution be economically reasonable? Is there a vital need for their implementation? The answer to all these queries is *yes*. There is historical precedent for the idea of a National Commission of Literacy. The National Commission of Excellence in Education (in 1983) endorsed the merit-pay-for-teachers plan. There is widespread enthusiasm about the merits of the voucher system. Private sector training is successful.[2] These four proposals thus have respectability, legitimacy, and feasibility. They represent reforms that are badly needed around which lay citizens, and, it is to be hoped, reading professionals should rally to help rid school reading programs of practices based on uncritically-examined beliefs.

These four proposals thus have respectability, legitimacy, and feasibility.

References

1. National Commission on Excellence in Education. *A Nation at Risk.* Washington, DC: U. S. Department of Education, 1983.

2. Groff, P. *Private Sector Alternatives for Preventing Reading Failure.* Washington, DC: U. S. Government Printing Office, 1987.

3. Finn, C. E. "A Call for Radical Changes in Ecucational Delivery." *Education Digest,* 1987, 52 (No. 5), 2-5.

4. Carnegie Forum on Education and the Economy's Task Force on Teaching as a Profession. *A Nation Prepared: Teachers for the 21st Century.* New York, NY: Carnegie Corporation, 1986.

Bibliography of Reviews of Research on Phonics

Bibliography of Reviews of Research on Phonics

The following references to the merit of phonics in reading with a few exceptions are critical *surveys* of the experimental evidence that was available on this topic previous to the date each particular survey was published. There are only a few of the references to follow that are exceptions to this rule (Beck, 1979; Becker, 1977; Cane and Smithers, 1977; Maggs and Maggs, 1979; Perfetti, 1977a; Stebbins, 1977; Weber, 1983; Doehring, et al., 1981.). Although these few references are reports of research, and not surveys of experimental studies, they deserve a place in this bibliography. They cite large-scale studies which compared the effects of intensive as versus nonintensive phonics teaching on a school(s)-to-school(s) basis, or with other relatively oversized populations of subjects.

It is clear that some of the reference to follow offer more explicit endorsements of the teaching of phonics than do others. While all of the references given below cite research evidence that points to the importance of phonics in reading, many do not refer to any recommended form of instruction that should be given for the inculcation in children of this information.

Chall's three reviews of the research, given below, are examples of surveys which do indicate that intensive, direct, systematic and early teaching of phonics is the preferred approach in beginning reading instruction. On the other hand, it is notable that Levy in her survey refers only to the fact that research indicates the positive effects that phonics knowledge has on the acquisition of reading comprehension. It is judged reasonable to combine the information that can be gained from these two kinds of surveys of the research, first the surveys that conclude that phonics in important in reading, and second, the ones that conclude that the intensive, direct teaching of phonics is the preferred approach.

For several reasons the *surveys* of the pertinent research on phonics provide a more valid source of information about the relative merits of phonics than would an inspection of the *individual* studies made on this issue. The findings of individual studies of phonics at times have been found to disagree with one another. A survey of these various studies can ascertain to what extent there are common conclusions about phonics in the research literature. Individual studies of phonics vary in the quality of their design, management, and interpretation of findings. Critical surveys of these studies tend to accept for their purposes only the studies that demonstrate superior methodological qualities, however.

Individual studies can be misleading in that they involve relatively small or nonrepresentative populations of children. Surveys of individual studies combine these smaller groups of subjects, and accordingly make judgments based on larger numbers or better samples of children as a whole. An individual study of phonics is usually made by a scholar or scholars in a single academic field, e.g., education, psychology, or linguistics. Surveys of these investigations can compare the findings of scholarly inquiry of phonics done by academicians in various areas of expertise.

The less-than-perfect results of individual pieces of published research on phonics often are excused by authors as a consequence of the self-imposed or accidental limitations of their study's design. Surveys of research seek to conform to more rigorous standards of judgement. As a consequence they are often motivated to question whether to findings of certain flawed individual studies have any merit whatsoever.

As well, some individual reports of studies of phonics appear in journals which teachers ordinarily read; some do not. Surveys of these studies can bring to teachers' awareness research information about phonics about which they likely would be unaware. It is apparent that not all authors of individual studies of phonics seem aware of all the pertinent evidence on their subject. Those who conduct the critical reviews of this research are more likely to be acquainted with the global nature of this information.

Often the readers of individual pieces of phonics research find these studies difficult to comprehend, interpret, and judge critically. Those who made surveys of these studies for professional journals or books generally are more experienced and skilled in understanding and interpreting educational research.

In short, a more adequate judgment of the relative merits of phonics can be made if one can say, "I am familiar with x number of *surveys* of the research on the topic," than if one can say, "I know what *x pieces of research* say about this issue." It is not impossible, of course, to prevent those who critically review the research on phonics to "stack the deck" so as to select from this body of experimental studies only those that conform to some predetermined conclusion that a reviewer has made about this subject. This kind of survey of the empirical evidence in the long run rarely survives, however, to become a highly-regarded or well-accepted source of information for teachers and future scholars.

To the contrary, the weaknesses of a biased or slipshod review of the research generally are soon exposed and the review in question discredited. This eventuality usually occurs as a result of the traditional academic competition among scholars to discover vulnerable surveys of the research and to display their inadequacies. This form of academic discipline imposed by scholars, one on the other, has helped maintain a desirable level of quality in the reviews made of the relative value of phonics. It thus is safe to say that the following review are the best sources of judgment about phonics that are now available.

It is seen that the surveys of research in the list of references to follow endorse the use of phonics. While the reading experts, whose critiques of the research are given here, regard phonics as essential to reading development, they do not view it as the single kind of information needed for this purpose. They emphasize equally strongly that phonics is only one means to the ultimate goal of teaching reading: to help children gain understanding of the meanings of printed material. As important as phonics, they stress, is attention given in reading instruction to the development of thinking skills, such as inference and the ability to realize the sequential relationship of information. Many of these critics of the research thus view reading as an interactive process in which the child uses phonics knowledge and higher-order thinking in a combined manner to provide for automatic word recognition as well as the comprehension of sentences and longer passages of written discourse.

Adams, M. J. "Failures to Comprehend and Levels of Processing in Reading." In R. J. Spiro; B. C. Bruce and W. F. Brewer (Eds.), *Theoretical Issues in Reading Comprehension*. Hillsdale, NJ: Lawrence Erlbaum, 1980.

> Research indicates that "children who have been taught to read without due emphasis on the mechanics of decoding are found to be at a disadvantage in the long run" (p. 15).

Adams, M. J.; Anderson, R. C. and Durkin, D. "Beginning Reading: Theory and Practice." In C. M. McCulloch (Ed.), *Inchworm, Inchworm: Persistent Problems in Reading Education*. Newark, DE: International Reading Association, 1980.

> Studies indicate that "readers must identify words automatically. Beginners, however, are still working on that requirement. To assist them, phonics is taught." "Although some might take it for granted that children sufficient and prolonged practice in decoding, classroom observations reveal something else" (p. 154).

Alexander, L. and James, H. T. *The Nation's Report Card: Improving the Assessment of Student Achievement*. Cambridge, MA: National Academy of Education, 1987.

> Research indicates that "individuals who cannot decode written texts with facility have great difficulty using printed information to expand their knowledge." "Reading as an enabling skill should be sufficiently automatic that the student can concentrate on the meaning of the text" (p. 53).

Allport, A. "Word Recognition in Reading." In P. A. Kolers, M. E. Wrolstad and H. Bouma (Eds.), *Processing of Visible Language*. New York, NY: Plenum, 1979.

> Research shows that "phonological coding in reading provides additional temporary storage after lexical access, until the meaning of larger syntactic units, phrases and sentences, has been satisfactorily analyzed" (p. 232).

Anderson, R. C., et al. *Becoming a Nation of Readers: The Report of the Commission on Reading*. Washington, DC: National Institute of Education, U.S. Department of Education, 1985.

> "Classroom research shows that, on the average, children who are taught phonics get off to a better start in learning to read that children who are not taught phonics. The advantage is most apparent on tests of word identification, though children in programs in which phonics gets a heavy stress also do better on tests of sentence and story comprehension, particularly in the early grades" (p. 37). "'The picture that emerges from the research is that phonics facilitates word identification and that fast, accurate word identification is a necessary but not sufficient condition for comprehension" (p. 37).

Balmuth, M. *The Roots of Phonics*. New York, NY: McGraw-Hill, 1982.

> "The simple fact is that, for those who are learning to read and spell, phonics is the inescapable essence of every word" (p. 2).

Banks, W. P.; Oka, E.; and Shugarman, S. "Recoding of Printed Words to Internal Speech: Does Recoding Come Before Lexical Access?" In O. J. L. Tzeig and H. Singer (Eds.), *Perception of Print*. Hillsdale, NJ: Lawrence Erlbaum, 1981.

> The evidence indicates that "speech recoding seems to be one mechanism by which words are kept available for short periods." "Research on speech recoding in reading . . . gives, we think, very good evidence that inner speech is an important part of mental processing in normal reading" (p. 167).

Baron, J. "Mechanisms for pronouncing printed words: use and acquisition." In D. LaBerge and S. J. Samuels (Eds.), *Basic Processes in Reading: Perception and Comprehension*. Hillsdale, NJ: Lawrence ERlbaum, 1977.

> "Orthographic rules are important in fluent reading. Their availability is helpful in reaing words out loud. Given this, it is likely that they are just as helpful in converting print into the kind of surface phonological representation that seems useful when short-term memory is required." "We have shown so far only that

he [the child] must learn them [phonics rules] eventually if he is to have a full battery of reading skills" (p. 204). "Aside from such empirical evidence, there are practical arguments for the importance of [phonics] rules in early learning. The most convincing of these is the fact that the beginning reader who knows the rules can in essence teach himself to read" (p. 205).

Barron, R. W. "Access to the Meanings of Printed Words: Some Implications for Reading and Learning to Read." In F.B. Murray (Ed.), *The Recognition of Words.* Newark, DE: International Reading Association, 1978.
The evidence suggests "that phonetic recoding plays a critical role in the comprehension of printed connected discourse by providing the reader with a strategy for maintaining in memory the wording of, for example, a sentence long enough for that sentence to be comprehended" (p. 36).

Barron, R. W. "Development of Visual Word Recognition: A Review." In G. E. Mackinnon and T. G. Waller (Eds.), *Reading Research: Advances in Theory and Practice,* Vol. III. New York, NY: Academic, 1981.
"There appears to be evidence challenging the adequacy of theories of word recognition that are based upon wholism at the feature level, particularly when the unit of processing is a word" (p. 147). "Children who are having trouble acquiring reading skill seem to be specifically deficient in their use of print-to-sound translation procedures" (p. 145). "Programs which emphasize analytic spelling-to-sound translation strategies (e.g., phonics) seem to be the most successful in teaching word recognition to the widest variety of children" (p. 148).

Barron, R. W. "Reading Skill and Reading Strategies." In A. Lesgold and C. Perfetti (Eds.), *Interactive Processes in Reading.* Hillsdale, NJ: Lawrence Erlbaum, 1981.
"The available evidence suggests that the less skilled readers . . . are primarily deficient in their use of a phonographic strategy" (p. 321).

Bateman, B. "Teaching Reading to Learning Disabled and Other Hard-to-Teach Children." In L. B. Resnick and P. A. Weaver (Eds.), *Theory and Practice of Early Reading,* Vol. 1. Hillsdale, NJ: Lawrence Erlbaum, 1979.
The research indicates that "Like other children, they [the learning disabled] do need to be taught the separate, or at least separable, skills of decoding sound-symbol correspondences."

Bateman, B. A. "Commentary on John's Critique of Gurren and Hughes's Study: Measuring the Effects of Intensive Phonics vs. Gradual Phonics in Beginning Reading." In L. M. Gentile; M. L. Kamil, and J. S. Blanchard (Eds.), *Reading Research Revisited.* Columbus, OH: Charles E. Merrill, 1983.
"Of the many children in this country today who do not learn to read well easily, the evidence is abundantly clear that their chances would have been far better had they had more early phonics instruction. Gurren and Hughes's review is a good example of that evidence" (p. 111).

Beck, I. L. "Reading Problems and Instructional Practices." In T. G. Waller and G. E. Mackinnon (Eds.), *Reading Research: Advances in Theory and Practice,* Vol. II. New York, NY: Academic, 1981.
"The independent conclusions of these prominent researchers are remarkably similar as they both point out that: (1) there is evidence that a code-emphasis approach teaches the word recognition aspect of reading more effectively, and (2) . . . there is no evidence that it inhibits comprehension" (p. 74).

Beck, I. L. *What Do We Know About Teaching and Learning in Urban Schools?* St. Louis, MO: Central Midwestern Regional Educational Laboratory, 1979.
The code-emphasis method produces the best results.

Beck, I. L. and McCaslin, E. S. *An Analysis of Dimensions That Affect the Development of Code-Breaking in Eight Beginning Reading Programs.* Pittsburgh, PA: University of Pittsburgh Learning Research and Development Center, 1977.
Jeanne Chall's judgment, from a survey of the research, that phonics intensive

reading approaches are superior to look-say methods "was a well-organized and insightful interpretation of a massive amount of data" (p. 5). It follows that "the primary objective of beginning reading is the acquisition of word attack skills and word recognition abilities" (p. 7).

Becker, W. C. "Teaching Reading and Language to the Disadvantaged--What We Have Learned From Field Research." *Harvard Educational Review,* 1977, 47, 518-543.

The direct instruction model, DISTAR, which emphasizes phonics "has demonstrated that children from low-income homes can be taught at a rate sufficient to bring them up on most achievement measures to national norms by the end of third grade" (p. 540).

Bennett, W. J. *First Lessons: A Report on Elementary Education in America.* Washington, DC: U. S. Department of Education, 1986.

"Research of the past two decades has confirmed what experience and common sense tell us: that children learn to read more effectively when they first learn the relationship between letters and sounds. This is known as *phonics.*" (p. 22).

Berliner, D. C. and Rosenshine, B. "The Acquisition of Knowledge in the Classroom." In R. C. Anderson, R. J. Spiro, and W. E. Montague (Eds.), *Schooling and the Acquisition of Knowledge.* Hillsdale, NJ: Lawrence Erlbaum, 1977.

Research shows that "the classroom behavior of the successful teacher is characterized by direct instruction, whereby students are brought into contact with the curriculum materials and kept in contact with them until the requisite knowledge is acquired" (p. 393).

Bryant, P. L. and Bradley, L. "Why Children Sometimes Write Words Which They Do Not Read." In U. Frith (Ed.), *Cognitive Processes in Spelling.* New York, NY: Academic, 1980.

There is "a great deal of evidence which does suggest that this sort of phonological awareness [understanding, "for example, that the word CAT can be broken down into the sounds *c-a-t*"] is essential for any one learning to read" (p. 357).

Bryant, P. L. and Bradley L. *Children's Reading Problems.* New York, NY: Basil Blackwell, 1985.

Finds the research to say that "sensitivity to the sounds in words plays an important part in most children's success or failure in reading. Any child's skill with sounds will play a significant part in deciding whether he reads better or worse than would be expected" (p. 153). Thus, "backward readers are bad at dealing with the sounds imbedded in speech: (p. 74).

Calfee, R. C. "Memory and Cognitive Skills in Reading Acquisition." In D. D. Duane and M. B. Rawson (Eds.), *Reading, Perception and Language.* Baltimore, MD: York, 1975.

Studies show that "the acqustion of decoding skills is one of the primary goals of beginning reading instruction." The child "has to learn certain basic symbol/sound correspondences from the set that form the alphabetic foundation of English writing" (p. 60).

Calfee, R. C. and Drum, P. A. "Learning to Read: Theory, Research and Practice." *Curriculum Inquiry,* 1978, 8, 183-249.

"We have examined typical research put forward in support of the 'decoding but not comprehending' position, and found it actually supports the opposite position." "We have yet to encounter a student who could decode fluently but failed to comprehend" (p. 238).

Cane, B. and Smithers, J. *The Roots of Reading: A Study of Twelve Infant Schools in Deprived Areas.* London: National Foundation for Educational Research, 1971.

The major difference between successful and unsuccessful schools in reading development "was the lack of systematic instruction in the unsuccessful schools. There was a considerable neglect of phonics here" (p. 75).

Carnine, D. and Silbert J. *Direct Instruction Reading.* Columbus, OH: Charles E. Merrill, 1979.

"The various findings suggest that good comprehenders decode accurately, rapidly, and use context cues. The implication is that training should foster accurate, rapid, and context-related decoding" (p. 264).

Carroll, J. B. and Walton, M. "Has the Reel Reeding Prablum Bin Lade Bear? Summary Comments on the Theory and Practice of Early Reading." In L. B. Resnick and P. A. Weaver (Eds.), *Theory and Practice of Early Reading,* Vol. III. Hillsdale, N.J.: Lawrence Erlbaum, 1979.

"The weight of evidence favors the positive recommendation that children should explicitly be taught to convert print to speech in beginning reading instruction" (p. 328).

Chall, J. S. *Learning to Read: The Great Debate.* New York, NY: McGraw-Hill, 1967.

The phonics approach (code-emphasis) "produces better results, at least up to the point where sufficient evidence seems to be available, the end of the third grade. The results are better, not only in terms of the mechanical aspects of literacy alone, as was once supposed, but also in terms of the ultimate goals of reading instruction--comprehension and possibly even speed of reading" (p. 307).

Chall, J. S. "The Great Debate: Ten Years Later, With a Modest Proposal for Reading Stages." In L. B. Resnick and P. A. Weaver (Eds.) *Theory and Practice of Early Reading,* Vol. I. Hillsdale, NJ: Lawrence Erlbaum, 1979.

"Would my conclusions regarding the benefits of code-emphasis be the same today--after ten more years of research? I would tend to say yes, since I do not see any viable data to disconfirm it" (p. 33).

Chall, J. S. *Learning to Read: The Great Debate* (second edition). New York, NY: McGraw-Hill, 1983.

"The research evidence from the classroom, the clinic and the laboratory is also stronger now for a code-emphasis than it was in 1967" (p. 37).

Cohen, K. M. "Eye Activity in the Study of the Reading Process." In F. B. Murray (Ed.), *Models of Efficient Reading.* Newark, DE: International Reading Association, 1978.

Notes that "much evidence has been accumulated to demonstrate sub-vocalizing activity during reading, even in the mature reader" (p. 22).

Crowder, R. C. *The Psychology of Reading.* New York, NY: Oxford University, 1982.

"There is research relevant to the issue of how good and poor readers balance meaning against decoding; it suggests that inadequate decoding skills are to blame for the poor readers" (p. 220).

Cruttenden, A. *Language in Infancy and Childhood.* New York, NY: St. Martin's, 1979.

Research supports the idea that "decoding to sound is involved in the early stages of reading; that is, that the child needs to say the words in order to get meaning from the printed text" (p. 145).

Danks, J. H. and Fears, R. "Oral Reading: Does It Reflect Decoding or Comprehension?" In L. B. Resnick and P. A. Weaver (Eds.), *Theory and Practice of Early Reading,* Vol. III. Hillsdale, NJ: Lawrence Erlbaum, 1979.

The evidence regarding the likelihood that phonics teaching causes word-calling indicates that "there is considerable dispute . . . over whether word callers readily exist and over what the criteria should be for so labeling a child" (p. 92).

Desberg, P. and Berdiansky, B. *Word Attack Skills: Review of Literature.* Los Alamitos, CA: Southwest Regional Laboratory for Educational Research and Development, 1970.

The revelant findings from research are "that: a) letter cues, and not whole-word shape cues, are the basis by which non-readers and beginning readers recognize words; and b) training in making grapheme-phoneme associations has more transfer value than does whole-word training" (p. 63).

Diederich, P. B. *Research 1960-1970 on Methods and Materials in Reading.* Princeton, NJ: Educational Testing Service, 1973.

"One of the few conclusions of reading research in which we can have a high degree of confidence is that earlier and more systematic instruction in phonics is essential" (p. 7).

Doehring, D. G.; Trites, R. L.; Patel, P. G.; and Fiedorowicz, C. A. M. *Reading Disabilities.* New York, NY: Academic, 1981.

"Previous research had suggested that reading comprehension was limited by poor word-reading skills in all types of reading disabilities" (p. 115). This book is the report of scores of 88 subjects on 31 different reading tests. The correlations found between oral reading and sentence comprehension "were in the .80 - .90 range" (p. 79).

Downing, J. and Leong, C. K. *Psychology of Reading.* New York, NY: Macmillan, 1982.

"The complimentary findings suggest that facility in decoding and extraction of word meaning are related. Less skilled comprehenders are deficient or inefficient in the utilization of decoding skills" (p. 313).

Dykstra, R. "Research in Reading." In C. C. Walcutt, et al., *Teaching Reading..* New York, NY: Macmillan, 1974.

Children taught intensive phonics "tend to do somewhat better than pupils enrolled in meaning-emphasis (delayed gradual phonics) programs in reading comprehension at the end of the first grade. Furthermore, second- and third-grade pupils in code-emphasis [phonics] instructional programs are at least as capable in reading comprehension as those whose instruction has been characterized by delayed gradual phonics instruction" (p. 397).

Ehri, L. C. "Linguistic Insight: Threshold of Reading Acquisition." In T. G. Waller and G. E. MacKinnon (Eds.), *Reading Research: Advances in Theory and Practice,* Vol. I. New York, NY: Academic, 1979.

From research "it is apparent that phonological segmentation and reading ability are closely related" (p. 97).

Ehri, L. C. "The Development of Orthographic Images." In U. Firth (Ed.), *Cognitive Processes in Spelling.* New York, NY: Academic, 1980.

The research indicates that the task of beginning readers "is to assimilate the word's printed form to its phonological structure" (p. 313).

Ehri, L. C. "How Orthography Alters Spoken Language Competence in Children Learning to Read and Spell." In J. Downing and R. Valtin (Eds.), *Language Awareness and Learning to Read.* New York, NY: Springer-Verlag, 1984.

"The importance of phonemic analytic skills in learning to read has been documented and discussed by a number of researchers" (p. 129).

Farnham-Diggory, S. "Introduction to the Third Revised Edition." In R. B. Spalding and W. T. Spalding, *The Writing Road to Reading.* New York, NY: William Morrow, 1986.

"Children can easily learn isolated phonemes, and once they have learned them, they can easily identify them in words. Once they understand what they are supposed to be listening *for*, they can readily categorize a wide range of /p/ sounds as all being represented by the same letter *p*. The research evidence on this point is absolutely beyond dispute" (p. 12).

Finn, C. E. *What Works: Research About Teaching and Learning.* Washington, DC: U. S. Department of Education, 1986.

"Recent research indicates that, on the average, children who are taught phonics get off to a better start in learning to read than children who are not taught phonics" (p. 21).

Fowler, C. A. "Phonological Coding in Beginning Reading." In M. L. Kamil and A. J. Moe (Eds.), *Reading Research: Studies and Applications.* Clemson, SC: National Reading Conference, 1979.

Research bears out the fact that "the child has to learn explicitly what he already knows tacitly--namely that words are sequences of phonological segments" (p. 291).

Fowler, C. A. "Some Aspects of Language Perception by Eye." In O. J. L. Tzeng and H. Singer (Eds.), *Perception of Print.* Hillsdale, NJ: Lawrence Erlbaum, 1981.
"Studies suggest that children do exploit the spelling-to-sound route of access to the lexicon in their reading" (p. 188). Research also verifies that "the sound system must be critically involved in the reading process independently of level of reading skill" (p. 184). Thus, "holistic association of a written word to a spoken word would seem to have little to recommend it" (p. 185). Studies also show that "phonetic or phonological units are normally involved in the procedures surrounding the memory and comprehension of text" (p. 193).

Gibson, E. J. "Theory-Based Research on Reading and Its Implications for Instruction." In J. B. Carroll and J. S. Chall (Eds.), *Toward a Literate Society.* New York, NY: McGraw-Hill, 1975.
Research says that "the heart of learning to read would seem to be the process of mapping written words and letters to the spoken language" (p. 298).

Gibson, E. J. and Levin, H. *The Psychology of Reading.* Cambridge, MA: MIT, 1975.
Studies on decoding indicate that it "must become smooth and automatic before attention can be strongly concentrated on the meaning to be extracted" (p. 378).

Glushko, R. J. "Principles for Pronouncing Print: The Psychology of Phonography." In A. M. Lesgold and C. A. Perfetti (Eds.), *Interactive Processes in Reading.* Hillsdale, NJ: Lawrence Erlbaum, 1981.
Based on research findings "it seems undeniable that phonic or analytic instruction works for beginning readers" (p. 80).

Golinkoff, R. M. "A Comparison of Reading Comprehension Processes in Good and Poor Readers." *Reading Research Quarterly,* 1975-1976, 11, 623-659.
This review of the research found that good readers "seem to have automatized basic decoding skills" (p. 653).

Golinkoff, R. M. "Critique: Phonemic Awareness Skills and Reading Achievement." In F. B. Murray and J. Pikulski (Eds.) *The Acquisition of Reading.* Baltimore, MD: University Park, 1978.
Found that "phonemic awareness skills--both analysis and synthesis--have been shown in a number of studies to be predictive of early and extended reading achievement" (p. 38). They "bear a clear relationship to the reading skill" (p. 39).

Gough, P. B. "One Second of Reading." In J. F. Kavanagh and Mattingly, I.G. (Eds.), *Language by Ear and by Eye.* Cambridge, MA: MIT, 1972.
Investigations indicate that "the [mature] reader is a decoder; the child must become one" (p. 348).

Gough, P. "A Comment on Kenneth Goodman." In M. L. Kamil (Ed.), *Directions in Reading: Research and Instruction.* Washington, DC: National Reading Conference, 1981.
From his survey of the research concludes "that Goodman is dead wrong about what separates the skilled adult from the beginning reader, and hence what must be accomplished in reading acquisition. The most conspicuous difference between good and poor readers is found in the swift and accurate recognition of individual words, in decoding, and the mastery of this skill is at the heart of reading acquisition" (p. 95).

Gough, P. B. and Cosky, M. J. "One Second of Reading Again." In N. J. Castellan, D. B. Pisoni and G. R. Potts (Eds.), *Cognitive Theory,* Vol. II. Hillsdale, NJ: Lawrence Erlbaum, 1977.
Analysis of the research indicates that "the letter-by-letter hypothesis is the strongest (i.e., the cleanest and richest) idea anyone has had about word recognition. In our view, it has not been done in, for most of its wounds have been superficial and easily treated" (p. 282)l.

Great Britain Department of Education and Science. *A Language for Life* (The Bullock Report). London: HMSO, 1975.

Experts in Great Britain's survey of the evidence found that "competence in phonics is essential both for attacking unfamiliar words and for fluent reading" (p. 88). Groff, P. *Phonics: Why and How.* Morristown, NJ: General Learning, 1977.

"Phonics teaching does, in fact, offer the child significant help in learning to read and spell. The research on the teaching of reading makes this clear" (p. 4).

Groff, P. *Phonics: Why and How.* Morristown, NJ: General Learning, 1977.

"Phonics teaching does, in fact offer the child significant help in learning to read and spell. The research on the teaching of reading makes this clear" (p. 4).

Groff, P. and Seymour, D. Z. *Word Recognition.* Springfield, IL: Charles C. Thomas, 1987.

"The research indicates we cannot merely say that children should learn phonics. To the contrary, the indications are they must learn it if they are to recognize words" (p. xii).

Gurren, L. and Hughes, A. "Intensive Phonics Vs. Gradual Phonics in Beginning Reading: A Review." In L. M. Gentile, M. L. Kamil, and J. S. Blanchard (Eds.), *Reading Research Revisited.* Columbus, OH: Charles E. Merrill, 1983.

"Since the results of this comprehensive and objective review of rigorously controlled research indicate that a gradual phonics approach is significantly less effective than an intensive phonics approach in beginning reading instruction, the authors recommend that an intensive 'phonetic' approach be generally accepted as one of the most essential components of a good reading program" (p. 92).

Guthrie, J. T. "Reading Comprehension: Processes and Instruction." In J. T. Guthrie (Ed.), *Cognition, Curriculum, and Comprehension.* Newark, DE: International Reading Association, 1977.

The investigations note that "a frequent and efficient method for understanding written materials is to decode the print into spoken language." The research emphasizes "the fact that reading comprehension usually requires decoding" (p. 285).

Guthrie, J. T., et al. *A Study of the Locus and Nature of Reading Problems in the Elementary School.* Newark, DE: International Reading Association, 1976.

Survey of "first grade studies illustrated that skill-based instruction which emphasizes decoding had an edge in efficiency over language-based approaches" (p. 120). "Low achievers seem to be inferior to higher achievers on: decoding accuracy, decoding speed" (p. 130). Accordingly, "acquisition of proficient decoding represents the major problem in early stages of reading" (p. 117).

Guthrie, J. T.; Martuza, V.; and Seifert, M. "Impacts of Instructional Time in Reading." In L. B. Resnick and P. A. Weaver (Eds.), *Theory and Practice of Early Reading,* Vol. III. Hillsdale, NJ: Lawrence Erlbaum, 1979.

The findings of research "validated one feature of many exemplary reading programs, a considerable devotion of time to teaching the basics of reading" (p. 175).

Henderson, L. *Orthography and Word Recognition in Reading.* New York, NY: Academic, 1982.

Studies indicate "that look-say methods lead to an early acquisition of a small sight vocabulary and then little progress beyond this" (p. 166).

Henderson, L. and Chard, J. "The Reader's Implicit Knowledte of Orthographic Structure." In U. Firth (Ed.), *Cognitive Processes in Spelling.* New York, NY: Academic, 1980.

"There is a fair amount of evidence that phonological recoding presents much of the difference in reading acquisition" (p. 97).

Holland, J. G. "Analysis of Behavior in Reading Instruction." In L. B. Resnick and P. A. Weaver (Eds.) *Theory and Practice of Early Reading,* Vol. I. Hillsdale, NJ: Lawrence Erlbaum, 1979.

The research makes it "clear that intensive, systematic decoding programs result in better reading achievement than do other kinds of beginning reading programs" (p. 243).

Hume, C. *Reading Retardation and Multi-Sensory Teaching.* London: Routledge and Kegan Paul, 1981.

Research in this field suggests that "an application of phonics enables a child to utilize this knowledge by supplying a strategy for translating written language into its spoken form." This allows new words to be deciphered; self-instruction may take place." Without phonics "each new word must be learnt as a unique entity, greatly increasing the load on memory" (p. 36). "An impairment in accessing the lexicon via phonological route may provide an explanation for the retarded reader's problem" (p. 169).

Jenkins, J. J. and Pany, D. "Instructional Variables in Reading Comprehension." In J. T. Guthrie (Ed.), *Comprehension and Teaching: Research Reviews.* Newark, DE: International Reading Association, 1981.

"Most reading authorities agree that some level of decoding proficiency is necessary for adequate reading comprehension," in other words, that "inefficient decoding can detract from comprehension" (p. 173).

Johnson, D. D. and Baumann, J. F. "Word Identification." In P. D. Pearson (Ed.). *Handbook of Reading Research.* New York, NY: Longman, 1984.

The research indicates that "programs emphasizing early, reasonably intensive phonics instruction produce readers who are more proficient at word pronunciation than programs emphasizing meaning . . . . The message is clear: if you want to improve word-identification ability, teach phonics" (p. 595).

Johnson, G. D. and Lefton, L. A. "Reading Comprehension: Essential Skills Are Not Sufficient." In D. F. Fisher and C. W. Peters (Eds.), *Comprehension and the Competent Reader.* New York, NY: Praeger, 1981.

"In summary, it appears that poor decoding skills can contribute significantly to poor comprehension" (p. 120).

Jorm, A. F. and Share, D. L. "An Invited Article: Phonological Recoding and Reading Acquisition." *Applied Psycholinguistics,* 1983, 4, 103-147.

"Our review of the available evidence leads us to conclude that phonological recoding plays a critical role in helping the child become a skilled reader" (p. 137). "Phonological recoding is vital to the acquisition of reading skill, because it acts as a self-teaching mechanism which enables the child to learn to identify words visually" (p. 139). "The evidence from classroom and laboratory research favours initial instructional programs which emphasize the acquisition of the alphabetic code" (p. 139). "We propose that such programs give children a self-teaching mechanism which permits them to decode new words independently" (p. 138).

Juola, J. F., et al. "What Do Children Learn When They Learn to Read?" In L. B. Resnick and P. A. Weaver (Eds.), *Theory and Practice of Early Reading,* Vol. II. Hillsdale, NJ: Lawrence Erlbaum, 1979.

Inquiries make clear that "beginning students of reading must be taught the left-to-right ordering of the letters and words in the text and their sometimes arbitrary relationships to the spoken language. Thus, the teaching of reading is focused mainly on the acquisition of basic visual recognition and decoding skills" (p. 91).

Kinsbourne, M. "Looking and Listening Strategies and Beginning Reading." In J. T. Guthrie (Ed.), *Aspects of Reading Acquisition.* Baltimore, MD: Johns Hopkins University, 1976.

A review of the evidence that says that "beginning reading is decoding visual symbols into their auditory-vrbal referents. Graheme-phoneme correspondence is the critical unit" (p. 147).

Kintsch, W. "Concerning the Marriage of Research and Practice in Beginning Reading." In L. B. Resnick and P. A. Weaver (Eds.), *Theory and Practice of Early Reading.* Vol. I. Hillsdale, NJ: Lawrence Erlbaum, 1979.

    The evidence indicates that "obviously, decoding here [in beginning reading] is crucial" (p. 327).

Layton, J. R. *The Psychology of Learning to Read.* New York, NY: Academic, 1979.

    The research tells that phonics is one of the "truly independent techniques . . . that will serve children into adulthood" (p. 126).

Lesgold, A. M. and Curtis, M. E. "Learning to Read Words Efficiently." In A. M. Lesgold and C. A. Perfetti (Eds.), *Interactive Processes in Reading.* Hillsdale, NJ: Lawrence Erlbaum, 1981.

    "There is no evidence to substantiate any strong claim that children having trouble learning to read will, if taught in a phonics-loaded program, become 'word callers' " (p. 357).

Lesgold, A. M. and Perfetti, C. A. "Interactive Processes in Reading: Where Do We Stand?" In A. M. Lesgold and C. A. Perfetti (Eds.), *Interactive Processes in Reading.* Hillsdale, NJ: Lawrence Erlbaum, 1981.

    Investigations have found that "speech processes are important for beginning reading because the child must learn to map print to speech sounds" (p. 402).

Levy, B. A. "Speech Processing During Reading." In A. M. Lesgold, J. W. Pellegrino, S. D. Fokkema, and R. Glaser (Eds.), *Cognitive Psychology and Instruction.* New York, NY: Plenum, 1978.

    An examination of the research indicates that "phonemic representation is important in reading, largely because it acts as a good memory representation from which message comprehension can occur" (p. 127). "Speech recoding is useful when details of the presented message must be held in memory to complete a comprehension task . . . or when memory for detail is required" (p. 143).

Liberman, A. M.; Mattingly, I. E.; and Turvey, M. T. "Language Codes and Memory Codes." In A. W. Melton and E. Martin (Eds.), *Coding Processes in Human Memory.* Washington, DC: V. H. Winston, 1972.

    Experiments have shown that "when language is presented orthographically to the subject's eyes, the information seems to be recoded into phonetic form." It is clear "on the basis of considerable evidence" that "the information can be stored (and dealt with) more efficiently in phonetic form" (p. 327).

Liberman, I. Y., et al. "Phonetic Segmentation and Recoding in the Beginning Reader." In A. S. Reber and D. L. Scarborough (Eds.) *Toward a Psychology of Reading.* New York, NY: John Wiley, 1977.

    From the research it can be seen that "by converting print to speech the beginning reader gains two advantages: he can read words he has never seen before, and he can, as he reads, fully exploit the primary language processes of which he is already master" (p. 223). There is "the possibility that working from a phonetic base is natural and necessary if the reader . . . is to take advantage of the primary language processes that are so deep in his experience and, indeed, in his biology" (p. 216).

Liberman, I. Y. and Shankweiler, D. "Speech, the Alphabet, and Teaching to Read." In L. B. Resnick and P. A. Weaver (Eds.), *Theory and Practice of Early Reading,* Vol. II. Hillsdale, NJ:Lawrence Erlbaum, 1979.

    The evidence shows that "the child's fundamental task in learning to read is to construct a link between the arbitrary signs of print and speech" (p. 110). These "readers must realize that speech can be segmented into phonemes, and they must know how many phonemes the words in their vocabulary contain and the order in which they occur." Then, "they must know that the letter symbols present phonemes" (p. 111).

Liberman, I. Y., et al. "Steps Toward Literacy: A Linguistic Approach." In P. J. Levinson and C. Sloan (Eds.), *Auditory Processing and Language.* New York, NY: Grune and Stratton, 1980.

    "Despite widely varying school populations . . . and quite diverse experimental procedures, each of these studies shows a high and significant correlation between success in phoneme segmentation and early reading ability" (p. 197).

Liberman, I. Y.; Liberman, A. M.; Mattingly, I. G.; and Shankweiler, D. "Orthography and the Beginning Reader." In J. F. Kavanagh and R. L. Venezky (Eds.), *Orthography, Reading, and Dyslexia.* Baltimore, MD: University Park, 1980.

    "There is, then, considerable support for the assertion that . . . poor readers do not rely as much on a phonological strategy as good readers do." The evidence indicates that "failure to use the phonology properly may be a cause, as well s a correlate, of poor reading" (p. 153).

Liberman, I. Y. and Shankweiler, D. "Phonology and Problems of Learning to Read and Write." *Remedial and Special Education,* 1985, 6, 8-17.

    The research suggests that "difficulties in the phonological domain are sufficient to cause problems in sentence understanding" since phonics ability helps the reader "retain the words in the sentence and their order, briefly, while the information is processed through the several levels from sound to meaning" (p. 18).

Lovett, M. W. "Reading Skill and Its Development: Theoretical and Empirical Considerations." In G. E. MacKinnon and T. G. Waller (Eds.), *Reading Research: Advances in Theory and Practice,* Vol. III. New York, NY: Academic, 1981.

    Experimental data indicate that "all reading behavior must be modeled along a continuum which encompasses both the minimal skills of earliest acquisition and the consumate product of adult fluency" (p. 29). The data "clearly demonstrate the continuity between the early [reading] behavior and its mature form" (p. 28).

McCuster, L. X.: Hellinger, M. L.; and Bias, R. G. "Phonological Recoding and Reading." *Psychological Bulletin,* 1981, 89, 217-243.

    The research evidence "suggests the importance, for the early reader, of decoding the graphemic information into a phonological form" (p. 241).

McGuinness, D. *When Children Don't Learn.* New York, NY: Basic Books, 1985.

    Finds that research indicates that "phonemic decoding and encoding is the central problem in the mastery of any phonetic writing system" (p. 58). "A system based on phonetic and orthographic rules is far more efficient than memorizing each word separately" (pp. 58-59).

Maggs, A. and Maggs, R. K. "Direct Instruction Research in Australia." *Journal of Special Education Technology,* 1979, 2, 26-34.

    An eight-year study of Direct Instruction in reading, the phonics intensive Distar program, indicated that "the results exceeded the usual expectations held for these populations [of pupils] in relation to academic and intellectual achievement" (p. 26). "There is no other major output of acceptable educational research in Australia that has shown the results obtained by this body of Direct Instruction research" (p. 32).

Mason, J. M.; Osborn, J. H.; and Rosenshine, B. V. *A Consideration of Skill Hierarchy Approaches to the Teaching of Reading.* Urbana, IL: University of Illinois Center for Study of Reading, 1977.

    Research studies "suggest that phonemic segmentation and/or letter-sound regularity need to be made accessible to beginning readers because they are closely related to later reading success" (p. 14).

Massaro, D. W. "Primary and Secondary Recognition in Reading." In D. W. Massaro (Ed.), *Understanding Language.* New York, NY: Academic, 1975.

    Models of reading that propose that the reader can go from visual features directly to meaning "simply do not have the machinery to describe what is known about reading" (p. 278). "We are not aware of any support for the notion that a phrase can be recognized before any of its component words" (p. 276).

Mathews, M. M. *Teaching to Read.* Chicago, IL: University of Chicago, 1966.

The findings of research "indicate clearly that phonics methods in which letters and sounds are taught initially and persistently give results superior to those obtained by other approaches" (p. 186).

Mazurkiewicz, A. J. *Teaching About Phonics.* New York, NY: St. Martin's, 1976.

Agrees with Chall's conclusion that an analysis of the research "tends to support Bloomfield's definition that the first step in learning to read one's national language is essentially learning a printed code for the speech we possess" (p. 29).

Menyuk, P. "Relations Between Acquisition of Phonology and Reading." In J. T. Guthrie (Ed.), *Aspects of Reading Acquisition.* Baltimore, MD: Johns Hopkins University, 1976.

Research indicates that "written language comprehension presumably proceeds from analysis to meaning, at least at the beginning stages." "Conscious awareness of phonemic segments is presumably required in the acquisition of written language comprehension" (p. 107).

Miles, E. "A Study of Dyslexic Weaknesses and the Consequences for Teaching." In G. T. Pavlidis and T. R. Miles (Eds.), *Dyslexia, Research and Its Applications.* New York, NY: John Wiley, 1981.

Research with the dyslexic child suggests that "the risk [from teaching phonics] that he will be merely 'barking at print'--that is, reading accurately without understanding--is minimal since typically he is a child of good comprehension but inaccurate word attack. If, therefore, he is reading without understanding it is probably because the phonic difficulties of that particular text are so great that he cannot consider the meaning as well as make the right sounds" (p. 260).

Mitchell, D. C. *The Process of Reading.* New York, NY: John Wiley, 1982.

Research indicates that "in the case of unfamiliar words it is almost certain that subjects use a pronunciation strategy to convert the [written] stimulus into a phonemic form so that it can be recognized in terms of its sound" (p. 72). "There is also some evidence that other units, particularly those associated with pronunciation and orthographic rules, may play a role in tasks that are related to word recognition. . . . A reasonable working hypothesis for the time being is that they may be used for this purpose under suitable conditions" (pp. 48-49).

Mosse, Hilda L. *The Complete Handbook of Children's Reading Disorders,* Vol. I. New York, NY: Human Science Press, 1982.

Agrees that the research says that "teachers who used a method that the new anti-phonics movement would recommend found that the pupils they so instructed developed significantly less ability in reading than pupils of teachers who gave early, intensive phonics to their beginning readers" (p. 122).

Naidoo, S. "Teaching Methods and Their Rationale." In G. T. Pavlidis and T. R. Miles (Eds.), *Dyslexia Research and Its Applications.* New York, NY: John Wiley, 1981.

Investigations show that "children cannot become independent readers able to give sound to unknown printed words, unless they master the code." "The dyslexic child without such instruction has little chance of achieving literacy" (p. 269).

National Advisory Council on Adult Education. *Illiteracy in America: Extent, Causes, and Suggested Solutions.* Washington, DC: U. S. Government Printing Office, 1986.

"Since 1911, a total of 124 studies have compared the look-say/eclectic approach with phonics-first programs. Not one found look-say superior." "These major reviews . . . 124 in all--revealed the superiority of the phonics method" (p. 23).

Nickerson, R. S. "Speech Understanding and Reading: Some Differences and Similarities." In O. J. L. Tzeng and H. Singer (Eds.), *Perception of Print.* Hillsdale, NJ: Lawrence Erlbaum, 1981.

Studies indicate that "perhps there are no better ways to teach reading" than through phonics approaches (p. 286).

Perfetti, C. A. "Comments on Five Exemplary Reading Programs." In J. T. Guthrie (Ed.), *Cognition, Curriculum, and Comprehension.* Newark, DE: International Reading Association, 1977 a.

From the research "it is possible to suggest some principles applicable to reading comprehension instruction. One is that fast decoding is critical . . . . Decoding has to be fast and automatic" (p. 281).

Perfetti, C. A. "Language Competence and Fast Decoding: Some Psycholinguistic Prerequisites for Skilled Reading Comprehension." In J. T. Guthrie (Ed.), *Cognition, Curriculum, and Comprehension.* Newark, DE: International Reading Association, 1977.

On the basis of research findings it is known that "the basic skills of decoding are better developed in skilled comprehenders than less skilled comprehenders." "It also appears not to be true that decoding is dependent on meaning only for less skilled readers but not for skilled readers" (p. 30).

Perfetti, C. A. and Lesgold, A. M. "Coding an Comprehension in Skilled Readers." In L. B. Resnick and P. A. Weaver (Eds.), *Theory and Practice of Early Reading,* Vol. I. Hillsdale, NJ: Lawrence Erlbaum, 1979.

"There is evidence that general verbal coding facility is substantially correlated with reading achievement" (p. 81).

Perfetti, C. A. *Reading Ability.* New York, NY: Oxford University, 1985.

Concludes that the research says that "learning to read is learning associations between print stimuli and oral language presponses" (p. 216). "In learning to read an alphabetic language, a major factor is the abstractness of the phonemes onto which letters are to be mapped" (p. 230). "Successful readers . . . advance, with practice at reading, to a stage of facility that is characterized by speeded word processes." This "word-processing efficiency leads to better comprehension, rather than being a by-product of comprehension" (p. 231).

Pollack, C. and Martuza, V. "Teaching Reading in the Cuban Primary Schools." *Journal of Reading,* 1981, 25, 241-250.

"For the most part, this research indicates that phonemic training of beginning readers tends to produce superior performance in later reading acquisition than does the use of visual or non-phonemic methods" (p. 243).

Raynor, K. and Posnansky, C. "Learning to Read: Visual Cues to Word Recognition." In A. M. Lesgold, J. W. Pellegrino, S. D. Fokkema and R. Glaser (Eds.), *Cognitive Psychology and Instruction.* New York, NY: Plenum, 1978.

"All of the differences we have found between beginning readers and skilled readers relates to the idea that beginning readers must learn to process higher-order features of words" (p. 187). (For example, letters and spelling constraints.)

Resnick, L. B. "Theories and Prescriptions ofr Early Reading Instruction." In L. B. Resnick and P. A. Weaver (Eds.), *Theory and Practice of Early Reading,* Vol. II. Hillsdale, NJ: Lawrence Erlbaum, 1979.

"The review of field research in reading has suggested an advantage for code-oriented teaching roughly through the primary school years." "We need to include systematic, code-oreinted instruction in the primary grades, no matter what else is also done." "The charge . . . that too early or too much emphasis on the code depresses comprehension finds no support in the empirical data" (p. 329). "Empirical evidence appers to support the code-first position. Initial emphasis on the code in a direct instruction program produces initial advantages and no long-term disadvantages" (p. 333).

Resnick, L. B. and Beck, I. L. "Designing Instruction in Reading: Interaction of Theory and Practice." In J. T. Guthrie (Ed.), *Aspects of Reading Acquisition.* Baltimore,

MD: Johns Hopkins University, 1976.

"The large majority of scholars--both psychologists and linguists--argue that a fundamental task of initial reading is learning the structural relationships between written and spoken language--i.e., the grapheme-phoneme mapping" (pp. 182-183).

Rispens, J. "Reading Disorders as Information-Processing Disorders." In R. N. Malatesha and P. G. Aaron (Eds.), *Reading Disorders: Varieties and Treatments.* New York, NY: Academic, 1982.

A survey of the research led this critic to the conclusion: "We think verbal coding is very important for reading. This verbal coding implies the use of phonemic recoding as well as some for of internal speech" (p. 194).

Rozin, P. and Gleitman, L. R. "The Structure and Analysis of Reading II: The Reading Process and the Acquisition of the Alphabetic Principle." In A. S. Reber and D. L. Scarborough (Eds.), *Toward a Psychology of Reading.* New York, NY: John Wiley, 1977.

The research reveals that "it is no wonder that poor reading and poor reading and poor phonological recoding skills are found to be so highly correlated among young readers" (p. 201). The value of phonics "seems primarily one of facilitating retention for the words of the text until the complete phrase or sentence in which they occur has been read and comprehended" (p. 202).

Samuels, S. J. "How the Mind Words When Reading: Describing Elephants No One Has Ever Seen." In L. B. Resnick and P. A. Weaver (Eds.), *Theory and Practice of Early Reading,* Vol. I. Hillsdale, NJ: Lawrence Erlbaum, 1979.

"A behavioral task analysis of reading would strongly suggest that accuracy in decoding skills and automaticity are important prerequisites for skilled reading" (p. 349).

Samuels, S. J. and Schachter, S. W. "Controvrsial Issues in Beginning Reading Instruction: Meaning Versus Subskill Emphasis." In S. Pflaum-Connor (Ed.), Aspects *of Reading Education.* Berkeley, CA: McCutchan, 1978.

Research indicates that "one important prerequisite is the development of decoding skills. These skills must be brought beyond the level of mere accuracy to the level of automaticity. When these skills become automatic, the student is able to decode the printed symbols without the aid of attention, thereby freeing attention for the all-important task of processing meaning" (p. 60).

Samuels, S. J. and Eisenberg, P. "A Framework for Understanding the Reading Process." In F. J. Pirozzolo and M. C. Wittrock (Eds.), *Neuropsychological and Cognitive Processes in Reading.* New York, NY: Academic, 1981.

Research shows that for the beginning reader "first, attention is used for decoding. After decoding is done attention is switched to the comprehension task" (p. 52).

Shankweiler, D. and Liberman, I. Y. "Misreading: A Search for Causes." In J. F. Kavanagh and I. G. Mattingly (Eds.), *Language by Ear and by Eye.* Cambridge, MA: MIT, 1972.

Investigations have shown that the child's "reading of connected text tends to be only as good or poor as his reading of individual words" (p. 291). This survey of the research asked "whether the major barrier to achieving fluency in reading is at the level of connected text or in dealing with individual words." It was found "that the word and its components are of primary importance" (p. 313).

Shuman, R. B. *Elements of Early Reading Instruction.* Washington, DC: National Education Association, 1979.

"Perhaps the most valuable book to date to deal extensively with the subject of phonics is Jeanne Chall's. This book is carefully, indeed meticulously researched. It has examined every significant research study in reading done during the period upon which it focuses, 1910 to 1965. Its conclusions and recommendations, objectively arrived at, cannot be ignored--although many of them have been" (p. 46).

Singer, M. H. "Competent Reading: A Laboratory Description." In M. H. Singer (Ed.), *Competent Reader, Disabled Reader: Research and Application.* Hillsdale, NJ: Lawrence Erlbaum, 1982.

The evidence indicates that "competent readers, despite their extensive experience with letters and words, still attend to the component parts (e.g., features) of written words" (p. 4).

Singer, M. H. "Insensitivity to Ordered Information and the Failure to Read." In M. H. Singer (Ed.), *Competent Reader, Disabled Reader: Research and Application.* Hillsdale, NJ: Lawrence Erlbaum, 1982.

"Orthographic rules specify ordered relations among letters as well as the order of letters within a word. Experiments revewed indicated that good but not poor readers utilized this ordered information" (p. 78).

Smith, E. E. and Kleiman, G. M. "Word Recognition: Theoretical Issues and Instructional Hints." In L. B. Resnick and P. A. Weaver (Eds.), *Theory and Practice of Early Reading,* Vol. II. Hillsdale, NJ: Lawrence Erlbaum, 1979.

The empirical data indicates that "perhaps converting words to some sort of speech code is a necessary first step in the development path that culminates in fluent reading" (p. 67).

Stanovich, K. E. "Individual Difference in the Cognitive Processes or Reading: 1. Word Decoding." *Journal of Learning Disabilities,* 1982, 15, 485-493.

"There is a large body of experimental evidence indicating that the ability to use a phonological code to access the lexicon is strongly related to reading fluency" (p. 488). "There is considerable evidence that phonemic segmentation and analysis skills that depend on explicit phonemic awareness are related to early reading success" (p. 489). "There is now much evidence indicating that the cognitive processes that support word decoding are also significant contributors to variance in reading ability" (p. 486).

Stanovich, K. E. "Word Recognition Skill and Reading Ability." In M. H. Singer (Ed.), *Competent Reader, Disabled Reader: Research and Application.* Hillsdale, NJ: Lawrence Erlbaum, 1982.

"The bulk of the research evidence suggests that word recognition ability represents a causal factor in the development of reading skill" (p. 86). "Most children with reading difficulties have problems decoding words" (p. 87). Experimental results "indicate that skilled readers, but not unskilled readers, exploit a phonological code" (p. 88). "There is a strong relationship betwen word recognition speed and reading ability, particularly in early grades" (p. 83). So, "in order to get *started*, to *begin* to attain the levels of practice that make fluent reading possible, the child must engage in an effort to break the spelling-to-sound code" (p. 90). That is the "evidence suggests that phoneme segmentation skill is a prerequisite or facilitator of reading ability" (p. 92).

Stebbins, L. B., et al. *Education as Experimentation: A Planned Variation Model, Volume 4-A: An Evaluation of Follow Through.* Cambridge, MA: Abt Associates, 1977.

"Most Follow Through interventions produced more negative than positive effects on basic skills test scores. The only notable exception to this trend was the Direct Instruction Model." "On the whole children served by basic skills models scored at least as well in tests of self-esteem and achievement responsibility as have children in models that aim directly to develop these outcomes" (p. 23).

This evaluation of Follow Through (designed to provide follow through programs after Head Start) showed that "models that emphasize basic skills succeeded better than other models in helping children gain these [reading] skills" (p. 143). The Direct Intruction Model, which emphasized the teaching of phonics, "had a distinctly higher average effect on basic skill scores than did any other model, of whatever type" (p. 146). "Models that emphasize basic skills produced better results on tests of self-concept" (self-esteem and achievement responsibility) (p. 147).

Sticht, T. G. "Literacy at Work." In B. A. Hutson (Ed.), *Advances in Reading/Language Research,* Vol. I. Greenwich, CT: JAI, 1982.

Research points out that "the literacy skills of reading and writing utilize the same cognitive content as is used in auding and speaking, plus the special decoding skills and encoding skills of reading and writing" (p. 223).

Taylor, I. "Writing Systems and Reading." In G. E. MacKinnon and T. G. Waller (Eds.), *Reading Research: Advances in Theory and Practice,* Vol. II. New York, NY: Academic, 1981.

From research evidence "one may conclude that phonics is better than the look-say method in teaching children to read new words" (p. 39).

Treiman, R. and Baron, J. "Segmental Analysis Ability: Development and Relation to Reading Ability." In G. E. MacKinnon and T. G. Waller (Eds.) *Reading Research: Advances in Theory and Practice,* Vol. III. New York, NY: Academic, 1981.

"There are many reports that children's performance on tests of segmental analysis correlates with reading skill." (Segmental analysis: "the knowledge that spoken words consist of smaller units, units that can be disassembled and re-arranged to form other words" (pp. 160-161). "The reading of individual words seems to be the major hurdle in the early grades" (p. 162). "What is crucial is that the child represents the word not as an individual whole but in terms of potentially separate parts" (p. 192).

Troike, R. C. "Linguistics and the Language Arts in Elementary and Secondary Education." In T. A. Sebeok (Ed.), *Currents Trends in Linguistics.* The Hague: Mouton, 1974.

"After a long and unfortunate enchantment with a 'whole-word' approach to the teaching of reading . . . schools have now begun to swing back to phonics-based instruction" (p. 2125).

Vellutino, F. R. *Dyslexia: Theory and Research.* Cambridge, MA: MIT, 1979.

Reports of studies indicate that "the child's task in learning to read is to decode print to his spoken language" (p. 334). "The child who is not only familiar with the meanings of given words and knows something of their use in sentences but who also knows the sounds associated with individual letters or combinations of letters in those words . . . will have little difficulty discriminating between them" (p. 330).

Vellutino, F. R. "Perceptual Deficiency or Perceptual Inefficiency?" In J. F. Kavanagh and R. L. Venesky (Eds.), *Orthography, Reading, and Dyslexia.* Baltimore, MD: University Park, 1980.

"Research data were reviewed that strongly contradicted perceptual deficit explanation, while providing both direct and indirect evidence for verbal processing deficiencies as a central problem in learning to read" (p. 269).

Venezky, R. L. "Theoretical and Experimental Bases for Teaching Reading." In T. A. Sebeok (Ed.), *Current Trends in Linguistics.* The Hague:Mouton, 1974.

"Letter-sound generalizations are important for learning to read alphabetic or syllabic writing systems" (p. 2074). "Utilization of letter-sound generalizations, for example, appears to be essential for acquiring word recognition abilities" (p. 2095). In applying phonics "the pronunciation of the printed form must only approximate in most circumstances the actual pronunciation for the appropriate match to be made" (p. 2074).

Venezky, R. L. "Reading Acquisition: The Occult and the Obscure." In F. B. Murray and J. Pikulski (Eds.), *The Acquisiton of Reading.* Baltimore, MD: University Park, 1978.

Research shows that "the ability to apply letter-sound generalizations continues to develop at least through grade eight" (p. 13).

Wallach, M. and Wallach, L. *Teaching All Children to Read.* Chicago, IL: University of Chicago, 1976.

Research suggests "that the child must be thoroughly trained to 'break' the code, to transform the visual forms of letters into the sounds they represent" (p. 57). "Comprehension difficulties seem to disappear when the child becomes competent at decoding" (p. 63).

Wardhaugh, R. *Topics in Applied Linguistics.* Rowley, MA: Newbury House, 1974.
"Valid research evidence to support look-and-say and other whole-word methods over phonics methods does not exist and fair comparisons nearly always show phonics instruction to result in the development of superior reading achievement" (p. 69).

Weaver, P. (Ed.). *Research Within Reach: A Research-Guided Response to Concerns of Reading Educators.* Washington, DC: U. S. Department of Health, Education and Welfare, 1978.
"We suggest that decoding be a primary objective of early reading instruction" (p. 59). "We recommend for teaching purposes that reading be viewed as a set of subskills that can be taught and integrated" (p. 7).

"Research has demonstrated the importance of word recognition skill for overall reading performance" (p. 19). It shows that "There are some skills that seem to be very important for learning to read." Among these are "being able to manipulate phonemes in words and understanding the conventions of printed language" (p. 32). The research "results tend to favor early and systematic code instruction over a whole word approach" (p. 65). "Consequently, we recommend that expert and automatic decoding be a primary goal of early grades reading instruction" (p. 60)I.

Weber, G. "Inner-City Children Can be Taught to Read: Four Successful Schools." In L. C. Gentile, M. L. Kamil, and J. S. Blanchard (Eds.), *Reading Research Revisited.* Columbus, OH: Charles E. Merrill, 1983.
Found eight factors common to successful schools but usually not present in unsuccessful schools. All of the successful schools were "using phonics to a much greater degree than most inner-city schools." After the "publication of Jeane Chall's book, *Learning to Read: The Great Debate,* there is a widespread recognition of the superiority of the phonics, or decoding, approach" (p. 545).

McPhail, I. P. "A Critique of George Weber's Study." In *Reading Research Revisited.* "The hypothesis of Weber's study was proven . . . it will remain a classic study of the assertion that low-income minority children can learn to to read if taught" (p. 556).

Weigl, E. "On Written Language: Its Acquisition and Its Alexic-Agraphic Disturbances." In E. H. Lenneberg (Ed.) *Foundations of Language Development.* New York, NY: Academic, 1975.
Research indicates that "written language can be learned only as a consequence of the rule governed correspondence between graphic and acoustic structures" (p. 384).

Williams, J. "The ABD's of Reading: A Program for the Learning Disabled." In L. B. Resnick and P. A. Weaver (Eds.), *Theory and Practice of Early Reading,* Vol. III. Hillsdale, NJ: Lawrence Erlbaum, 1979.
"More and more studies have corroborated this point of view": an "instructional program which develops word analysis skills to a high level of proficiency shows some transfer of these skills to the reading task." Thus, "it is clear that progress in beginning reading is related to proficiency in those auditory skills that can be identified as components of the decoding process" (p. 183).